Creative Writing Innovations

Also Available From Bloomsbury

Can Creative Writing Really Be Taught?, edited by Stephanie Vanderslice and Rebecca Manery
Composition, Creative Writing Studies, and the Digital Humanities, Adam Koehler
Creative Writing in the Digital Age, edited by Michael Dean Clark, Trent Hergenrader, and Joseph Rein

Creative Writing Innovations

Breaking Boundaries in the Classroom

Edited by
Michael Dean Clark, Trent Hergenrader,
and Joseph Rein

BLOOMSBURY ACADEMIC
LONDON • NEW YORK • OXFORD • NEW DELHI • SYDNEY

BLOOMSBURY ACADEMIC
Bloomsbury Publishing Plc
50 Bedford Square, London, WC1B 3DP, UK
1385 Broadway, New York, NY 10018, USA

BLOOMSBURY, BLOOMSBURY ACADEMIC and the Diana logo are
trademarks of Bloomsbury Publishing Plc

First published in Great Britain 2017
Paperback edition first published 2018

A catalogue record for this book is available from the British Library.

A catalog record for this book is available from the Library of Congress.

ISBN: HB: 978-1-4742-9717-2
PB: 978-1-3500-8163-5
ePDF: 978-1-4742-9719-6
ePub: 978-1-4742-9718-9

Typeset by Newgen Knowledge Works (P) Ltd., Chennai, India.

To find out more about our authors and books visit
www.bloomsbury.com and sign up for our newsletters.

Contents

Introduction: Creative Writing Innovations
Michael Dean Clark, Trent Hergenrader, and Joseph Rein 1

Part 1 Rethinking the Workshop

1 Notes Toward an Inventive, Process-Oriented Pedagogy for Introductory Multigenre Creative Writing Courses *Tim Mayers* 7

2 The Unworkshop *Graeme Harper* 21

3 *The Gum Beneath God's Shoe*: A Testimony in Favor of the Sequence or Series Graduate Workshop *Derrick Harriell* 33

Part 2 Expanding Genre

4 The Empathy Project: A Research Assignment for Fiction Writing Students *Rachel Haley Himmelheber* 45

5 Musico-Literary Miscegenations: Word and Sound Relationships in Creative Writing Pedagogy *Hazel Smith* 57

6 The Poetry of Music, the Music of Poetry: An Annotated Syllabus *Tom C. Hunley* 73

7 Words With Borders, Projects Without: Screenwriting, Collaboration, and the Workshop *Joseph Rein and Kyle McGinn* 89

8 Sequential Experiences: Course Design as Resistance in Creative Nonfiction *Michael Dean Clark* 103

Part 3 Creative Collaborations

9 Collaborative Story Writing and the Question of Influence *Mary Ann Cain* 119

10 Steampunk Rochester: An Interdisciplinary, Location-Based, Collaborative World Building Project *Trent Hergenrader* 133

11 Place-Based Pedagogy and Creative Writing as a Fieldwork Course *Janelle Adsit* 149

12 Our Town: Teaching Creative Writing Students to Love Research and Collaboration *Cathy Day* 163

13 For WB: When Our Students Write Us *Katharine Haake* 177

Part 4 Identity and the Creative Writing Classroom

14 Radical Imperfectionism *Tonya C. Hegamin* 193

15 Gender Identity and the Creative Writing Classroom *Ching-In Chen* 211

16 Pedagogy and Authority in Teaching *The Waste Land*: What We Do With Authorial Voices and the Postcolonial Body in the Writing Workshop *Prageeta Sharma* 223

List of Contributors 235

Index 241

Introduction: Creative Writing Innovations

Michael Dean Clark, Trent Hergenrader, and Joseph Rein

Creative writing has evolved. We realized this when, at a recent Association of Writers and Writing Programs (AWP) conference, all of our discussions with colleagues revolved not around the same old topics—publication and print, literary prizes, the fundamentals of craft—but around the exciting innovations in our classrooms. Few of us discussed recent events in our workshops; none worried over whether we had properly trained the next generation of literary geniuses. Our excitement in teaching stemmed from inventive classroom practices that engaged and energized students about novel, trailblazing opportunities in creative writing. And although there seemed to be much of this work happening, we also quickly realized that, without these conversations, we would know nothing about them. We were all working in isolation. Thus, we set about creating a formalized place to bring these approaches to the fore. We set about creating this very collection.

In some ways, the theories and practices described in this book also stem from a sort of collective frustration. Those of us deeply entrenched and invested in creative writing as a discipline tire of the assumptions placed upon us, not least of all that our success somehow directly correlates to our students' future publishing careers. In this line of thinking, creative writing in the academy serves a singular purpose: to train the next generation of writers for literary excellence as demonstrated by publishing award winning creative works that transform our culture.

The public debate over whether creative writing workshops, particularly in Master of Fine Arts (MFA) programs, advance or impede progress in the literary arts seems unlikely to end anytime soon. We find this disappointing because it represents a mere fraction of the kinds of activities happening in creative writing courses in the academy, especially in undergraduate classrooms. Before the year 2000, scholarly examinations of creative writing were scarce and underappreciated. Since then, however, the number of single-authored books and edited collections that interrogate the practices of creative writing has dramatically increased. Another significant event occurred in 2016 with the formation of the Creative Writing Studies Organization (CWSO), which publishes the *Journal of Creative Writing Studies* and holds an annual conference dedicated to this topic. As scholars as well as creative writers, we are now more than ever invested in questions of the possibilities of our field. If we decouple creative writing from the goal of literary publishing, what else can we accomplish? And perhaps equally importantly, how do we go about accomplishing it?

With this collection we hope to capture some answers to these questions, and to perpetuate those stimulating classroom activities beyond our own individual careers. The contributors herein view the time and space afforded in creative writing classrooms as a laboratory for experiments: in language, in genre, in methods, in tools. They cast aside the safety nets of traditional creative writing and instead choose different high wire acts of their own invention.

The first section of this book begins, as many innovative discussions in creative writing do, with questions on rethinking the workshop. In the first chapter, Tim Mayers addresses the often-problematic nature of the workshop model at the introductory level by encouraging a multigenre and process-based approach to the course. Next, Graeme Harper discusses the benefits of recasting creative writing as an "unworkshop" that focuses not on the collective but the individual experience. And to conclude the section, Derrick Harriell presents an alternative notion of employing the workshop for students as a meta-workshop foregrounding several response models. In doing so, Harriell's students can broaden their understanding of the process of creating collections of poetry at the MFA level.

The second section of the book is concerned with notions of expanding genre, beginning with Rachel Haley Himmelheber's examinations of empathy and its employment in the fiction classroom. This discussion is followed by Hazel Smith's exploration of the often-overlooked expression of sound in creative writing by requiring students to work in intermedia contexts. Tom Hunley follows with an annotated syllabus discussing a course that puts students of poetry and their instructor in the role of songwriters to challenge their understanding of self-expression. Keying their chapter to the importance of providing concrete expectations and representations on student work, Joseph Rein and Kyle McGinn describe the benefits of a project in which screenwriting students wrote screenplays for production by film students at their university. And finally, Michael Dean Clark discusses the difficulties addressing student expectations in creative nonfiction classes and proposes ways of sequencing course work that both de-emphasizes product and encourages greater creativity in the process of expanding their understanding of the genre.

Section three presents a variety of perspectives on creative collaborations to explore the educational benefits of resisting the intrinsically solitary notion of the artist communicated by traditional pedagogies. To this end, Mary Ann Cain describes the way in which creating a collaborative collection provides her students opportunities to discuss unspoken assumptions about influence, originality, creativity, and ownership that are equally exciting and challenging to the class dynamic. In his chapter, Trent Hergenrader describes the interdisciplinary opportunities created by the process- and genre-oriented Steampunk Rochester project that brings together the work of approximately seventy-five students from the Liberal Arts and Computing and Information Sciences. The next two chapters of the section address the power of place in creative writing courses. Janelle Adsit advocates using the place-based pedagogies of ecopoetics and environmental writing to push, literally, beyond the four-walled classroom common to creative writing classes. Cathy Day illustrates ways in which research and collaboration, underdeveloped aspects of creative writing pedagogy, can create real opportunities for writing growth when connected to the unique culture and history of place. And finally, Katharine Haake offers an eloquent tribute to Wendy Bishop while also describing the process of having our students "write us."

The final section of the book addresses issues of identity in the creative writing classroom. Tonya Hegamin describes helping students with basic writing and literacy levels to improve their skills by rejecting the idea of "the perfect draft" and creating a culture more inclusive of diverse expressions of identity, authority, and privilege. Ching-In Chen's chapter is also interested in expanding classroom culture, discussing frameworks and strategies from

LGBTQIA research that creative writing instructors can incorporate to nurture early explorations of gender and sexuality that students so often explore in writing courses. And finally, Prageeta Sharma discusses how applying post-colonial criticism to canonical texts like "The Wasteland" can help students expand their perceptions of what constitutes "good writing" by challenging the cultural frameworks that inform those perceptions.

Creative writing has indeed evolved. Universities and the publishing industry have changed; so too has the student population, both in terms of diversity and demographics, but also in terms of the experiences these students want and need from today's college degree. Traditional approaches to creative writing—namely workshopping distinct genres for print publication—remain core to the identity of our field, and have represented its trajectory for nearly a century. This collection, however, presents a shift in that trajectory: a different type of creative writing, a type unburdened by the weight of tradition and expectation that might limit the potential of the contemporary student, a type more in tune with the exciting, vast possibilities of our field.

Part One

Rethinking the Workshop

1

Notes Toward an Inventive, Process-Oriented Pedagogy for Introductory Multigenre Creative Writing Courses

Tim Mayers

Creative writing in the academy has been a site of contest and controversy ever since courses and programs in the field were first developed. But at the end of the twentieth century and the beginning of the twenty-first, these contests over creative writing have intensified. Paradoxically, perhaps, creative writing's greatest strengths appear sometimes to open up its greatest weaknesses. One obvious strength of creative writing is its popularity with students. When courses and programs in creative writing are offered, they very often get filled (which tend to make them popular with college university administrators also). Yet this very popularity seems to invite—for degree programs especially—questions about what students are going to do with those degrees. What kinds of jobs are they going to get? How are their identities as writers going to fit into the larger arcs of their careers? The number of MFA and PhD graduates in creative writing far outpaces the number of available tenure track academic jobs in the field. And in the case of undergraduate BA or BFA degrees in creative writing, aside from graduate school, there is no *obvious* post-degree career track. Beyond such monetary and pragmatic concerns, questions arise also about what students will do with the knowledge and ability they acquire via creative writing programs. A common complaint about creative writing programs—so common now as to have become its own sort of cliché—is that they produce students who flood the literary marketplace with technically adept but uninspired works. Graduates of creative writing programs, according to this line of thinking, write homogenized and bland poems, stories, novels, and memoirs, thereby robbing contemporary literature of its verve, its daring, its edginess. And yet another question about creative writing, stemming also in part from its popularity with students, asks whether it is sufficiently "scholarly" or "rigorous" to merit a place in higher education. Questions about creative writing's academic legitimacy or validity sometimes even come from within the very English departments where creative writing courses and programs are housed; traditional literary scholars, for example, often express these concerns. Creative writing is, in the eyes of some critics from within academia but outside the field itself, too "soft," too "easy," too appealing to students' narcissism or self-absorption, and insufficiently rooted in a scholarly or intellectual tradition that might give it weight.

Arguably of greater concern to those of us who actually teach creative writing at the college or university level are the questions that come from *within* our ranks. Creative writing seems in many ways to have outgrown its origins (especially in the United States, where it began to develop during the first half of the twentieth century primarily at the graduate level, and to serve students who arrived with a significant amount of experience and aptitude in writing) and yet to have retained too many of the accidental features of those origins. Foremost among these features is *workshop pedagogy*, which has served as an epicenter for both critiques and defenses of creative writing in the academy.

During the past decade, roughly speaking, a new subfield of English often called *creative writing studies* has emerged and begun to develop (though one could certainly argue that its roots reach back into the latter decades of the twentieth century). Practitioners and scholars of creative writing studies tend to share in common some form of background in creative writing proper;[1] the vast majority have MA, MFA, or PhD degrees in the field. Some have associations only with creative writing, while others are hybrid figures, also having graduate education and/or scholarly background in other areas of English studies, like composition-rhetoric or literary studies. Creative writing studies thus far have produced a wide range of questions about, and critiques of, many of creative writing's traditional institutional practices and configurations. A detailed overview of these critiques is far beyond the scope of this chapter. In the following section, then, I will simply note some key features of these critiques and point to a few representative examples. This will provide context for my ultimate goal here: to outline a pedagogy for introductory multigenre creative writing courses that pays heed to potential "problem spots" in these areas and seeks to provide an alternative to traditional practices.

Critiques of creative writing's traditions

From around the mid-twentieth century onward, graduates of major creative writing MFA programs (the oldest and most prestigious of which had formed in the first half of the century at universities in Iowa, Oregon, and a few other places) were hired as professors in increasing numbers as other colleges and universities sought to develop creative writing programs to meet student demand.[2] The workshop pedagogy that many of these new professors brought with them to their new jobs was not subjected to serious scrutiny from within the field until almost the last decade of the century (by which time the job market for tenure track creative writing professors had also become glutted). In 1989, Joseph Moxley's edited collection, *Creative Writing in America: Theory and Pedagogy*, brought to the national scholarly stage conversations which, perhaps up until that time, had been isolated in faculty lounges, university hallways, and occasional discussions at conferences. In the preface, Moxley noted, "Despite the rapid growth and popularity of courses and programs in creative writing, pedagogical techniques have not evolved all that much."[3] The first chapter in that book, Eve Shelnutt's "Notes From a Cell: Creative Writing Programs in Isolation," argued that creative writers in academia (many of them, at least) had cut themselves off from the currents of intellectual discourse flowing elsewhere in the academy, especially in literary theory. Five years later, the first chapter in another major edited collection, Wendy Bishop's and Hans Ostrom's *Colors of a Different Horse: Rethinking Creative Writing Theory and Pedagogy*[4], struck a similar note. François Camoin's "The Workshop and Its Discontents"[5] also characterized the relationship between creative writing and literary theory as strained, with many creative writers concerned about literary theory yet unable to engage with it. From the very beginning of what later would be called "creative writing studies," then, academically employed creative writers expressed concern about potential inadequacies and blind spots within the practices handed down from those who first brought creative writing to the academy. And as practices such as the creative writing workshop have been questioned and critiqued, it has become evident to creative writing studies scholars—as it had become evident in earlier decades to scholars in composition studies—that such practices are rooted in and replicate ideas (whether these are held consciously or not, and whether those who work within their purview can articulate them or not) about *what writing is* and *how it works*. And since writing is so deeply woven into the fabric of a hyperliterate society such as ours, these ideas are never *merely* about writing; they have philosophical, psychological, social, economic, and political implications.

Although creative writing is often criticized for being too isolated from the rest of English studies,[6] its sharp focus on individualism is not (or at least has not always been) a problem unique to it. In 1987, composition scholar Karen Burke LeFevre published an important book called *Invention as a Social Act* in which she noted that the teaching of composition had long been characterized by a hyper-individualistic focus likely due to its institutional proximity (i.e., its placement within college and university English departments) to literary study.[7] From the late 1980s onward, composition scholarship has developed a rich strand of work devoted to histories and theories of rhetorical invention that move "outward" from an individualist focus to account for social and environmental elements that factor into writing processes. Critics of creative writing's excessive focus on individuality have sometimes looked toward scholarship in composition studies or literary studies for theoretical groundwork.

Inventive, process-oriented pedagogy: An outline

The university where I work does not have a creative writing program, per se. Creative writing is folded into a larger curricular option called *writing studies*, which also includes technical writing, business writing, visual rhetoric, and a capstone experience, for which a significant number of students choose to write some sort of creative senior thesis (such as a novel manuscript, a collection of short stories or poems, a memoir, or some sort of hybrid critical/creative document). The introductory multigenre creative writing course that I often teach attracts not only students who are pursuing the degree option or minor in writing studies, but also students from across the university seeking a general education elective in the humanities. Class size is capped at twenty-five; the class always fills, and is occasionally overfilled when students are in dire need of the course to fulfill their graduation requirements. The class size, along with the range and diversity of students (it is quite common to have in the same classroom students who have been writing creatively for years—some of whom have already completed one or more novel manuscripts, or reams of short stories or poems—along with those who have never before attempted anything they would call "creative writing") make the traditional workshop untenable.

The challenge I have faced (and that others in similar institutional situations face), in attempting to address some of the critiques of creative writing outlined above and to deal with the size and diversity of the student population, is twofold—to develop an introductory creative writing pedagogy that (1) widens the course focus beyond complete-draft revising and editing, thereby embracing more of the writing process than most traditional workshop models do, and (2) widens the course focus beyond the written products of individuals, thereby acknowledging the social and collaborative dimensions of creative writing more than most traditional workshop models do. To be clear: I do not mean that late-stage revising and editing or the work or the individual dimensions of creative authorship should be ignored.[8] The concern instead is that these focuses should not be allowed to *dominate* the class, thus obscuring or distorting the importance of other focuses. I characterize the pedagogy I have developed as *inventive* and *process-oriented* because it focuses most of the instructor's and students' attention on how and where works of creative writing *start* (invention) and how they *develop in their earliest phases* in ways both guided by and sometimes outside of or contrary to the writers' intentions (process).

This pedagogy relies heavily on writing prompts and exercises. It should be noted that there is nothing particularly new about prompts and exercises per se; a certain segment of undergraduate creative writing instructors at the college and university level has probably used prompts ever since creative writing courses were inaugurated. The main "innovation" in my practice lies in *how the prompts are used* and *how extensively they are woven into the course's day to day functioning* in support of the semester's larger goals. I almost always begin the course by focusing on fiction (because experience indicates that fiction is the preferred genre of most of my students), then move to poetry, and then fold other genres into the mix. The model is flexible, however, and can be reordered to change the generic emphasis (by placing poetry first, for instance) or to de-emphasize genre separation and thus to become multi-generic from the start.

In the description that follows, I do not outline the entire semester in detail. I tend to use several more exercise sequences than the ones I will describe. For the purposes of this chapter, I have chosen specific ones that best illustrate how the inventive and process-oriented focus to an introductory multigenre creative writing course might work.

The first fiction exercise is called "The Three Elements Story." I get it underway during the first week of a course, and sometimes even on the first day. The exercise sequence begins during a class period, during which students are actively writing for all but the final ten minutes (and the amount of time necessary at the beginning to present and explain the exercise). These are the "elements" that must be included in the story, as I present them to students:

1. A young woman (in her early 20s), while repairing a framed photograph, finds another photograph underneath the one that was displayed. In this photo, her father (as a young man) has his arm around a woman the daughter does not recognize.
2. A man, walking out of a pizza place, discovers that he has received more money in change than he should have.
3. A child, four years old, has an imaginary friend. The child sits on a picnic bench and watches a plane fly overhead.

   In class today, you may begin working any way you wish: the opening paragraphs of a first draft, an outline, a character sketch, or anything else that may work for you.

The final ten minutes of class, after writing, are spent on discussion of any questions the students have about the experience and where the prompt took them. Then students have one week to continue writing on their own, after which they are required to submit a draft at least five pages long. The draft need not be a "complete" story; it can be a fragment of a potentially much larger one.

After the drafts have been submitted, instead of conducting workshops focused on individual drafts, I invite all students into a discussion of their experiences with the assignment, beginning with the following questions:

1. Do you feel that you have a complete draft of the story you composed for the Three Elements assignment? In other words, have you told the whole

story? (Please note that having a complete draft does not necessarily mean that the story is finished, as it may still require more revision to get to that point; it simply means that the narrative parameters—beginning, middle, end—are already fully contained within your draft.)
2. Or, on the other hand, do you feel that your story is not yet finished? That it needs to be longer? That it might ultimately become a longer short story, a novella, or a novel? Why so? With regard to the story as it stands, what specific aspects make you believe it could or should be longer?
3. If you could continue this story and you were allowed to remove any (or all) of the required elements, which one(s) would you remove, and why? How would this help you make it a better story or a different story?
4. Do you want to continue working on this story? Why or why not? If you were to continue working on it, what would you plan to do?

In some ways, the ensuing discussion might sound very much like traditional creative writing workshop discussion, insofar as students talk about details of their own emerging stories and (at least at the outset) often ask questions about minor technical issues. But the overall focus of the discussion is grounded in the shared, collective practice in which the students have just engaged. They have all struggled with the same constraints. They have all worked to attempt to connect three initially unrelated plot "elements" into a narrative (or alternatively antinarrative) framework. Interesting discussions can emerge from any of the questions listed above, and also from similarities and differences between students' efforts:

- How many people felt that they generated complete (even if highly flawed) drafts of short stories? In what ways were these pieces similar? What features did they seem to have in common?
- How many people felt that their drafts were only fragments of potentially much longer stories? What did these drafts have in common, if anything? What features distinguished them from the efforts of other students who felt their drafts were complete?
- Did any of the assigned plot elements feature more prominently in students' stories than the others? If so, which ones? And why might these have seemed more promising as inventive tools than the others?
- How many stories seemed to be in a realist mode as opposed to those that may have leaned toward fantastic or speculative modes? Were those

modes chosen—at least for those students for whom the choice seemed conscious as opposed to accidental or organic—because of preexisting student preference, or because the elements seemed to lead in that direction.

After this part of the prompt exercise is complete, I offer students the option to expand or revise the story, with the option of removing one or two of the originally required plot elements. I do not *require* that students do so, in large measure because we move on immediately to a new exercise sequence after this. But since the course requires students to submit an end-of-semester portfolio, they can choose to continue working on the story throughout the semester, or come back to it later. This "three elements story" is usually a popular one for portfolio inclusion; many students choose to continue it in some way. (In one memorable case, a student's effort extended beyond the end of the course, and she expanded it into a complete novel manuscript that served as her undergraduate honors thesis.)

After the "three elements story," the class usually goes through one or two more fiction-oriented exercise sequences. Very often, I follow up the "three elements" prompt with a "three paragraphs" prompt that gives students the opening three paragraphs of a story and asks them to continue it. Again, students are given one week after the prompt is given (and the writing begun) in class to submit a draft in response. Again, our class discussions once the drafts are submitted focus on the challenges faced in responding to such a prompt, and on similarities and differences between the story drafts students produced. Depending on the level of student interest in fiction as opposed to poetry, the "three paragraphs" exercise sequence may be followed up by another fiction exercise, or the class focus may shift, for a time, toward poetry.

Probably my favorite in-class writing prompt (and one I usually use at the beginning of the poetry unit in a multigenre introductory creative writing course) is designed to generate the complete draft of a twenty-line poem in thirty or thirty-five minutes. It becomes a "new" exercise with each class, for reasons that will shortly become obvious. The exercise begins when I ask students if any of them have brought books with them to class—either books they are reading for pleasure or texts from other classes. Since I no longer use any textbooks in my own creative writing classes, I do not have to exclude the course textbook(s) from this list, as I used to do. If your course employs any required texts, you can decide whether you would like to exclude them from this exercise. Ideally, I like to get five books for this exercise, and I like for the books to differ significantly in topic and genre. Seemingly discordant collections of books—say, for example, a nutrition textbook, a teen paranormal romance novel, a course textbook on statistical methods, a book about Chinese history, and a collection of Irish short stories—can often lead to fascinating and challenging results.

I then choose ten words at random from the five books. To do so, I simply lay the books open, on a desk or table, to a random page, look away, and point with my index finger. Whatever word my finger points to becomes one of the poem's designated words. (If the first book is Book 1, I choose one word from it, then move on to Book 2, then Book 3. Once I have chosen a word from each of the five books, I begin the process over again, so that Word 1 and Word 6 both come from Book 1, and Word 5 and Word 10 both come from Book 5.) The words are numbered 1 through 10, and written on the blackboard and/or typed into a Word document that is projected onto a display screen.

Then I instruct the students that we will each be composing a poem using these ten words, and that rules for composing the twenty-line poem are as follows:

1. The ten words chosen at random must appear at the ends of the poem's even-numbered lines. So, for instance, "Word #1" must appear at the end of the poem's second line, "Word #2" must appear at the end of the poem's fourth line, and so forth, until the poem concludes, with "Word #10" appearing at the end of the poem's twentieth line—and serving as the last word in the poem.
2. Slightly altered forms of the chosen words are acceptable. For example, if one of the chosen words is "draw," the poet may choose to use it as "draws" or "drawn."
3. Each line must be no shorter than eight syllables, and no longer than seventeen syllables.
4. No more than eight of the poem's lines (including the final line) can be end-stopped. (In other words, the poem must employ a significant amount of enjambment.)

The object is to produce the *complete first draft* of a twenty-line poem in half an hour, or slightly longer. I usually teach in fifty-minute class periods. So if setting up the exercise takes ten minutes, and the writing time is thirty minutes, there are usually about ten minutes at the end of class for students to discuss the challenges they faced in completing the exercise, and (if they wish) read aloud some of the poems they have produced. I always complete this exercise along with my students, composing my poem draft in a Word document projected on a screen at the front of the classroom, so that students can watch (at least the visible part of) my composing process while they take brief breaks from their own writing or after they have completed their own drafts.

Writing a complete draft of a poem in such a short period of time, and under such constraints, can be challenging. Not all students are able to finish, though many are, and for those who produce incomplete drafts during class, I allow them to continue working on the poem draft and submit it by the beginning of the next class—which is an offer I extend also to those students who managed a complete draft; the poem is not due until the next class, although I do not tell students that when the prompt is first given. I want the time crunch to be part of the initial challenge. Discussion for the last few minutes of the class, and most or all of the next class, can focus on issues of process, which in this case often involves the sheer challenge of completing the exercise:

- Which constraint was the most difficult to meet?
- Which words were most difficult to fit into the poem? Which were easiest?
- How many people wrote drafts in a linear fashion (beginning with the first word and moving line-by-line until the last word)?
- How many wrote in a non-linear fashion (beginning somewhere other than the poem's first word, perhaps writing in small "chunks" that had to be connected together later to make a whole draft)?

These discussions usually highlight something that has likely started to become obvious to students during the fiction exercise sequences: There is no single, universal "writing process" that works for everyone, all the time. Different people approach the same task differently, and sometimes the same writer needs to abandon a process that has worked in the past in order to face a new challenge. At the same time, students will often find that their processes are similar to those of *some* of their classmates, so that if writing processes do not follow a singular, universal set of rules, our attempts to step back and describe them may reveal recognizable patterns and possibilities.

After we have worked through a series of fiction *and* poetry exercises, I use a prompt that highlights *genre* as one of the choices students must make. Similar in some ways to the "Three Elements Story" prompt, this one specifically allows students to choose a genre, either at the beginning of the process or at some point during the first draft. The assignment instructions specifically state that the piece can be composed in any genre the student prefers: fiction, poetry, screenplay, song lyric, and the like. Here are the parameters:

1. The opening scene must take place on board a plane, bus, or train.
2. The piece must be narrated by someone much older, or much younger, than you currently are.
3. Someone in this piece should be looking for something (or someone) that has been "lost."
4. The color green must play a prominent role in this piece of writing.

As with most of the other exercise sequences, students begin this one during a class session, and are given one week to submit a draft. The follow-up discussion focuses primarily on what genres the students chose, and their reasons for doing so. These reasons are not always easy for students to articulate, and sometimes it is helpful to break students into small groups, based on the genres they chose, to discuss this issue for a while. Discussions around this exercise sequence often extend earlier discussions in interesting ways, layering in genre as one choice among other types of writerly choices with which students have previously struggled. I have often wondered what it might be like to begin the semester with a genre-optional exercise sequence, but have not yet done so.

Conclusion: In service of writing, in service of writers

The primary object of my introductory multigenre creative writing course is to offer students extensive practice in writing and a space in which to discuss issues that arise during the earliest (i.e., the inventional) stages of their writing processes. In that regard, the course differs from one of the most traditional models of creative writing workshop pedagogy in which the primary focus is on complete (though not "finished") drafts of individual student work. The course, then, operates in service to writing at least as much as it operates in service to writers, if not more so. The most important "work" of the course is shared and collaborative, undertaken in an environment of open-ended questioning.

Student resistance is an issue to be considered, since some students may arrive expecting the course to include some time specifically analyzing their own individual works. Some students may complain that the writing prompts are formulaic, or that they are not "creative," because they do not originate within their own minds, from the sources of their own "inspiration." (During the time in which I have structured my creative writing courses in the manner described in this chapter, I have been surprised by how few of my students have actually made this complaint, though it has arisen on two or three occasions.) This kind of resistance, I believe, offers a wonderful opportunity to discuss exactly what "creativity," "originality," and "inspiration" really are. Students protesting that the prompts are not "creative" enough might simply be asked, "What do you mean by *creative*?" And this question can be posed to the entire class. Discussion will likely reveal that students have differing ideas of what this key term means, and that can lead to discussion of what other terms relevant to creative writing tend to be contested. Students thus leave the course at the semester's end not only having written a great deal, but having also seen their writing practice generate theoretical discussions—and even, at times, arguments—about writing that will serve them well if they wish to continue writing on their own or in future creative writing courses.

Notes

1 For a more detailed description of the distinction between "creative writing" and "creative writing studies," see my 2009 *College English* article, "One Simple Word," *College English* 71(3): 217–28.

2 D. G. Myers's *The Elephants Teach* (Englewood Cliffs, NJ: Prentice Hall, 1996) is the standard history of creative writing in the United States; Stephen Wilbers's *The Iowa Writers' Workshop* (University of Iowa Press, 1980) provides a detailed look at the nation's most influential single MFA program.

3 Joseph Moxley, *Creative Writing in America: Theory and Pedagogy* (National Council of Teachers of English, 1989):xiii.

4 Bishop, Wendy, and Hans Ostrom. *Colors of a Different Horse: Rethinking Creative Writing Theory and Pedagogy* (Urbana, IL: NCTE, 1994).

5 In Bishop and Ostrom, *Colors of a Different Horse*, 3–7.

6 See, for example, Eve Shelnutt's "Notes from a Cell: Creative Writing Programs in Isolation," in *Creative Writing in America*, ed. Joseph M. Moxley (NCTE, 1989), 3–24.

7 LeFevre, *Invention as a Social Act* (National Council of Teachers of English, 1987), pp. 15–17.

8 My experience, in fact, is that these things are virtually impossible to ignore, as so many students' prior conceptions of what "creative writing" is are firmly rooted in individualist, even Romantic, presuppositions.

2

The Unworkshop

Graeme Harper

Destructive construct

A man walks into a bar. Hey, it happens! The bar is a social space, a construct, an assemblage, a community, a body politic. A man walks into a bar, and quietly joins a TV audience for basketball. A man walks into a bar and recognizes many of his friends already there. A man walks into a bar and meets his future life partner. A man walks into a bar and discusses political unrest. A man walks into a bar and is asked if he wishes to eat. A man walks into a bar and gets into a bar fight. A man walks into a bar, gets drunk, falls down, and appears to lose consciousness. Now he's both in the bar and not in the bar. His mind, his consciousness, his subconscious, his perspective is elsewhere. He's individualized the experience to such an extent that he has transcended it. Let's ignore his mode of transcendence for the moment. He is, we'd agree, not entirely there: he's in his own space and time, his world connected by mind and imagination to others but not completely to the spatiotemporal assemblage around him. There's an immediate tension in this. The social construct of the bar, while certainly engaging economically and socially with his mode of transmogrification, does not accept such a complete transcendence. It's a social faux pas. Some of the assembled are clearly thinking it's a travesty, even a kind of attack. "Had he done this at home, alone, it would be okay," says the bartender.

No workshop

A man walks into a creative writing workshop … The reader will recognize where I'm going with this.

Though I have regularly taught creative writing for some time now, I have not conducted a creative writing workshop for many years. I believe that creative writing is a transcendence. I therefore cannot impose an incongruous social construct on this transcendence for the purposes of matching the structural or systemic needs brought about by institutionalized education, yet not specifically related to the needs of each individual creative writer. Instead, for some time I have been subtly developing the unworkshop.

The unworkshop begins with the premise that a creative writer is such because she or he writes creatively; and so, at some point, each creative writer must write. It is informed by the idea that in writing creatively the creative writer takes action and joins up individual actions, and that these actions are informed by kinds of critical understanding drawn not from one disciplinary or epistemological perspective but most often from many. The unworkshop is creative writing focused and bears *only* the relationship with what some consider cognitive fields, such as literary study, critical theory, aesthetics, education or psychology, offer to the situation. The situation, that is, of writing creatively.

Situational understanding comes about by way of applying, evolving, responding, considering, and coping. It is a form of address to creative writing conditions, a mode of engaging a creative writer's natural human instincts of survival, an element of our life narratives whereby we draw upon understanding to respond or advance conditions of living. In other words, we face writing situations and we seek to overcome, engage with, benefit from, and employ tactics and skills that have the measure of those particular situations. To give a simple creative writing example, consider the circumstance in which a poet cannot find the best word or words to express an emotional state related to an observation about an annual town parade. Seeking to address this, the creative writer concludes that the celebratory nature of the parade could be related figuratively to other conditions of celebratory excess. Finding this response produces a pleasing result: they thus come to understand that figurative or metaphoric shifts in plane of reference can overcome the limitations of the literal, that productive dissonance might play a role in such overcoming, and that the effect of such an approach is to deepen a narrative of emotional engagement.

Situational understanding produces and develops what I have called "situational knowledge"[1]—knowledge drawn from empirical conditions and related to acts of creative writing that require address and resolution to reach a final satisfactory text. By "satisfactory text" I am referring to that text which the creative writer feels is in some way complete or successful for them, given also that creative writing is also communication and that they respond to, even if mostly implicitly in some instances, the notion that such a text might at some point find itself exchanged with a reader or audience.

The unworkshop combines explorations concerned with what the individual creative writer defines as successful or complete with questions about their purpose in writing creatively. It does not assume that every creative writer seeks the same thing in undertaking creative writing. Nor does it assume that a shared group or methodological holistic sense of achievement is the defining sense of achievement for all creative writers—this sense being one that prevails in the workshop. The unworkshop is responsive, individualized, contextualized, pragmatic yet engaged with ontological and epistemological variation. The result is that the majority of creative writers involved in unworkshop activity believe they have learnt something about creative writing, both their creative writing and creative writing generally, and that while on some measure the result of their creative writing might not match definitions of success offered by others, or preferred by others, the close association between their aspirations and the results of the unworkshop provide a platform on which their current and future creative writing can wonderfully build.

Entering the unworkshop

A woman, man, or child decides to participate in an unworkshop. This unworkshop is part of a program of study; alternatively, perhaps it is a free-standing activity, undertaken for any number of reasons. In either case, this unworkshop professor offers the student or students options.

While we might meet to discuss creative writing, the options could just as often include an individual meeting rather than a group one, attending a public event like a reading or screening, or some kind of social engagement. If there is conversation it is open, though the implicit purpose of the unworkshop launching is to consider what creative writing is for the individual creative writer and how the unworkshop might assist them in their goals and aspirations.

The construction of a curriculum in the unworkshop is synaptic—in other words, from conversation and direct individual interaction sparks of interest produce nodal possibilities that might lead to recommendations on compositional actions, textual examples (of emulation or comparative purposes), aesthetic or anthropological considerations, psychological or transcendental behaviors, and empirical or theoretical investigations. It might be that this unworkshop professor suggests a book of poems to read, or a novel to explore, but it could just as readily be that the suggestion is to take a trip downtown, or talk to family members or visit a factory or take a hike in the forest, or watch some TV or gather a group of colleagues or friends together and initiate a discussion or . . . .

The unworkshop is not a structural or systemic juggernaut. It does not seek to overwhelm by the size of its enterprise, group validity descending upon individual creative writing practice, or by basing judgments on the significance of success or failure (things along the lines of "B+ in this class would be a good result," or "Last semester around 50% of students maintained a GPA above 3.7," or "A good grade in this class is a prerequisite for proceeding further in the fiction concentration," or even "Failure or failing grade in this class can be used to create a strategy for future success."). The role of the unworkshop professor, who by virtue of the nature of the enterprise is a creative writer who has also engaged critically through research and through creative writing practice with the practice and understanding of creative writing, and thus has developed situational understanding and situational knowledge (albeit individually generated, for their own purposes) is not defined by pyramidal leadership concepts.

While it is true that the unworkshop professor operates in a leadership position, any unworkshop can be orchestrated according to its membership, whether that membership involves one person, several, or a great many, and the horizontal or complexity paradigm involved[2] encourages and supports interconnectivity, and authority based on knowledge, on sustainable value, and on sharing. The unworkshop does not assume rules; rather, it assumes networks and synapses. In other words, while compositional studies might suggest a rhetorical decree, a regimen or guidelines, the unworkshop, focused as it is on the actual individual acts and results of creative writing, suggests intrinsic and extrinsic value will be related to the creative writer's decisions on what is fit for purpose, as well as on an accompanying sense of what constitutes nodes of exchange. A node of exchange is a synaptic point in the network of activities where unworkshop professor and creative writer student have defined a goal or goals and how they will gauge progress toward these. To give an example, the unworkshop professor and the student determine that one goal will be to create resonance in an original work of creative nonfiction. This resonance will be reflective of the condition of uncertainty that is bound up as a theme in the subject of the creative nonfiction investigation. As the work evolves, both student and professor determine the extent to which an undertaking of resonance and modes of incorporating and advancing resonance are developing. Either in the completed piece of work and/or in drafts and responses to drafts and/or in discussions concerning situational understanding and the evolution of situational knowledge a sense of achievement toward this one goal is determined.

An unworkshop might have one or many goals or outcomes for the participant. No unworkshop will necessarily be like any other, even if it is located in institutional education where systems and structures demand such things as the use of a fixed number of weeks for study and the submission of grades. The unworkshop professor can also set out what they expect the outcomes in their case will be. Those outcomes might have direct pedagogic focus, they might be related to the mutuality of the learning relationship between professor and student or students, or they might be related to subject, themes, or practices that assist the professor to continue to grow their own situational knowledge. With synapses in mind, and the energy that such a cellular reference suggests, the unworkshop is a continuity where conjunctions occur whether socially or pedagogically and where the participant is in the position of student or teacher.

Tools of the unworkshop include conversation, visual or aural stimuli, experiential immersion in the form of participant observation, action research or similar techniques, the providing of textual examples (these texts might not necessarily be literary texts), and the use of contrasting representations in other fields of ideas being considered in creative writing (e.g., how does neuroscience consider the mechanism of human belief as opposed to philosophy's consideration of it? How does a cinematographer or set designer "compose" a scene?). The unworkshop operates on more than one plane of reference. Exploratory, organizational, and conjunctive metaphors provide further means of discovery here. Taking into account the relationship between synapses and memory, in terms of a key procedural metaphor the unworkshop seeks at its highest level of possibility evidence of parallelism (i.e., more than one person is seeking a solution to the same or similar situation or a same or similar situation is identified by more than one person and is being resolved in a variety of ways).

In a creative writing workshop a solution to any situational conundrum is most often resolved either by an agreed approach being superior, as determined by the workshop's group reaction, or by the workshop professor offering majority disciplinary opinion on the most likely solution, or by provision of examples of success based on extrinsic evidence (most often published work that is offered us as an exemplar of good practice even though it is not the actual practice but physical evidence of creative writing having occurred in the past). Contrastingly, in the unworkshop, situational understanding brought about by considering directly and indirectly related approaches—that is, both actions and ways of thinking—offers guidance to forming greater understanding. Any parallelism suggests possible cognitive bridges, even emotional or dispositional contexts, that enhance the potential success of a solution both in terms of the humanities generally and in terms of the communicative work of creative writing. Thus solutions in the creative writing unworkshop, while most certainly open to wider range of reference points for success, also have the potential to be deeper, more sustainable, and repeatable than those in the creative writing workshop.

Practicalities: Creative writing without borders

The unworkshop does not necessarily require a classroom—physical or virtual. Neither does it reject the use of such a physical or virtual space. All manifestations of the unworkshop are optional and all are open to interpretative application. It might be that you—as a creative writing professor—will schedule a space on campus, simply to have the option of using it. It could be that you provide a way of allowing students access to such a space and encourage them to consider its uses, if any.

Because experiential learning involves experiences, by definition, will you initiate or direct a student or students toward these experiences, and will they be entirely individualized based on your assessment of the student or students' needs? You might use a metonymic approach to this, using the activities of a street or a neighborhood or a city as a mode of experiencing aspects of greater life. Metonymy might be employed in other instances to provide experiences reduced in dimension but applicable to subject, theme, compositional conditions of structure, tone, address, and so forth.

The unworkshop, practically, requires choices in modes of interaction and connectivity. This means adopting an approach to participation that is open while using experience and comparative judgment to determine if an approach might work or is working. To explore this: one student joining the unworkshop would rather join it via email, visit you occasionally with work in progress, and attend the occasional social event with other unworkshop participants that semester. Later, elements of the student's understanding do not seem to be developing well, based on discussions and on work seen by you so far. The question becomes: how do you act responsibly in your role as teacher to improve the positive impact of the unworkshop? Several options open up: the use of the unworkshop cohort in some way to bring about peer learning (a technique drawn from the workshop model but not limited by its systemic rigidity); the suggestion of further experiential exploration to inform cognitive or imaginative growth; the direct presentation of related textual evidence, with the instruction to consider how it might have been brought about (again, a technique drawn from the workshop but not limited by suggestions of post hoc critical judgments prevailing, but simply by way of consideration of physical manifestations of technique); shadowing, or the provision of a one-to-one exploration of turning thoughts and feelings into text, working alongside the professor. These are just a few examples. Each consideration of what interactions, when, where, and how might produce best results relates the individualistic approach to the holistic, the action-based to writing results.

Procedurally, also, the unworkshop does not need to begin and end according to the timeframes established by formal education. In other words, while by the nature of much current education we seek to provide a platform for comparative judgment (i.e., one person's achievements in comparison to another, how far one person comes to understand something compared to another, how much someone achieves within a similar timeframe to that provided for another), the unworkshop can commence according to an agreement between professor and student as to what will be achieved with a timeframe, how that relates to situational understanding and situational knowledge, and to what extent that involves a manifestation of these things in completed creative texts and what might indeed be presented as evidence otherwise produced (so, e.g., the basic notion of draft materials or the less basic notion of critical materials produced and related to goals in a figurative, connective, or investigative manner).

Used in the unworkshop, visual, aural, and experiential stimuli can be presented in a variety of ways, and their impact recorded for future use by the participant either in a manner by which they can review how action and reaction were related or by the use of writing in the manner of a rehearsal of ideas and reactions in an alternative form to that used in creative writing or, indeed, directly into the production of a work or works of creative writing. This approach can be explicit or be implicitly manifest through a discussion between the student and the professor of themes and/or subjects and orchestrated to assist exploration of these specifically.

The unworkshop extols flexibility and is fit for purpose as core ideals—individualism being notable in any creative writer's practice and thinking—with consideration of the practice of creative writing and what might become of its results. With this in mind, the unworkshop professor can consider unworkshopping at a micro level and include in this consideration of such things as the use of mnemonics, so that the individual creative writing might improve their access to their situational knowledge, those mnemonics can be model based, so that methods of approach draw regularly on a set of conceived principles of action. Or they might be connection based so that what is learnt is reverse-engineered toward previous knowledge, both providing new insights and further enhancing previous ones. Other micro applications can include spatiotemporal changes in individual and/or group activities—for example, where a different location might be used to stimulate new ideas, or an alternative time for discussion can draw on the established intellective or psychical patterns and in this way stimulate newness. Further, the unworkshop (simply by the fact of education being delivered most often in group environments) can suggest group activities, and can stimulate thought on how events occur, how they are related to the creative writing of each likely participant, what role external involvement might undertake, whether closely monitored or less closely encouraged, and what ways in which a group event might bolster individual discussions and peer led activities, in whatever ways these are occurring.

Finally, to ground the unworkshop in direct evidence, two examples of students of mine who have emerged from the unworkshop are as follows: *Student A* joined the unworkshop in her senior year. She had an interest in writing fiction well, but was unmoved by literary studies discussions in formal English classes and felt restricted by what she thought of as conservative ideals associated with "reading like a writer," in the way these ideals were expressed in a workshop. Reminded that the construction of a curriculum in the unworkshop is synaptic—conversation and direct individual interaction producing nodal possibilities that might lead to recommendations on compositional actions, textual examples (of emulation or comparative purposes), aesthetic or anthropological considerations—*Student A* was encouraged to consider what it was that did motivate and excite her when she thought of creative writing. The answer was the pace and structure and aesthetic of television crime series. Her unworkshop activities thus included watching and analyzing television crime series, and mapping out what it was that made them work. Using this unworkshopping she went on to write, and discuss with the unworkshop leader, the nature of narrative and story as she discovered it, and to produce what was ultimately a published and, indeed, celebrated short story based on her new knowledge. She received for her creative writing one of the highest grades in her graduating group. *Student B*'s unworkshopping is more related to the fact that the unworkshop does not assume that every creative writer seeks the same thing in undertaking creative writing. Nor does unworkshop assume that a shared group or methodological holistic sense of achievement is the defining sense of achievement for all creative writers—this sense being one that prevails in the workshop. *Student B* was in his second year at college and wanted to explore creative writing because of his primary interest in psychology. He enjoyed writing both fiction and poetry but had no particular interest in being a published creative writer, or even being identified as a creative writer; he simply wanted to know more about creative writing, to be more skilled at it, and to relate doing it to what he was learning in the field of psychology. Because it was understanding of the human mind, its functions and behaviors, that was his primary interest, and creative writing was seen by him as something reflective of such things, he wanted to find ways of interacting with other creative writing students. With that aim, his unworkshopping included participating in small group discussions with other creative writing students around the subjects of form and structure and theme and subject and intention and meaning—concepts and physical attributes that others discussed with him and that he considered, and discussed, in relation to how they related to the activities of the mind. Ultimately, he produced both a range of poetry and prose fiction, while also taking to his psychology professors the idea that concepts and physical attributes seen in creative writing might offer insights into the relationships between human actions and the operations of the mind, and that his work as a psychologist might be further enhanced by embracing a sense of how observing action and analyzing physical evidence could represent certain definable activities of the mind.

Roll the unworkshop

The unworkshop is far more attuned to the networked synaptic post-digital world of the twenty-first century than the workshop can ever be, "post-digital" meaning here the social nodal world that has evolved from the initial impact of late twentieth-century digital technologies. If we accept that mass education is unlikely to become individualized in the near future, but that creative writing is frequently if not solely based in individualism, then we need to seek out ways of making our teaching productive in a learning context that does not favor the individual. The unworkshop does this, and it provides a better mode of engagement with the *actual* practices of creative writing than the workshop has done in the past, almost universally, and for some time. It is also, interestingly, more in tune with the social media practices of the majority of students arriving in higher education today, and it is considerably well placed to build on the strengths of individual creative writing teachers as well as to provide modes of strengthening those professors' own creative writing, their pedagogic inventiveness, and their connections with others who can become part of the creative writing teaching and learning experience. The unworkshop is an exciting social space, an individualized construct, a productive assemblage, a proactive community, a powerful body politic, and systemic evolutionary activity of our times and of our discipline. Roll on, the unworkshop!

Notes

1 For a discussion of situational knowledge see "Creative Writing Research" in *Key Issues in Creative Writing*, ed. Dianne Donnelly and Graeme Harper (Multilingual Matters: Bristol, 2012), 107.

2 Vlatka Hlupic offers further ideas about the "complexity paradigm" in *The Management Shift: How to Harness the Power of People and Transform Your Organization for Sustainable Success* (Palgrave: London, 2014), 22–3.

3

The Gum Beneath God's Shoe: A Testimony in Favor of the Sequence or Series Graduate Workshop

Derrick Harriell

In recent years I've been pleasantly surprised at the rising quality of poetry collections written by first time authors. Many of these collections contain the technical prowess of the writer who's already written that embarrassing first book. Young poets today are dedicated to pushing formal boundaries and eager to respond to our complicated political, social, cultural, and global concerns. In the last decade the number of traditional and low residency creative writing programs has risen. Additionally, social media has allowed for shop conversations to extend beyond the classroom and coffee shop. Online writing interactions transcend our geographical limitations. This has created an exciting climate for writing. Independent presses are more abundant and dedicated to publishing diverse voices. As a result, more poets are publishing books. As a teacher of creative writing and poetry it's important that I provide my students with the most effective tools to produce quality work. In particular, I want to ensure that my graduate students are able to examine the pragmatic function of the work they produce. This means considering how the work will exist beyond the workshop. It is not enough to simply workshop individual poems. Rather, we must think about the direction of our aesthetic and its connection to how the work is presented holistically. I spent very little time thinking about this as a graduate student. It was rarely emphasized in my graduate programs. So when Aquarius Press solicited a poetry manuscript from me, I was completely unprepared.

The opportunity to submit my collection came outside a Chicago hotel in 2009. It was the dead of winter, and I was a young writer who wanted to prove that all my years of schooling and writing had not been a waste. Snow covered the downtown Chicago streets and buried cars hummed in concert with streetlights. It was cold. It was Chicago cold. I was a fourth year doctoral student and had two remaining years of funding. I'd already completed a bachelor's and master of fine arts degree in creative writing but hadn't published much. For the majority of my cohort a collective paranoia hovered as we inched closer to the dreaded job market. They weren't giving tenure track jobs away. They especially weren't giving them to folks with minimal publications. We knew we needed books. We knew we needed books bad.

I don't remember the name of the Chicago hotel we stood outside of. I do remember talking to Randall Horton. Horton had recently solicited two of my poems. He worked as poetry editor for Aquarius Press and their new literary journal *Reverie.* I was completely enthralled when those poems were accepted because for some time I didn't believe anyone wanted the poems I wrote—and not because they weren't good—but because most journals weren't interested in the misogynistic voices of hustlers and pimps that I pursued. But Horton and the folks at *Reverie* saw beyond the mere tragedy of these voices and wanted to hear more about the soul of these personas and the spaces they represented. I'd been warned for quite some time that my poems might be difficult to place. Still, I found these voices worthy of exploration. They were the voices of men I'd known and worshipped growing up. These were stories of real and learned uncles.

Randall talked about his connection to the voices in my poems. He told me how these were men he'd also known. I felt validated because the poems did reach someone. This wasn't storage bin work but poems about people, places, and a subculture worthy of further investigation. Horton asked about the direction of a fuller body of work. "How does your larger manuscript read?" I highlighted a hopeful direction. I hadn't thought of my poems as connected. To me they were an amalgam of inspiring forces that shifted depending on the weather. If there were connections, they weren't deliberate. Randall said he'd love to see an entire manuscript, and told me Aquarius Press could be interested in publishing it. I told him I'd mail him a copy in the coming weeks. I left that conversation honored and floored and severely unprepared.

* * *

Four months after standing outside of that Chicago hotel, I found myself on my apartment floor doing that thing I was taught. I was told by more than one workshop instructor to "spread all of your poems on the floor and the order of your manuscript would come to you." I embraced this mysterious part of the process. It felt romantic. I felt like a real writer spreading out those ninety plus pages of poems. I threw poems in the air and made it rain poems. I placed ten-year-old poems next to ones I'd written a week ago and waited. I stared at them like some jigsaw puzzle and waited for something magical. I tried channeling all my poetic heroes and waited for divinity. I don't know who initially came up with the poems on the floor idea, but I embraced it. I thought of Randall's excitement when he said that Aquarius Press had a book division, Willow Books. This conversation happened after the one outside. It happened later on at the hotel bar. Chicago was hosting the annual Association of Writers and Writing Programs (AWP) Conference and writers and student writers moved with exuberance and intention. The bar was packed with writers and students of writing. Everyone seemed to be channeling their heroes, in search of opportunity the same way we were as kids walking our neighborhood.

Randall asked more questions about my imaginary manuscript. I wanted to tell him that I didn't have a manuscript because that was the truth. I had a bunch of poems I'd written in graduate school that had gone through workshop and revisions. I had a couple of poems that had been published in some measly online journals and one or two that had found a home in established literary journals. I didn't have a manuscript though. I wasn't even sure what the concept entailed. I knew I couldn't reveal this to Randall. I was taught not to pass up life altering opportunities, especially coming from where I'm from and the compromised streets of Milwaukee. We don't have the luxury to pass up opportunities. They may never come back around. I would figure it out, as I always had, as I always did.

All I ever wanted was to author a book of poems, and now Randall Horton and Aquarius Press was providing me the chance. When nothing happened as my poems lay on the living room floor, I began organizing them in the most logical narrative order. I assumed that at the very least, I would tell a story. Everyone loves a good story. But I found difficulty in creating a neat narrative; the poems I'd written years ago carried a distinctly different voice and tone than the recent ones. Furthermore, placing persona poems next to coming-of-age poems next to one-night-stand poems seemed impossible. But I tried. I tried making every "good" poem I'd written fit in a manuscript called *The Gum Beneath God's Shoe*.

During that spring of 2009 when Randall would call or email about *The Gum Beneath God's Shoe*, I responded with more excuses than a homeboy who owes you money. I'd either tell him I was still playing with order, or that there were a few poems that needed tweaking. The truth was that I hadn't forwarded the manuscript because I had very little confidence in those ninety pages. Even though I'd followed every piece of advice and gone over old workshop notes, something felt off. I did have enough pages for a poetry collection, but I didn't have a book. I felt it. I spent weeks combing through celebrated poetry collections for clues. I consulted past professors and peers who'd advise me to spread the poems on the floor. Finally, after months of staring at poems on the floor, and writing last-minute ones, I drove to FedEx and bound two copies of *The Gum Beneath God's Shoe*. Somehow within the chaos of my uncertainty, I'd accepted the book for what it was. I convinced myself that it was a good book; no, I convinced myself it was a great book. I mailed and accompanied Randall's copy with a note: "This book goes good with bourbon." I spent days reading through the pages of the copy I'd bound for myself. I'd written an exceptional first book.

When weeks went by and I hadn't heard from Horton, I didn't worry. I figured he'd been moving slowly through the manuscript and all of its brilliance. It takes time to get through that kind of genius. I understood. In the interim, I purchased a bottle of relatively expensive scotch and awaited the pending affirmation. I figured it'd go something like this: Horton would call, and I'd play modest as he shouted superlatives about my book. We'd share our favorite moments and begin discussing potential publishing dates and cover ideas. He'd tell me the book would ensure me a tenure track job. It would be a coronation. I waited.

It was summer when Randall finally called. It'd been weeks since I'd sent the manuscript. I was ready for the coronation and eagerly stared at the caller ID; however, Horton's tone was not one of elation. He thanked me for sending the manuscript and said there were good moments. He spoke glowingly about the poems that reflected those that *Reverie* had published. I paid attention to the holes in our conversation. This wasn't how I assumed coronations were supposed to go. I asked about a publication date for the collection. He paused.

In most of my graduate poetry workshops, during the last week of class, the instructor would go over final manuscript requirements. Usually this meant revisions of eight to twelve pages of poetry. In most workshops there was typically a variation of themed and non-themed assignments. For example, one week we'd turn in a persona poem and then a free form poem the following week. We rarely discussed how these assignments were related or their significance on the course schedule. We rarely built toward a final manuscript. In determining manuscript order, we were told to either spread the poems on the floor or arrange them thematically. I usually placed poems arbitrarily. When I collected my manuscripts post-semester, instructor comments normally emphasized line edits and technical stuff (e.g., how imagery could be worked with, where a long stanza could be broken, etc.). While these comments helped me become a better writer, they didn't assist me in becoming a more effective assessor of my work holistically—didn't help me see, as Robert Frost suggests, the book—or manuscript in this case—as the final poem. My graduate poetry workshops hadn't trained me to discuss the macro function of poems.

Before Horton answered my question about a publication date for *The Gum Beneath God's Shoe*, he asked about the process in determining order. I told him what I did. He then asked about the different creative periods the poems had been written. I responded. He lastly questioned the overall scope of the manuscript, "What are you trying to say to my reader?" I didn't know how to answer that. I had no idea. While I could discuss a micro ambition for each poem, the manuscript had no deliberate macro direction—by macro I mean a stepping out of the smaller concerns of individual poems and evaluating the collection as one singular piece of art and the impression it leaves on the reader holistically. You may want to think about a favorite album, especially concept albums, and how they sometimes feel like one long song; or, how a collection of songs might leave one lasting impression. I often think of D'Angelo's *Voodoo* or Marvin Gaye's *Here, My Dear* as examples of tightly crafted bodies of music.

After some skating around Horton's question, he eventually said, "Look, we're going to publish the book, don't worry about that. The problem is you have two or three books here, and right now, we need to figure out a way to focus on just one." While I wasn't prepared to hear this and it began the shattering of my pretty coronation, it made sense. There existed several possible collections in those ninety some-odd pages I'd handed over. We talked more about the poems *Reverie* had published and those in the manuscript that mirrored that direction. We talked for over an hour about major and minor characters, temporal and narrative arcs. We discussed personas and some that could and should invade the landscape. We began unearthing a vision and a possible real book from those ninety pages.

Once Randall and I ended our call, I reflected for hours on what had just occurred: our conversation, the ruins of what I'd previously thought was an excellent first collection, the work that lay ahead of me. I remember thinking to myself, what if Randall hadn't been gracious? What if my manuscript was being read by some editor who had no stake in the work? I was embarrassed I'd submitted such mess. I thought about the ten or more graduate workshops I'd had a seat in and wondered about the "putting your manuscript together" workshop. How come in all my years of graduate school I never had the "putting your manuscript together" workshop? How come none of my graduate workshops explicitly placed emphasis on the macro? In that moment I knew exactly the kind of poetry graduate workshop I'd teach if I was someday fortunate enough to. I'd teach the "putting your manuscript together" workshop.

* * *

I began fleshing out my graduate poetry workshop in the fall of 2012. I was in an Oxford bar brainstorming with some of our MFA poetry students. It was my first year working as an assistant professor of English and African American Studies at the University of Mississippi. I'd finally landed one of those tenure track jobs. I was scheduled to teach my first graduate workshop in the spring. I can't lie, I was nervous about it all. Just two years ago I'd been a student in a graduate workshop. Just a year ago I'd been finishing a dissertation. I wanted to bring my student experience to the classroom. I felt connected to our MFA students. Their experiences were still fresh for me. I made sure to remember and reconsider not only the components I found productive, but to also underscore those things that were missing. I wanted to create a workshop that focused on the sequence and series without completely abandoning craft. How could we discuss manuscript composition and line breaks? In addition to these questions, I wondered if students would find it a valuable class.

At the bar I asked the students if a workshop emphasizing the macro sounded like something beneficial. They shared stories about the traditional workshop (where every student workshops his or her poems in each class meeting) and how it often felt rushed for them. They discussed the time constraints that usually amounted in an unproductive experience: ten students, two and a half hours, fifteen-minute break, ten to twelve minutes spent on each student's work. Oftentimes, once we become familiar with a writer and her work, it's reactionary to situate old tendencies against new work. Meaning, more times than not aesthetic connections and trend observations will naturally occur (e.g., "this reminds me of that one line in your other poem we workshopped"). Rather intentional or not, the workshop wants to evolve the work of its writers. The time restraints associated with traditional workshops can undermine this.

As the students and I further brainstormed a macro workshop, we agreed that limiting the number of workshopped writers each class would alleviate the rushed sensation. If the workshop required students to submit six to eight pages of poetry, then each class could only highlight a few students. We found this a productive obstacle, a way to have fewer writers but more work discussed. And while this wouldn't allow students to have poems workshopped weekly, it would allow for a more full and holistic commentary. Students would receive more recommendations on the overall scope of their work: where it's been, where it is, where it's headed. MFA poetry students in most academic programs are required to submit a thesis of forty-eight to sixty pages before graduating. How do we expect them to successfully organize these theses without training? While I do believe some of this work can be accomplished through the direction of thesis advisors, a workshop placing emphasis on the macro is more useful for all students.

The morning after our conversation, I started developing a course description and framework. I knew the idea could fall flat, and perhaps that was the reason I hadn't seen it done. A macro poetry workshop seemed obvious and I couldn't have been the first person to think of it. I'd taken a lot of workshops, but none focused on sequence or series. Perhaps this was already happening at other universities. I found no peers or colleagues who either taught or was taught in a workshop of this kind. These sequences or series would be minor projects and connected. Students wouldn't have the luxury to write individually unconnected poems. At the outset of the semester, a brief essay explaining their aesthetic and the direction of their work would be handed in; afterwards, they'd propose a project for the semester in which a common idea, aesthetic, direction, or ethos would be pursued. And to avoid completely pigeonholing students, I decided to allow for slight deviations if they could articulate its utility.

Two student writers would be workshopped each class. Given that thirteen of our class meetings would be dedicated to workshop, each student writer would be workshopped twice. And while this initially sounded like a low number, each student writer would have the same total number of pages discussed as in a more traditional workshop (12–16). I decided to invite student commenters to make additional mechanical comments, but the bulk of our class discussion would be dedicated to larger concepts like arcs, patterns, voice, consistency, direction, major and minor characters, and the like. Additionally, we would speculate what preceding and proceeding poems could and should look like. To this end the workshop would have a conceptual function, a tool for the student writer post workshop. In my student experience, once the workshop was over, all I was left with was a bunch of revised poems and nothing more to explicitly think about. In thinking about things like unwritten or possible poems, the student gets to reflect directions for their larger manuscript, or work-in-progress graduate thesis.

* * *

I taught my first macro workshop in the spring of 2013, and again a year later. Each time I've been thrilled by how productive they have been. The emphasis on only two students for each class has proved extremely beneficial. Poetry students aren't normally used to having a full hour that has allowed for more nuanced aspects of their work to be discussed and evaluated. One of the most effective ways for my students to think about the series or sequence has been through the use of the music metaphor: what's your favorite album and why, what kind of work does each song do, what's the function of interludes or background noise. It's helped my students gain a firmer handle on their aesthetic tendencies and direction. I've introduced Katrina Vandenberg's essay "Putting Your Poetry in Order: The Mix-Tape Strategy" to my classes, in which she compares the organizing of a poetry manuscript to that of a mix-tape and the various connections between the two. Vandenberg says, "[o]rdering poems becomes a familiar act if you consider the lyric poem in its original form—the song."[1]

In the two times I've taught the class, the majority of my students have celebrated its usefulness. To this end, several students have gone on to have fuller versions of their class writings accepted by credible poetry presses. One of the misconceptions I've made clear when I've taught the workshop is the idea that narrative poems or a neat narrative order are the priority. Rather, the goal is to simply consider the larger practical function of the poems. Many of my students have been self-proclaimed elliptical poets wanting nothing to do with narrative. In these cases our conversations have dealt with symbolism, images, voice, themes, and the like.

* * *

The Gum Beneath God's Shoe was never published. One third of the manuscript was pulled and carefully worked with. New voices and subworlds were pursued and a family tree investigated. It became personal work. Additional layers of aunts and uncles were unearthed and the aftermath dealt with. Putting the manuscript together eventually turned into something rewarding. I began to revel in organizing as much as writing and became obsessed with themes and subthemes and arcs and sub-arcs, and getting rid of superfluous pages. This was its own master class. The collection would become my first, *Cotton*. In 2011, I started working on a second collection. Ironically, the seed for this collection was also planted in *The Gum Beneath God's Shoe*. Among those pimp and hustler poems had been Jack Johnson persona poems. Horton recognized those poems as a separate body of work. While moving through this manuscript, I was able to anticipate mistakes. Experiencing the bumps and embarrassment of the first manuscript allowed for a more concentrated focus. Organizing the new collection was similar to putting together a familiar puzzle. I realized a body of work has a pulse; it's our jobs to locate it. I didn't spread my poems on the floor this time. I never needed to. I'd been so obsessed with order that most of the poems were placed before they were written. The last poem had a home before I'd written the first word. The framework and structure of the manuscript had been exhaustedly deliberate. Aquarius Press-Willow Books would publish my second collection, *Ropes*, as well. *Ropes* would go on to be acknowledged by the Mississippi Institute of Arts and Letters as the 2014 poetry book of the year. Regarding her decision to choose *Ropes*, judge and acclaimed poet Sandra Beasley wrote, "*Ropes* uses a smart structure of four 'rounds,' staged in reverse chronological order, to embrace the spectacle of Mike Tyson and then to track the boxing tradition back to Jack Johnson, the first black heavyweight champion." The inception of how these poems would be structured or arranged was a result of previous failure.

While I do believe that the more traditional workshop model has its merits, I think it's important that as teachers of poetry we consider alternative approaches: especially as it relates to graduate workshops. I'm sure most programs and or graduate workshops may inadvertently place an emphasis on the macro, but a more directive and explicit weight will likely have a more profound impact. If nothing else, it will create a climate for fresh discourse and offer the students a new way of approaching the larger pulse of their work. I can't say I know for sure that without my workshop those students would not have gone on to have their first books accepted by credible presses anyway. I can say that those collections did begin and grow out of our workshop. In a time of such talented young writers publishing such glowing first collections, I'm interested and dedicated to providing my students with as many skills as possible to produce the highest quality work. I'm additionally dedicated to making sure I'm transparent with them in all the ways they can learn from my previous shortcomings and failed manuscripts like *The Gum Beneath God's Shoe.*

Note

1 Katrina Vandenberg, "Putting Your Poetry in Order: The Mix-Tape Strategy," *Poets and Writers* (May/June, 2008).

Part Two

Expanding Genre

4

The Empathy Project: A Research Assignment for Fiction Writing Students

Rachel Haley Himmelheber

I have always felt that the most crucial nontechnical skill for a fiction writer is empathy.[1] To tell a story is to rigorously and generously imagine what it is like to be someone else, and the employment of that rigorous, generous imagination depends on empathy. To skillfully imagine the particulars of being "someone else" is essential; after all, in fiction, the point of view *is* the story. But how do student writers loosen the grip of their own perspectives, their life experiences, and their values to empathize with and inhabit their characters?

And are there not many, many barriers to empathy that frequently impede us all? A small sampling of barriers to empathy might include our own idiosyncratic ethics and values, our prejudices and privileges, our values surrounding language, our culture, our social identities, and even our sense of loyalty. How might we anticipate and resist some of those barriers if we choose to focus on empathic development?

While some still conceptualize empathy as a natural and instinctive trait, social scientists and neuroscientists increasingly believe empathy is a developmental process. As a developmental process, it can be learned—and taught. Even in brains with deficiencies in empathic responses, such as people with neuroatypicalities like autism, there are behavioral and cognitive therapies that may help people compensate for these difficulties and find alternate ways to develop their own senses of empathy. Recent news stories cite studies that link reading literary fiction with increased empathy. I began to wonder how fiction writers interact with empathy. What might support writers who are working to develop empathy for their characters?

I considered these and other questions for several years before I incorporated a research project called The Empathy Project into my undergraduate introductory fiction writing course. This assignment aims to help students accomplish three goals: to research an identity that feels other as a purposeful means to develop more empathy for that identity, to have that research impact the student writer's process of characterization, and to introduce or reinforce an academically unconventional research process fiction writers employ. It is also meant to serve as a means for student fiction writers to articulate, validate, question, and begin to formalize an empathic process that will serve their fiction writing far past the assignment.

As part of their participation in this research assignment, students completed readings, writing exercises, and discussions chosen to highlight some aspect of empathic development or empathic barrier. They each chose an identity to research that corresponded with a way one of their characters identified but which was a difficult identity for the writer to feel empathy; then they researched this identity from a variety of angles and using a variety of academically conventional and unconventional methods. Fiction-writer research is a meandering form of inquiry. It is not bound to peer-reviewed sources or some static sense of reliability; in fact, sometimes the best sources are highly unreliable, totally opinionated, first-person accounts such as blogs, messages on message boards, comments in an article, or social media postings. For the fiction writer researcher, "anecdotal" ought never be preceded by "merely." My students' goal is not to find answers or formulate taut opinions, as it can be with a traditional research project. The goal is to discover more questions. The goal is to have more awareness of how vast any individual identity is and to acknowledge how much one does not know about it. The goal is to get really fascinated with imagining what it is like to be this other. The final product is a narrative research essay tracking what they discovered in their research processes and reflecting on its efficacy in their characterization process and in their own process of empathic development. While I do require my students to cite at least one peer-reviewed or otherwise traditionally scholarly source, they are also required to cite at least one first-person account. Their remaining sources can be conventional or unconventional.

The creative writing classroom, as an inherently interdisciplinary space, is open to incorporating social science and neuroscience findings, and I have found such sources helpful in convincing some students at the beginning of this project that empathic development is both possible and measurable. Recent studies in social science and neuroscience concerning empathy have received a lot of mainstream media attention and have clear implications for the creative writing classroom. A study from a group of researchers at Mount Sinai School of Medicine in New York, published in the September 2012 volume of *Brain*,[2] demonstrates that the anterior insular cortex is where feelings of empathy originate in the brain. This study has major implications for people with neuroatypicalities like autism who have deficits in empathetic response. Another study published in the December 2013 volume of *Brain Connectivity*[3] showed that reading literary fiction improves people's ability to empathize with others and is thus a factor in supporting prosocial behaviors. Supporting prosocial behaviors and writing better characters are not at odds, although it can be uncomfortable for some creative writing teachers to align themselves with any activity perceived as holding primarily therapeutic or moral value.[4]

While some in creative writing may want to emphasize writerly rather than social or ethical development, the whole-person(al) aspect of empathic development does align with the origins of creative writing as an academic discipline. In *Negotiating the Personal in Creative Writing*, Carl Vandermeulen concedes that "concern for the becoming of persons characterizes composition more than creative writing," but notes that "a concern for the growth of persons was a generative force in creative writing" and cites Paul Dawson's work that asserts that "creative writing got its start, at least in the schools, because doing artistic work was believed to be good for learners, not because of a perceived need to help outstanding writers become published authors."[5]

My pedagogy is a feminist one, and so the research project's central tenet—that the goal of this research process is to develop questions rather than answers—aligns with my pedagogy and decenters many forms of authority, including the authority of sources that are conventionally included in academic research. My students cite online journalism, and they also cite the sometimes inflammatory and bigoted comments below the article. The project values first-person accounts as much as it values peer-reviewed scholarship. As Pamela

Annas and Joyce Peseroff note in "A Feminist Approach to Creative Writing Pedagogy,"

> It is important to keep in mind that what feminist and other radical approaches to teaching writing have at their center is a combination of inclusion and disruption—to *include* a multiplicity of ways of seeing and saying from a multiplicity of experiences and to *disrupt* a hegemonic, or prevailing systemic, ruling class discourse and world view.[6]

Nisi Shawl and Cynthia Ward's *Writing the Other: A Practical Approach*[7] can be seen as a seminal text in the underdeveloped field of research-based empathic development for fiction writers. In the chapter "Beautiful Strangers: Transracial Writing for the Sincere," which I have my students read and discuss, Nisi Shawl affirms the research-based approach in a feminist pedagogy and counsels writers who want "to go beyond the level of just assigning different skin tones and heritages to random characters" to do research "[b]ecause yes, all people are the same, but they're also quite different."[8] Shawl recommends including general reading in this research process but advises writers to "use as many primary sources as possible."[9] Using primary sources may help disrupt stereotypes the writer may have encountered. Shawl reminds writers that "black people don't spend their whole lives thinking of themselves as black. We're Ghanaians and editors and diabetics, and lots of other –ians and –ors and –ics."[10] Shawl's chapter "Appropriate Cultural Appropriation" also offers lessons for the writer interested in an unfamiliar identity. She discusses larger issues like the dangers of exoticism and offers specific advice about craft choices such as using dialect. Shawl tells writers "to be honest about the fact that [they're] outsiders" and ask for help but also cautions that "all transcultural writers can hope for is understanding and acceptance by readers in general and by individual members of the culture they're attempting to represent in particular."[11]

In summary, neuroscience and social science researchers have made recent discoveries about empathy that impact creative writing. A feminist pedagogy welcomes the sort of inquiry my research project undertakes, especially in its ability to disrupt hegemonic sources of knowledge, and there is support with creative writing's academic origins for a pedagogy that takes the whole person into account. And while there are some extraordinary how-to manuals that discuss writing about other identities, there is an opportunity in creative writing pedagogy for research-based investigation into best practices for facilitating empathic development in a fiction writing course. After noticing patterns and themes emerge during my teaching of six previous iterations of this project, I decided to formalize my inquiry into a research study. This chapter tracks some selected themes from data I gathered during this pilot study, which involved six students who focused their various empathy project research on a wide range of identities: burn victims/survivors; morticians; prostitutes; Shintoists; spiritualists/mediums; and the American painter Andrew Wyeth. Each student had a character she was writing who somehow aligned with the identity they chose to research. (In the case of Andrew Wyeth, the student was writing a counterfactual fictional narrative with Wyeth as a central fiber.) For the purposes of this chapter, I will offer some abbreviated findings using selected pre- and posttest material of two student writers.

For this pilot study, I used a narrative pretest/posttest to capture data. The pretest was administered at the start of students' research process, and the posttest was administered after the projects were complete. Before answering the posttest questions, students had about an hour to complete a writing exercise that focused on the character they created using the identity from their research. My analysis process included an iterative reading of the data, and I began initial coding as patterns emerged.[12] I coded different portions of student reportage into groups. Within these codes, I was able to construct themes that will help me as I assess the assignment's efficacy and refine its presentation.

My data demonstrated that the students in this pilot group found the process of this research assignment effective for increasing their empathy for their chosen identity. In the posttests, students unanimously indicated they felt a greater sense of empathy than they did before they started their research. Five out of six students indicated their research had helped their final in-class drafting exercise, and all six students indicated that their research had helped them as they drafted their character and story outside of class.

In their pretests, students discussed why they chose their research topic. Two themes I identified had to do with a lack of personal experience with the identity or the identity's markers (traits or details within the identity) and with perceived distance from their own identity to the identity they would research. For example, student one, whose research centered on burn survivors, wrote: "I chose my topic because I have a character who is a burn survivor and I want to be able to write him better. [It's difficult for me to have empathy for this identity] because I've never had a severe burn and I don't have any debilitating or noticeable scars." And student two, whose research centered on the painter Andrew Wyeth, emphasized identity differences but also noted one common aspect of identity between the artist and herself: "I'm not an artist, a man, or any of the things/stereotypes of Wyeth, but he's supposedly quiet and aloof, which I can empathize with." Student two also noted other distances from Wyeth, including lack of familiarity with places where Wyeth lived (Maine, Pennsylvania), and included specific research about these places as part of the research plan.

Another theme I tracked in the pretest was the theme of cultural context and prejudices. Students discussed negative cultural connotations to this identity, stereotypes of this identity, or feelings of disgust or contempt for identity (markers). For example, student one noted that it might be difficult to have empathy for burn survivors because people may be "put off by a [survivor's] appearance." This student's research strategy included drawing her character and looking at photographs of burn survivors as a way to resist this negative response.

In the posttest, students cite specific examples from the research process that proved helpful to their empathic development. These responses are crucial to understanding which strategies or interventions worked in my pilot group so that I can continue to revise and refine this project. In these answers, students indicated what helped aid authentic, confident, knowledgeable characterization. Multiple themes emerged: factual knowledge, cultural stereotypes or connotations challenged, and ability to interact in some way with identity/use of first-person accounts.

The first theme in these responses is that of factual knowledge. Students cited facts they did not know before they began their research, and they explained how these facts aided confidence, detail, and discovery in their characterization process. Student one wrote: "One of the most helpful sources for me was the Phoenix-Society website. Phoenix Society is a national support group for burn survivors, and I found their forums particularly helpful in bringing up things I never would have thought of on my own such as scar itching and nerve damage. One of the most surprising things I learned was that burn survivors have difficulties with temperature control due to an inability to sweat from any regions of grafted skin." Student two, who had been concerned about her lack of knowledge about Maine and Pennsylvania, two states in which Wyeth lived, also noted that biographies of Wyeth provided "context and background to further develop [the character]."

Another way I categorized student responses in the posttest was within the theme of cultural stereotypes or connotations challenged. Student one described a particularly intense experience of this theme: "I think it's one thing to read about burn survivors like Labonya Siddiqui and Kim Phuc, but it's another thing entirely to see the person beyond the story of their burns. I think these articles [focusing on the identity of burn survivors] certainly serve a purpose as a jumping off point for people seeking to gain more empathy for this identity, but the articles are written with a particular purpose in mind and will almost always seek to show the individual in a good light and will focus on a very specific aspect of their life. This isn't a bad thing, but it doesn't give a full picture. I found that Tumblr actually offered one of the best windows into this identity. There would be maybe one or two entries by one user that were actually about their experience as a burn survivor, but the rest of the things I found scrolling through this blog would be just things they liked and cared about. A lot of it was stuff I loved too, and that made them instantly more relatable as people. Even though most of their content had nothing to do with being a burn survivor, I felt it was an important part of my own building empathy."

Two student responses were categorized within the theme of ability to interact in some way with someone with this identity (first-person accounts). Student two found this perspective beneficial: "Autobiographies and biographies of Andrew Wyeth helped me in that they provided both factual information and first-person accounts. The factual information didn't help me develop empathy as much as reading Wyeth's own thoughts did. … First person accounts were more helpful." Student two also noted in her pretest that part of her usual process of creation involves taking on a role: "It helps me to assume their character … to go about my business as that character, both mentally and physically. This allows me to feel, perceive, interact, etc. in the way that they might." In the posttest, she returned to this idea of assuming the identity in her interest in Wyeth's work and how it was made: "Examining the paintings also helped me a lot."

The posttest's final question asked students to consider what they learned that might help others develop more empathy. Four themes, all of which have corollary to the previous posttest and pretest questions' themes, emerged. These themes are as follows: factual information; cultural stereotypes, prejudices, or negative connotations challenged; the ability to interact in some way with someone with this identity/first-person accounts; and connections from researched identity to identities writer holds. Students one and two both demonstrated these four themes in their responses to the pre- and posttests. These themes represent how these six students were able to engage meaningfully with the project, and as I continue to reflect upon and research best practices in this assignment, I will consider how I might best emphasize and support these themes.

Because this pilot study was the seventh iteration of my teaching this assignment, I have had the opportunity to develop many teaching strategies designed to allow students to debrief during the research process and to engage in some meta-analysis of the project structure itself. For example, I have a large list of curated texts (articles, videos, speeches) available for this project. I largely allow identified need in the classroom to dictate which texts we will study that semester. If students articulate a good understanding of the concept of privilege, we skip some of those readings. If they do not, we concentrate on the concept more.

David Foster Wallace's 2005 commencement speech at Kenyon College is one reading and discussion assignment that is a part of my empathy project and which could be usefully adapted for fiction writing teachers wishing to incorporate some discussion of empathy and what I term "imaginative research." The speech went viral after Wallace committed suicide in 2008 and it was made into a book, and so the speech is now sometimes derided as a treacly entreaty to be a nicer human being. But that is a misreading of this text, which is actually a vigorous plea to resist barriers to empathy and to rigorously consider generous interpretations of others. It is a plea from a fiction writer using the principles of imagination and empathy.

In class, we listen to the speech while we read the text. (Both are easy to locate online.) We then have a discussion and a writing exercise that responds to its ideas.

In this speech, Wallace asks us to consider multiple obnoxious identities he encounters during a hypothetical trip to the grocery store. He admits he could be "angry and disgusted at all the huge, stupid, lane-blocking SUVs and Hummers and V-12 pickup trucks burning their wasteful, selfish, forty-gallon tanks of gas," but he could also imagine and consider other possibilities, no matter how unlikely: "It's not impossible that some of these people in SUVs have been in horrible auto accidents in the past and now find driving so traumatic that their therapist has all but ordered them to get a huge, heavy SUV so they can feel safe enough to drive; or that the Hummer that just cut me off is maybe being driven by a father whose little child is hurt or sick in the seat next to him, and he's trying to rush to the hospital, and he's in a way bigger, more legitimate hurry than I am—it is actually *I* who am in *his* way."

Wallace details several such mental exercises, all involving imagining someone (creating a character) in order to gain more empathy or even sympathy. Wallace wants us to offer our own sense of frustration and annoyance as a mirror: I am in a hurry, so I imagine the SUV driver's hurry. Wallace's exercise here can be interpreted as a way to activate your mirror neurons, the cells that activate when you witness someone else performing a similar action to our own.[13] Here, the "action" is in our imaginations. What Wallace does not do is reverse the exercise. His mental gymnastics serve as a way to see some of the self in the other: My self is in a hurry, and annoyed, so now I will imagine the other as in a hurry, and annoyed. I tell my students that Wallace has given us only half of the equation, that true empathy depends on also seeing the other in the self, including, perhaps especially, seeing the uglier parts. Wallace gives the SUV driver a sick child or a traumatic accident as a way to humanize and bring the other closer, but where does he locate in the self his own wasteful, selfish, gas-guzzler? Much of my students' projects depend on research outside the self, but interior examination is equally important.

After listening to and discussing the speech, I offer my students a writing exercise that enacts these two directions of empathic imagining and it is an easy one for them to adapt or replicate and repeat on their own. The exercise asks them to fictionalize an encounter with someone who offended them with speech or actions. They write the scene from their own offended perspective and then I have them switch the point of view and attempt to find nuance in and connection with the offense without changing any content of the encounter. I tell my students that this simple writing exercise is akin to lifting reps in the gym or playing scales on the piano: it strengthens your empathic ability as you jump back and forth from other to self, self to other.

Notes

1 "Empathy" is denotationally distinct from "sympathy" and "compassion," two terms with which it is often conflated colloquially. Parsing these terms and discussing their etymologies are among the first discussions I have with my students during this project. I also find it useful to offer some context for affective empathy and cognitive empathy. See Simone Shamay-Tsoory, Judith Aharon-Peretz, and Daniella Perry, "Two Systems for Empathy: A Double Dissociation between Emotional and Cognitive Empathy in Inferior Frontal Gyrus versus Ventromedial Prefrontal Lesions," *Brain* 132.3 (2009): 617–27.

2 Xiaosi Gu, Zhixian Gao, Xingchao Wang, Xun Liu, Robert Knight, Patrick Hof, and Jin Fan, "Anterior Insular Cortex Is Necessary for Empathetic Pain Perception," *Brain* 135.9 (2012): 2726–35.

3 Gregory Berns, Kristina Blaine, Michael Prietula, and Brandon Pye, "Short- and Long Term Effects of a Novel on Connectivity in the Brain," *Brain Connectivity* 3.6 (2013): 590–600.

4 Of course, there are benefits to empathic development to one's whole person and not only to one's fiction writing. A thorough discussion of the complexities inherent to this issue is not within the scope of this chapter, but I will briefly outline some broad considerations. Some teachers who facilitate this type of project will want to incorporate more emphasis on wellness, personal growth, and/or social justice and activism. This attention to ethical development in the person is a valid teaching goal and not mutually exclusive from growth as a student writer. If a writer becomes more empathic and thus perhaps even more compassionate, might her themes then become more complex, might the psychology of her characters deepen, might her attention to the details of the fictional world sharpen and become more sensitive? The pedagogical stance involved in attempting to explicitly facilitate development in the person is not without its risks though. For example, as a female-bodied teacher who presents as feminine and who teaches in a highly feminized field such as creative writing, the risks to perception of my coursework as soft, emotional, New Age-y, anti-intellectual, or not rigorous are great. How much time a teacher allots to such a project also results in constraints, as does the expertise level of the students. Some teachers will be more cautious than others about boundaries with students, and some will find it ethically distasteful to play the role of facilitator of personal growth.

5 Carl Vandermeulen, *Negotiating the Personal in Creative Writing* (Bristol: Multilingual Matters, 2011).
6 Pamela Annas and Joyce Peseroff, "A Feminist Approach to Creative Writing Pedagogy," in *Creative Writing Pedagogies for the Twenty-First Century*, ed. Alexandria Peary and Tom C. Hunley (Carbondale: Southern Illinois UP, 2015), 78–101.
7 Nisi Shawl, "Appropriate Cultural Appropriation," in *Writing the Other: A Practical Approach*, ed. Nisi Shawl and Cynthia Ward (Seattle: Aqueduct Press, 2005), 75–84.
8 Ibid., 76.
9 Ibid., 77.
10 Ibid., 83.
11 Ibid., 90–1.
12 Kathy Charmaz, *Constructing Grounded Theory* (Los Angeles: Sage Publications, 2014); Xiaosi Gu et al., "Anterior Insular Cortex."
13 V. S. Ramachandran, *The Tell-Tale Brain: A Neuroscientist's Quest for What Makes Us Human* (New York: W.W. Norton, 2011).

5

Musico-Literary Miscegenations: Word and Sound Relationships in Creative Writing Pedagogy

Hazel Smith

Since 2012 I have been teaching an evolving postgraduate unit about the contemporary literature–music relationship. The unit is part of a Master of Arts (MA) in Literature and Creative Writing based in the Writing and Society Research Centre at Western Sydney University. Generically called "Sounds, Images, Texts" for administrative purposes, it actually focuses on relationships between literature and music, words and sound in contemporary literature and experimental intermedia. The unit is unusual in that it concentrates on the intermedia relationship as the basis for both literary studies and creative writing. In addition, the unit has a strong critical and theoretical basis, it does not revolve (as many creative writing subjects do) around creative writing exercises (though such exercises are included), and the creative writing aspect of the unit is gradually evolving. The unit is based on the model of a one-hour lecture, followed by two hours of discussion and workshopping. It introduces students to the various ways in which sound and music can impact on literature and on their own creative writing. In addition, it demonstrates how word–sound relationships can facilitate ideas about disability, gender, and ethnicity.

The unit relies on the idea that most people enjoy and are responsive to some form of music, whether it is classical, popular, folk, or jazz, and therefore will be able to engage with the issues raised. The students do not have to have any musical expertise to take the unit, though clearly it is an advantage if they do. On the whole I have not found lack of musical expertise on the part of the students to be an overriding disadvantage. The music included in the unit ranges from classical music to contemporary music, jazz, and computer music, and potentially any kind of music can be included. One of the objectives of the unit is to introduce students to kinds of music and intermedia work with which they may not be familiar. However, for their assignment students can engage with music that particularly interests them, and do not have to be restricted to the musical styles central to the unit.

Sound is an aspect of creative writing that is often overlooked in favor of image, both in practice and in teaching. We are enculturated to respond more to the visual than the sonic, and most students will be more visually than sonically orientated. Even when intermedia work is included in creative writing courses, it very often focuses primarily on word–image rather than word–sound relationships, through the employment of collage, visual poetry, or screened texts. This is partly because academics and writing teachers are often more literate in visual rather than sonic media, but also because of a pervasive cultural bias. The unit I have evolved addresses these imbalances and absences, and highlights the way that students can experiment with the relationship between words and sound in their own creative writing.

The MA in Literature and Creative Writing: Practice-led research, research-led practice

The MA is a postgraduate degree that is currently undergoing a great deal of change in Australia and worldwide. Historically Masters degrees in Australia tended to be of two types: coursework or research. However, currently, there is a move to fuse the two different kinds of Masters degree. The aim is to make the degree the main preparation for a PhD (though some people may enroll for it simply as an end in itself) and to create some uniformity with Masters degrees in other countries. At Western Sydney University this combination of coursework and research takes the form of a new degree, the Master of Research, that has been recently introduced at the university. The MA in Literature and Creative Writing interacts with the broader Master of Research and is designed to address the specialized expertise and methodological approaches that students of creative writing require; it is a coursework MA with a small research/creative project component. Students from the MA in Literature and Creative Writing can join the Master of Research in the second year if they reach the required standard and are considered suitable; this means that they can undertake a more substantial yearlong research project that gives them a good foundation for a PhD or a Doctorate of Creative Arts (DCA) should that be their goal—the DCA is the equivalent of a PhD but puts more emphasis on the creative component. The research project for the Master of Research can be, if desired, a creative writing project with accompanying exegesis.

The MA in Literature and Creative Writing is intended for a range of abilities and experience in both literary studies and creative writing. It has a flexible basis so that students can either focus on Literary Studies or Creative Writing or on both. The course is 18 months long: coursework occupies the first year and the following six months are devoted to an individual research or creative project of the student's choice. The course runs one day a week. A two-hour unit in the morning, Applied Techniques in Literary Studies and Creative Writing, covers research skills, creative writing techniques, and workshopping. The afternoon consists of a succession of three-hour units, each of six weeks' duration, taught by my colleagues and myself. These units cover such diverse topics as awkwardness in Australian literature (taught by Ivor Indyk); philosophies of time in literature, art, and film (Gail Jones); play and form in French experimental writing from Dada to the Oulipo (Chris Andrews); and literary processes and methods in their relationship to philosophy and science (Anthony Uhlmann). Most of these units are critically based, but they allow the students to respond to the critical work with creative work.

The core idea of the MA is that creative writing will arise out of the strong intellectual basis of each unit. The units, such as mine, that combine critical and creative approaches have limited time for teaching creative writing techniques but can partly draw on the technical skills the students are learning in the Applied Techniques in Literary Studies and Creative Writing unit. The course has been evolving, and the creative writing component of it has been increasing. Most of the students are aspirant creative writers and we found that they needed more technical advice about creative writing than we were initially giving them. The MA is therefore built on the principle of the reciprocal relationship between academic endeavor and creative practice, a dynamic central to my own work.[1] In collaboration with Roger Dean I have previously theorized this relationship as an "interactive cyclic web"[2] in which practice-led research (creative work and its resulting research insights) and research-led practice (academic research that results in the production of creative work) are interwoven and symbiotic.[3]

This principle of practice-led research and research-led practice also underlies my contemporary literature–music unit. That is, the unit encourages students to obtain insights from studying and researching the literature–music relationship, which they can then apply to their own creative writing. At the same time the activity of creative writing will hopefully give them understanding into the literary and intermedia works we study in the unit, and why these writers write in the way they do. Nevertheless, one of the challenges of my unit, and the other afternoon units that comprise the course, is ensuring that the students take on the intellectual issues that are explored and address them in their creative work. The students often find it difficult to meld their own free-for-all creative impulses with the specific critical and theoretical issues that the course raises. To some extent this is a challenge of all creative writing courses that set specific tasks, rather than simply inviting the students to choose their own creative direction. The problem is much more pronounced, though, when the content of the course is primarily intellectual and critical, since the student will have to make a considerable mental effort to "translate" the critical/theoretical ideas into concepts or techniques for creative writing. As a teacher, I find I have to point out how the critical analysis we are undertaking can lead into specific creative writing strategies: for example, how understanding a structure can suggest ways to build one. It is advantageous for students to grasp this because focusing on a particular intellectual issue or technique—and learning to produce creative work as a result of exploring it—is a significant skill that any writer will benefit from acquiring, and is the reason why attentive readers are often good writers. Moreover, the subject matter of the unit opens out onto a wide range of formal, thematic, and cross-media pathways for creative writing, so the choice of approaches for the student is broad.

My unit started out in 2012 as largely critical and theoretical. It consisted of an hour-long lecture based on set readings followed by two hours of discussion. The overall idea then was that in their assessment task students could respond with creative writing to the ideas, forms, genres, and media raised on the course (though they could also respond with a critical essay if preferred).

Although this is a good format in many ways because it gives the unit a strong intellectual basis, I have found progressively that it is necessary to bridge the gap between the critical and creative in a more concrete way: only then can the concept of practice-led research, research-led practice be said to be fully operating. It soon became apparent that the students were anxious to respond creatively to the unit, but were sometimes rather lacking in skills to do so. This has been partly resolved by increasing the teaching of creative writing techniques on the MA course overall. However, I have also found it necessary to include more direct technical advice and specific writing tasks in my own unit, so that students can realize the content of the unit creatively.

The contemporary literature–music relationship as the basis of the unit

Designing a unit based on the relationship between words and sound was an obvious option for me: reciprocity between literature and music has been central to my own research and creative practice for some time. The unit exploits my expertise from my previous career as a professional musician, and therefore draws on my musical training, but also my practical and everyday experience of performing music. Many of my publications, but particularly my monograph on the contemporary literature–music relationship,[4] address the theoretical and critical issues I discuss in the unit. Similarly, much of my own creative work consists of collaborative contemporary experimental intermedia and multimedia work in which the relationship between words and sounds is pivotal.[5] Even my writing for the page is strongly influenced by the sonics of writing.

My approach to creative writing and to teaching creative writing has always been intermedia, and I have consistently welcomed off-the-page approaches to writing as well as on-the-page ones. Off-the-page approaches comprise two chapters of my volume *The Writing Experiment*: the book also has an accompanying website so that the students can listen to and watch intermedia and multimedia works. I believe that one of the hallmarks of being a good writer is the ability to think across the arts. And while every creative writing teacher wants their students to read books, it is just as important for writing students to listen to music, go to art galleries, watch films, and attend theatre and dance events as it is for them to read. It is also vital in the digital era that students become aware of, and participate in, electronic literature, which is intrinsically multimedia. I find it regrettable that there is still inertia about this in the literary establishment, which for the most part clings to the primarily literary. As a result, many students, even at postgraduate level, still tend to think of creative writing in a "words only" fashion, and it is not always easy to persuade them that writing is an intermedia and increasingly technologized activity. However, for this very reason, it is important to challenge these kinds of assumptions.

The content of the unit changes somewhat from year to year and the choice of texts is flexible. The unit divides into two halves, the first part is concerned with the representation of music and musicians in novels, the second part is committed to what I call contemporary experimental intermedia and multimedia (CEIM) work in which words and sounds are brought into close juxtaposition.[6] These two different approaches suggest very different forms of creative writing, from on-the-page narrative to oral or screen-based work. Throughout there is an emphasis on creative process and the kinds of question that preoccupy writers, though through the lens of the literature–music relationship.[7]

The unit begins with a discussion of the problematics of musical meaning, and the formal and cultural issues involved in word–sound relationships, drawing on the work of Wolf,[8] Benson,[9] Kramer,[10] and others. The first week of the unit addresses the issues of structure, sociopolitical context, and affect in relation to musical meaning. Thinking about musical meaning can give students a completely new way of considering literary meaning, and also a novel perspective on how they might behave and think as writers. What music means, and why it means, is complex, because music is less obviously referential than literature, and this certainly suggests that meaning cannot be reduced to the purely semantic. The power of musical meaning demonstrates that the sonic and visual can be forceful components in writing, that for writers the signifier is as important as the signified, and that meaning may sometimes be produced by subverting semantic and syntactic conventions. Another way of putting this is that studying musical meaning helps students to understand the more abstract, nonrepresentational aspects of writing, and to balance those with the more representational ones. The discussion of musical meaning in the first week of the unit is accompanied by in-class writing exercises that encourage students to write creatively in response to contrasting pieces of music. These pieces of music inhabit different points along the continuum from representational to abstract sounds, and may include environmental music, computer music, popular music, and classical music.

The unit then turns to the representation of music and musicians in novels, in this case Vikram Seth's *An Equal Music*,[11] which features a deaf musician, and Richard Powers's *The Time of Our Singing*,[12] which focuses on two American biracial brothers who become classical musicians. Here again, the issues raised in the discussion of the novels can be applied and adapted to the students' own creative writing. I interpret *An Equal Music* as a novel about musical meaning, but also as a novel about disability, since it features a deaf pianist Julia, and also Michael, a violinist who has a mental breakdown. I draw on Lacanian theory to talk about musical meaning in terms of the relationship between the real, imaginary, and the symbolic. In addition, to highlight how Julia manages her deafness and can still—despite her impairment—be a high-flying musician, I apply theoretical perspectives from music psychology. My focus here is primarily the work of Freya Bailes[13] and the idea of musical imaging or "tune on the brain" as it is more commonly known, the phenomenon by which we often hear music in our heads even though we are not listening to music at the time. Employing Foucault and Attali's concepts of "normalization,"[14] I also discuss the way that the musical profession is portrayed, and whether Seth romanticizes it. This highlights the important problem of how writers manage their own ideological positions.

The Time of Our Singing is a novel about music and ethnicity, and centers on two biracial boys (they are part African American and part German Jewish) who are attempting to be successful in the world of white classical music-making. The novel raises many issues about the essentialism or non-essentialism of ethnic identity and also the power of music: the degree to which music can transcend the social or is inevitably always grounded in it. I frame the discussion of the book with theories drawn from a number of fields including biracial theory, for example Zack[15] and Root,[16] and postcolonial theory from such works as that of Gilroy[17] and Bhabha.[18] Particularly important is the concept of hybridity, since the novel suggests that the way forward (both for society and art) lies in what I call musical miscegenation: the assimilation, collaging, and remixing of different musical styles and materials from diverse cultures. This can encourage students to think about hybridity in their own writing. Since Powers is neither African American, Jewish, nor a professional musician, the book also poses many pertinent questions about the role of the writer and the capacity of writers to project into cultural identities that are not their own.

The Seth and the Powers novels can be used as a basis for writing exercises that focus on techniques of representation and the relationship of musical experience and musical contexts to disability and ethnicity. Most students respond to this narratively, but they can also be shown how to approach it using a wider platter of writing techniques: for example collaging/remixing material about music and disability, or music and ethnicity, from a variety of academic and nonacademic sites on the Internet. The Seth and Powers novels also have a structure that can be read as analogous to a musical structure. Seth's novel seems fugal in structure, while the Powers novel adopts the more circular structures characteristic of African American music. The students, therefore, can also be encouraged to think about—and experiment with—ways in which literary structures can be built using musical structures as a model.

After the first three weeks the unit takes a different turn and moves to discussion of intermedia in the sense of the juxtaposition of words and music in creative works. The intermedia relationship is discussed in both formal and cultural terms. Important here is the concept of semiotic and perceptual exchange: that is, the idea that, when juxtaposed, words and music to some extent adopt each other's characteristics, so that the music seems more referential and the words more sonic and abstracted. We also discuss the different ways that words and music can be combined. These include coordination (where words and music are connected by association in various ways, including effects in the music that illustrate the import of the words), parallelism (where the music and words run in parallel to each other and are not consciously coordinated), antithesis (where the words and music sharply contrast with or even conflict with each other), and heterogeneous assemblage (where each medium is composed of a large number of different elements that come together into temporary configurations, fall apart, and then come together into other configurations). Similarly, we discuss the cultural consequences of these word–music juxtapositions, such as the formation of hybrid cultural artifacts that combine words and music from different cultures and ethnicities. Such hybrid entities have the capacity to create cross-cultural exchange in a process

I call musico-literary miscegenation.[19] Analysis of intermedia work gives the students a basis for thinking about intermedia strategies in their own creative works. The focus in the unit is on juxtapositions of spoken words and sounds rather than on songwriting, however if students wish to write songs they may do so. I also emphasize that they do not need to use elaborate technology but should try to produce work that is conceptually interesting, and students often respond by employing simple technologies that are at their disposal.

With theory of intermedia as a basis, we discuss voice, improvisation, and intermedia in the experimental work of two African Americans, sonic poet Tracie Morris[20] and composer-writer-performer Pamela Z.[21] The comparison of the work of Morris and Z is productive. Whereas Morris's remarkable sonic control of her voice is acoustic, Z's is computationally processed, multiplied, and transformed through digital technologies: she also frequently uses a digital delay to create a plethora of voices. This can lead to a discussion of the different ways in which voice can manifest itself in performance and on the page. It is also illuminating in terms of process because both Morris and Z improvise, Morris more acoustically and Z in conjunction with technological transformation. We look more closely at improvisation by contrasting three of Morris's performances of "My Great Grand Aunt Meets a Bush Supporter," all of which have slightly different improvised elements.[22] Improvisation is often a concept that is rather underplayed in literary studies. Very few students would think that their writing could take the form of an oral improvisation, but listening to such improvisations can make them think of ways of incorporating improvisation into their practice. Certainly the work of Morris and Z can be a starting point to think about writing sonic poems, using alliteration, assonance, sound association, and repetition in ways that bring out the sonic element of writing but do not resort to rhyming verse. It can also encourage students to explore the voice and manipulate it acoustically and—if the student has some familiarity with sound technologies or has a friend with some expertise in that area with whom they can collaborate—to experiment with sampling, transmuting words, and processing the voice. An important aspect of the discussion is about the way the work of both Morris and Z draws on different ethnic traditions. Morris, for example, is influenced by sound poetry and language poetry, but also by the African musical traditions of soul, blues, and jazz, creating musico-literary miscegenation.

This week of the unit also includes a wider discussion of the role of technology in word and sound juxtapositions and its cultural effects. Important here is the idea of sonic cross-dressing in which the voice is manipulated in such a way that a male voice becomes female or a female voice becomes male. This is a feature of some of my own collaborations, and I sometimes use examples from my own work, such as "the space of history"[23] and "Scaling the Voices"[24] to illustrate sonic cross-dressing for students. Referring on occasion to my own creative work is part of my teaching methodology. I think it is important that I lead by example and show that the writing strategies and theories I am promoting are not only realizable but are sometimes part of my own creative practice.

Week five of the unit involves analysis of works of electronic literature that explore the relationship between screened words, images, and sound through new technologies. These include John Cayley's "Translation."[25] This work continuously translates between English, French, and German by means of what Cayley calls "transliteral morphing," the gradual replacement of letters from one language with letters from another. However, it also translates between words and music, since both the words and the music share the same algorithmic process, producing what we have called algorithmic synaesthesia.[26] In addition, the unit includes "Operation Nukorea" by Young-Hae Chang Heavy Industries,[27] a work that juxtaposes a piece of music by pianist Bill Evans, titled "Peace Piece," with a terrifying narrative about an imagined invasion of South Korea by North Korea in response to American provocation. The words move on the screen rhythmically in response to the music in a way that suggests semiotic and perceptual exchange. But there is an antithetical parallelism between the words which convey acts of extreme aggression and the music which gestures toward peace. The study material for the unit also includes "Film of Sound,"[28] a piece by Will Luers, Roger Dean, and myself in which Will and I responded in images and words to music composed by Roger as part of the process of making the piece. In this piece, sounds, images, and words coalesce in heterogeneous assemblages, coming together into certain configurations, moving apart, and then linking together in alternative configurations. In relation to electronic literature we discuss the different ways in which the words and music can interrelate formally, but we also explore the way such works can create musico-literary miscegenation. Students can then use the analysis of formal principles and awareness of the cultural possibilities to construct their own work. The limitation here is the time constraint (the unit is only six weeks in length) and the fact that some students lack the technological skills to make such work, but the emphasis is on conceptual understanding rather than technological prowess.

The final week of the unit is devoted to workshopping and focuses on the development of the students' projects for their assignment; I also summarize the issues we have covered during the unit and emphasize their application to the students' work.

Writing tasks and assessment

For their assessment, the students can either respond with a critical essay of 5000 words or a creative piece with a 1000 word exegesis: most students choose the latter option. I usually give them a list of topics that they can use as the basis for their assignment. However, I invite them to think up their own topic and most of them do. The instructions for the assignment ask them to engage with an aspect of the unit that particularly interests them, but also to demonstrate understanding of other issues raised during the unit.

The exegesis that accompanies the creative piece should speak to the creative work, and there should be a symbiosis between the two. However, there is considerable flexibility about how the exegesis is written and what it will address. Ideally, it takes up some of the intellectual issues from the unit, discusses them, and shows how these relate to the creative work or are used as a foundation for developing it. The exegesis is very useful for helping the students to articulate some of the intellectual ideas that informed the piece, but also encourages them to be reflective about the work they have done. In addition, it can be a guide to the marker in terms of what they have tried to achieve (as opposed to what has actually been achieved which may be at a lower level).

Writing exercises

The following are some writing exercises that can be employed to encourage students to work creatively with words and sound.

1. Write creatively in response to three very different pieces of music. At least one piece of music should include some environmental sounds. You do

not need to write continuous sentences but can just write down words and phrases. Try to respond to the music, but also allow other thoughts and ideas to become part of the flow and to take you off in their own direction. You can then develop your responses to one piece or try to combine your responses to all three.

2. Write a fictional text that describes a place but focuses entirely on sounds not visual images. So if you were describing a kitchen you might focus on the sounds of vegetables being cut up or the fridge door slamming. Or write a text describing a place visually and then turn all the visual images (or most of them) into sounds.
3. Write a text about a musician with a disability. Think about the various effects different disabilities might have on playing an instrument. As a basis for the piece you might want to research instances of musicians with a disability. Some interesting examples are Evelyn Glennie, Horace Parlan, and Cyril Smith.
4. Create a narrative or poem that is about tensions/fusions between Western music and non-Western music. You might want to use Richard Powers's novel *The Time of Our Singing* as a trigger for thinking about this.
5. Cut and paste ideas about music from the Internet, or from articles about music, particularly focusing on what performers, composers, and critics say about music. See if you can produce a multivoiced text or "polylogue" in the first person that produces different points of view about music. This might just be a piece that works well on the page, but it might also be a performance piece.
6. Take the structure of a piece of music that you particularly like and base a piece of writing on it. The way that you map out the structure could be technical or could be your entirely nontechnical impression of it. The standard structure of a popular song for example is AABA (32 bars). So material A is repeated three times with minor variations and B supplies a contrast. This is one way to map out your structure (using letters of the alphabet to differentiate between different types of material) but there are other ways, for example you can draw a diagram to convey your impression of the structure.
7. Combine words and music in an intermedia, audio, or screen-based piece, using the ideas of semiotic exchange, parallelism, coordination, antithesis, or heterogeneous assemblage to create correspondences and contrasts. You can use preexisting music, compose your own music, or collaborate with a composer.

8. Create a sound poem, song, or intermedia piece that draws on more than one ethnic/folk tradition. You might, for example, want to explore folk song, jazz, or world music to suggest possibilities in the way you pitch the voice or for the rhythms you use. Or you might choose to draw on poetic traditions from other cultures such as the haiku or the ghazal, or use languages other than English.
9. Write a poem in which you interject environmental sounds or the sounds of objects into a poem, or use such sounds as a backcloth to the poem.
10. Record a text and then sample words, chop them into segments, join segments from different words together, and play them backwards. What are the effects on language of doing this? Do you find the words start to form sound textures?
11. Write a short poem and digitally process the voice in such a way as to change the gender of the speaker or to explore the continuum between male and female.
12. Improvise a text using a digital delay system. You may want to write down some words, phrases, or sentences from which you can improvise (this is sometimes called using a referent). Use the delay as a way to dialogue with yourself.

Notes

1 Hazel Smith and Roger T. Dean (eds.), *Practice-led Research, Research-led Practice in the Creative Arts*, (Edinburgh University Press, 2009); H. Smith, *The Writing Experiment: Strategies for Innovative Creative Writing* (Sydney: Allen and Unwin, 2005).

2 Hazel Smith and Roger T. Dean, "Introduction: Practice-led Research, Research-led Practice—Towards the Interactive Cyclic Web," in *Practice-led Research, Research-led Practice in the Creative Arts* (Edinburgh University Press, 2009), 19.

3 Ibid., 19–25.

4 Hazel Smith, *The Contemporary Literature–Music Relationship: Intermedia, Voice, Technology, Cross-cultural Exchange* (New York and London: Routledge, 2016).

5 Hazel Smith, Personal website. Available online: http://www.australysis.com (accessed June 7, 2016).

6 Smith, *The Contemporary Literature–Music Relationship*, 1–3; 20–23.

7 Although I outline the issues the unit addresses here, my monograph (Smith 2016) explores them in much more detail.

8 Werner Wolf, *The Musicalization of Fiction: A Study in the Theory and Historyof Intermediality*(Amsterdam-Atlanta, GA: Rodopi, 1999).
9 Stephen Benson, *Literary Music: Writing Music in Contemporary Fiction* (Aldershot, Hampshire: Ashgate, 2006).
10 Lawrence Kramer, *Musical Meaning: Toward a Critical History* (Berkeley: University of California Press, 2002).
11 Vikram Seth, *An Equal Music* (London: Phoenix House, 1999).
12 Richard Powers, *The Time of Our Singing* (New York: Picador, 2003).
13 Freya Bailes, "Translating the Musical Image: Case Studies of Expert Musicians," in *Sounds in Translation: Intersections of Music, Technology and Society*, ed. Amy Chan and Alistair Noble (Canberra: ANU E Press, 2009),41–60; Freya Bailes and Laura Bishop, "Musical Imagery in the Creative Process," in *The Act of Musical Composition: Studies in the Creative Process*, ed. Dave Collins (Farnham, Surrey: Ashgate Publications, 2012),53–77.
14 Jacques Attali, *Noise: The Political Economy of Music* (Minneapolis: University of Minnesota Press, 1985); Michel Foucault, *Discipline and Punish: The Birth of the Prison* (London: Penguin, 1991).
15 Naomi Zack, *Race and Mixed Race* (Philadelphia: Temple University Press, 1993).
16 Maria P. P. Root, *The Multiracial Experience: Racial Borders as the New Frontier* (London: Sage, 1996).
17 Paul Gilroy, *The Black Atlantic: Modernity and Double Consciousness* (Cambridge, MA: Harvard University Press, 1993).
18 Homi K. Bhabha, *The Location of Culture* (London and New York: Routledge, 1994).
19 Smith, *The Contemporary Literature–Music Relationship.*
20 Tracie Morris, Personal website. Available online: http://www.traciemorris.com (accessed June 7, 2016).
21 Z, Pamela, Personal website. Available online http://www.pamelaz.com/ (accessed June 6, 2016).
22 Morris, "Three versions of 'My Great Grand Aunt Meets a Bush Supporter.'" *PennSound.* Available online: http://writing.upenn.edu/pennsound/x/Morris-Tucson.php (accessed June 7, 2016).
23 Hazel Smith and Roger T. Dean,"the space of history,"in *The Erotics of Geography: Poetry, Performance Texts, New Media Works*, CD-Rom accompanying book, Kāne'ohe, Hawai'i: Tinfish Press, 2008. Also available online at *PennSound:* https://media.sas.upenn.edu/pennsound/authors/Smith-Hazel/Smith-Hazel_Dean-Roger_The-Space-of-History_2006.mp3 (accessed June 5, 2016).

24 Roger Dean and Hazel Smith,"Scaling the Voices,"*soundsRite, Four and More 2015.* Available online: http://soundsrite.uws.edu.au/soundsRiteContent/Four&More/FourAndMore2015Info.html (accessed June 5, 2016)

25 John Cayley, "Translation." 2011. Available online: http://programmatology.shadoof.net/index.php?p=works/translation/translation.html (accessed June 7, 2016).

26 Roger T. Dean, David Worrall, Hazel Smith, and Mitchell Whitelaw, "The Mirage of Real-time Algorithmic Synaesthesia: Some Compositional Mechanisms and Research Agendas in Computer Music and Sonification," *Contemporary Music Review, Special Issue, Musical Hybrids: Sonic Intermedia in Australia* 25.4 (2006): 311–26.

27 Young-Hae Chang Heavy Industries, "Operation Nukorea." Available online: http://www.yhchang.com/OPERATION_NUKOREA.html (accessed June 5, 2016).

28 Will Luers, Roger Dean, and Hazel Smith, "Film of Sound," *Cordite Poetry Review*, 2013. Available online: http://cordite.org.au/ekphrasis/film-of-sound/ (accessed June 5, 2016).

6

The Poetry of Music, the Music of Poetry: An Annotated Syllabus[1]

Tom C. Hunley

English 329/G: Special topics in creative writing: The poetry of music, the music of poetry

Spring 2015	Dr. Tom[2] C. Hunley
T 5:00–7:45pm[3]	Cherry 122

Course Description: The university catalogue describes ENG 329/G as "a semester-long, detailed study of a specified topic in language, literature, or composition." This term, we will write and workshop song lyrics and poems.

Prerequisite: ENG 200[4]

Texts and Materials: *Songwriting without Boundaries* by Pat Pattison[5]; *The Poetry Gymnasium* by Tom C. Hunley[6]; *Actual Air* by David Berman[7]; and *The Second Sex* by Michael Robbins.[8]

Late Work: Barring terrorist attacks on Bowling Green or extreme acts of God, I'm not going to accept late work.

Attendance: Every class session is going to be an event, a happening, and only a complete square would want to be anywhere else. Perfect attendance gets you 10/10 points. Missing once gets you 9/10. Missing twice gets you 7/10. Missing three times gets you 5/10. If you miss more than that, you risk failure on the grounds that you're not an active class participant.

Plagiarism: Representing someone else's words as your own is grounds for failure in this course. It will not be tolerated.

Minimal Course Requirements: At the least, you are required to:

- Attend class regularly.
- Participate in class discussions and writing exercises.
- Complete multiple drafts of six poems and the lyrics to six songs.
- Keep up with assigned reading and be able to intelligently respond to that reading orally and in writing.
- Provide your classmates with constructive criticism on their works in progress.
- *Grading*: The course will be graded on the following point system:
- Poems: 35 points
- Lyrics: 35 points
- Writing Challenges: 20 points
- Attendance: 10 points

I will determine your final grade based on your percentage of the total points possible, using the following table:
92–100: A
83–91.5: B
73–82.5: C
65–72.5: D
Below 65: F

I will not change your final course grade except in the case of a mathematical error. Please do not take up my time with last-minute requests for extra credit or tales about how you need a better grade so that you can get into law school, get into graduate school, get back into your parents' good graces (or other similar irrelevancies). I will not participate in any conversation or answer any email message whose subject is grade grubbing. If you wish for me to reconsider your grade on a given assignment, re-submit the graded copy of the assignment along with a one-page note explaining why you believe the grade should be raised. If I find your argument frivolous, I will lower the original grade. That said, I encourage students to come to me —early in the semester—asking for advice on how to raise their performance (and thus their grade) in future assignments.

Schedule

January 27: Discuss syllabus; Writing prompt based on two Leonard Cohen songs.[9]

Homework for February 3: Read *The Second Sex* by Michael Robbins.

February 3: Discuss *The Second Sex* by Michael Robbins; exercises from *The Poetry Gymnasium* tba.

Homework for February 10: Read Challenge 1 of *Songwriting without Boundaries.*

February 10: Challenge 1 in *Songwriting without Boundaries.*

February 17: Challenge 1 in *Songwriting without Boundaries* (continued).

February 24: Visiting poet/lyricist Gerry LaFemina,[10] author (most recently) of *Little Heretic* and rhythm guitarist of The Downstrokes (formerly in Expletive Deleted); Homework for March 3: Read *Actual Air* by David Berman.

March 3: Discuss poems from *Actual Air* by David Berman; Discuss lyrics by Silver Jews; exercise from *The Poetry Gymnasium* tba;[11] Workshop.

March 10: Spring Break.

March 17: Exercise from *The Poetry Gymnasium* tba; Workshop.

Homework for March 31: Read Challenge 2 in *Songwriting without Boundaries.*

March 24: Workshop; Develop criteria for song lyrics[12]; Challenge 2 in *Songwriting without Boundaries.*

March 31: Turn in Portfolio #1 (three poems developed from exercises in *The Poetry Gymnasium* + lyrics to three songs, developed from exercises in *Songwriting without Boundaries*) and/or from other in-class exercises; Challenge 2 in *Songwriting without Boundaries* (continued).

Homework for April 7: Read Challenge 4 in *Songwriting without Boundaries.*

April 7: Workshop; Challenge 4 in *Songwriting without Boundaries.*

April 14: Workshop; Challenge 4 in *Songwriting without Boundaries* (Continued).

April 21: Workshop (first half of class); Guest Panel featuring Madison Armor, Stephen Gordon, Chris Rutledge, and TBA (second half).[13]

April 28: Turn in Portfolio #2 (three poems developed from exercises in *The Poetry Gymnasium* + lyrics to three songs, developed from exercises in *Songwriting without Boundaries* and/or from other in-class exercises); Rehearse for Open Mic.

May 5: Open Mic (location tba).[14]

Grading criteria for lyric portfolios

On March 24, we will collaborate, as a class, on grading criteria for lyric portfolios. Stay tuned!

Grading

The following 100-point scale (ten points each) will be used to judge your poetry and songwriting portfolios.

95+ points = A
92–94 points = A-
88–91 points = B+
83–87 points = B-
79–82 points = C+
73–78 points = C
65–72 points = D
Below 65 points = F

Criteria for poetry

- Something important is at stake in the poems. The poems matter. They pack an emotional punch and evoke a visceral reaction in readers.
- The poems exhibit evidence of considerable revision.
- The poems are written in complete sentences, using proper grammar and standard punctuation. Any deviation from standard grammar must come in dialogue and/or must be clearly done intentionally and for a specific purpose. Any grammatical errors, whether intentional or not, should not make the poems unreadable or distract from their meaning.
- Spelling and capitalization must be used appropriately. You are not sending text messages (unless one of your poems is in the form of a text message, which might be kind of cool).

- The poems use images, concrete language, and figures of speech rather than wallowing in abstractions, generalizations, and various techniques better suited to analytical prose. Show, don't tell.
- The poet draws on an excellent lexicon and writes as though each word cost $1,000. The poet's use of language is playful, fresh, and precise.
- The poet has control of the poetic line. A poem is not simply broken off prose.
- Do you use the poem's line to modulate the speed of the poem? Are you choosing your end words for emphasis?
- The poems should be clear. If there are allusions and references in the poems, they are either clear in context or readily accessible via the magic of modern technology.
- (Wikipedia, Google, etc.). Private jokes and "you-had-to-be-there" references are absent.
- The packet includes at least one poem that displays mastery over rhyme or meter.
- Free verse poems in the packet demonstrate the poet's skill with sound effects including, but not limited to, assonance, consonance, onomatopoeia, internal rhyme, anaphora, and alliteration.

Criteria for song lyrics

- The lyrics evoke a powerful visceral and/or emotional reaction.
- The lyrics are arresting or at least entertaining. In a world in which everyone has remote controls and a lot of options, there's something in these lyrics that would enable them to compete for people's attention.
- The lyrics exhibit evidence of considerable revision.
- The lyrics are written in complete sentences, using proper grammar and standard punctuation. Any deviation from standard grammar must come in dialogue and/or must be clearly done intentionally and for a specific purpose (such as making the voice folksier). Any grammatical errors, whether intentional or not, should not render the lyrics inscrutable or distract from their meaning. There are no misspellings.
- The lyrics consistently appeal to the five senses, rather than wallowing in abstractions and generalities.
- Some of the lyrics appeal to Pat Pattison's sixth (awareness of inner bodily functions such as heartbeat and pulse) and seventh (kinesthetic sense,

such as the blurred vision that comes when one is seasick or drunk) senses.

- The lyrics draw on an excellent lexicon and writes as though each word cost $1,000. Minimum syllables, maximum meaning.
- The writer's use of language is playful, fresh, and precise.
- The lyrics should be clear. If there are allusions and references in the poems, they are either clear in context or readily accessible via the magic of modern technology (Wikipedia, Google, etc.). Private jokes and "you-had-to-be-there" references are absent.
- The lyrics are somewhat metrical. At the least, each verse should have roughly the same number of syllables.

Notes

1 True to its title, this chapter will take the form of an annotated syllabus. I will recall my goals and intentions, my missteps and mistakes, my "aha" moments and those of my students at Western Kentucky University (WKU) in a special topics course that I taught on poetry writing and songwriting.

2 Since completing my PhD at Florida State University and migrating to WKU in 2003, I have encouraged my students to call me Dr. Tom. The first name alone seems too informal to me; "Dr. Hunley" or "Professor Hunley" seems too removed and stuffy. This is part of an attempt to cultivate a classroom persona that will bring out my students' best writing. Highlighting my professional credentials with the "Dr." part of the appellation is an attempt to establish ethos, to say that I have experience critiquing poems and can respond to work professionally. Highlighting my humanness with my first name says that I'm also someone that students can trust with a side of themselves they may not have shared with anyone before. I love the story that Jean Valentine tells about Grace Paley's response to a college student who felt stymied as a writer because, in the student's words, "I have nothing to say." Paley's answer: "Yes, you do, you just don't have anybody to say it to. Say it to me." We each have to find our own teaching persona, and I think it's worth the effort of asking oneself, "How can I best come across as both an expert reader and a caring, attentive listener?" See: Jean Valentine, "What Remains Unseen," in *A God In The House: Poets Talk about Faith*, ed. Ilya Kaminsky and Katherine Towler (North Adams, MA: Tupelo Press, 2012), 73.

I am by no means an experienced or expert songwriter. Although I have written poetry and made it a cornerstone of my life and career for nearly thirty years, I turned to instrumental music and songwriting six years ago, at age forty. When some men reach their midlife crises, they have affairs or buy sports cars. I love my wife, our Toyota Corolla, and our Honda Odyssey way too much to do that. Instead, I turned to music, with a vengeance, scratching my balding head wondering why I hadn't done this decades before. This positioned me as a "co-learner" with my students, as my teacher Wendy Bishop had called herself on the first day of her "Rhetorical Theory and Practice" seminar (her specialties being Composition Theory and Creative Writing Pedagogy, not Rhetoric). I knew going into the special topics course, "The Music of Poetry: The Poetry of Music," that I would be less experienced as a musician and songwriter than some students in the class. This meant going out on a limb a little bit. It's easy to be the sage on the stage lecturing about something that one knows well; it's much harder to carry out one's own education in public. Part of the challenge is the surrendering of authority, as Katherine Haake well knows. In her essay "Dismantling Authority: Teaching What We Do Not Know," Haake explains how she creates her special topics courses, not drawing on her considerable knowledge and expertise but rather "with a sense of curiosity—a wondering—and each proceeded raggedly through unfamiliar texts and assignments to become what seemed real occasions for writing." That was my goal here: to learn alongside my students and to create an environment that would foster real discoveries and breakthroughs. See Katharine Haake, "Dismantling Authority: Teaching What We Do Not Know," in *Power and Identity in the Creative Writing Classroom: The Authority Project*, ed. Anna Leahy (Clevedon, UK: Multilingual Matters, 2005), 101.

Throughout my teaching career, I had found that some of my students were rock-and-rollers who signed up for my poetry writing classes because they hoped to write better lyrics. For years I think I served those students poorly, erroneously assuming that everyone who takes a poetry writing course wants to be a poet. It was only at the point of my midlife crisis, when I asked a student named Eddie Rogers to help me choose a bass guitar to buy with my tax refund, that I started to think hard about the connection between poetry and song writing.

3 I should have scheduled the class for Thursday nights. This college town considers that the beginning of the weekend, and there's always great live music on Thursday nights at local dive bars. Meeting on Thursday nights would have helped us extend the classroom conversation, experiencing the best songwriting performances available in our town, which boasted the top two new artists of 2011 (Cage the Elephant and Sleeper Agent), according to a Rolling Stone readers' poll. See: "Readers' Poll: The Best New Artists of 2011," in *Rolling Stone* (January 2, 2012), 9–10.

4 The only prerequisite for special topics courses in English at WKU is Introduction to Literature. Although some of the students in the class were

Creative Writing majors who had taken most of the required coursework for that degree already, I could not count on the students having taken any creative writing at all, which presented some challenges. Knowing some students would have already taken a couple of poetry writing classes in addition to a multi-genre introduction to creative writing class meant that I would have to design writing exercises that could challenge and inspire veteran poets while not frustrating students who had never studied poetry before. It also meant that I needed to seek out advanced students who could simultaneously reinforce their knowledge and help out their classmates by leading discussions and making presentations. I also knew that some students were advanced musicians and songwriters while others played no instruments and had never tried their hand at songwriting before, so I would further dismantle my teacherly authority by allowing the experienced songwriters to take on leadership roles during discussions of songwriting.

5 This book seemed like a natural fit for the course. Pattison, a professor at Berklee College of Music, has collected fifty-six writing prompts (which he dubs "songwriting challenges") along with sample free-writes by his students, who include Grammy winners John Mayer and Gillian Welch. I like his emphasis on sense-bound free association, and I find his claim that there are seven senses, not five, particularly intriguing. The sixth and seventh are "organic sense (body) … awareness of inner bodily functions, for example, heartbeat, pulse, muscle tension, stomachaches, cramps, breathing" and "kinesthetic sense (motion) … your sense of relation to the world around you" (6). There's also a very helpful chapter on rhyme and meter, covered better than it is in most poetry writing textbooks. The downside of Pattison's book is that he doesn't do much to show how to move from free-write to song; that is left to the writer to puzzle out. Here's a little review by my student Timothy Caldwell: "Though I balked at it a bit while I was in class, I think what was most helpful and generated the most material were the timed writings from *Songwriting without Boundaries*. At first the idea of so much freewriting was unbearable, but as the class went along, it really helped me to embrace the idea of generating large amounts of content without … thinking too much about creating perfect content." … The part of the class that I felt needed improvement was actual song creation. I had a lot of trouble bridging the gap between free-written bulk and lyrics. I think it might have helped to study the dynamics and structures of different genres of songs." I like Timothy's idea, and I wish I had found a textbook that did a better job of helping students move from free-write to first draft to revision to finished song lyric. See: Pat Pattison, *Songwriting without Boundaries: Lyric Writing Exercises for Finding Your Voice* (Cincinnati, OH: Writers Digest Books, 2011).

To be fair, some of my students did manage to make the leap from the free-writes of Pattison's image-based songwriting challenges to actual song lyrics. Here is a song that Derek Ellis, bassist for a band called Lady Grace, wrote in class:

> Phone Call
> *Intro:*
> I've been sitting in this cell alone,
> wastin' all my phone calls on anyone but You.
>
> *Verse 1*
> This bed is just too cold, the plastic just don't do.
> It sticks to my skin, as it pulls and tears.
> You forgive me of my sins and I'm still stuck in here
> I need light to lead me out –
> I promise my promises aren't empty now.
>
> *Verse 2*
> I've been wondering where you went;
> my body's tired and cold – and spent.
> I bruise my knees on this concrete floor –
> selfish prayers like I deserve more.
>
> *Bridge*
> It's a sad disposition and I take the blame,
> I'd dig myself out but I don't see the gain.
> Be the compass to my lost heart,
> and rest my soul and give me strength to trust who you are.
>
> *End Refrain/Chorus*
> Douse my body in holy oil – burn off my flesh.
> I'll know I was right, when I reach the end.

Despite Derek's success here, Pattison's book does not make the leap from freewriting to songwriting a very simple, intuitive process. Students like Derek and his classmates Collin Hancock and Riley Finwood (members of a great band called Heron and Crane), didn't have any trouble, but I should have either found a supplemental songwriting textbook or found ways of my own to help students turn their free-writes into song lyrics. Natalie Rickman had a great idea, which I might implement if I were to teach the course again: "One thing I wished we had done in your song writing class was pair up, or group up, with people in the class who play instruments and actually try to write a song, or even just a chorus. For me, because I don't play an instrument, this would have been a really engaging exercise! Of course this wouldn't always work as an exercise because you might not always have students who play, but if you did, I think your students would have a lot of fun with that!"

6 My book includes ninety-four of my writing exercises, along with examples of poems by well-known poets such as Sherman Alexie, Dean Young, Denise Duhamel, and Billy Collins, and, more importantly, examples written by my students. It seems to me that the exercises in most poetry writing textbooks are afterthoughts that have not been proven to result in good poems; it was important to me that the exercises in my book be student-tested. Additionally, each exercise comes with a specific learning objective, a rationale for why the exercise is written as it is, and some historical background on the subgenre of poetry being attempted. The exercise from *The Poetry Gymnasium* most germane to this poetry/songwriting class is probably "Restoring the Music" which prompts each student to play a favorite song for the class while delivering a mini-lecture about the song's imagery, wordplays, uses of repetition and variation, or any other techniques that make the song poetic. The students then rewrite the song line for line, replicating its meter and any other features such as the use of a refrain. The goal of the assignment is to make meter less daunting for students and to get them to trust their own ears. See: Tom C. Hunley, *The Poetry Gymnasium: 94 Proven Exercises to Shape Your Best Verse* (Jefferson, NC: McFarland & Co., 2012).

7 Some in the poetry world are disdainful of songwriting and believe that poets and lyricists have nothing to learn from one another. No naysayer says nay more eloquently than William Logan: "Song lyrics and poems work in such divergent ways, it's not surprising that a man might be the master of one and the fool of the other." Logan goes on to argue that lyrics, separated from their music, rarely approach the level of poetry. "Cut out the tune, and lyrics are just words that look annoyed … I'd rather read the Des Moines phone book" (4–5). See William Logan, "Collateral damage," in *The New Criterion* (June 2013). But Berman, poet and leader of alt-rock legends Silver Jews, wrote this poetry collection that inspired former US Poet Laureate Billy Collins to enthuse "so this is the voice I have been waiting so long to hear, a voice, I wish in some poems, were my own," and he's written song lyrics like these, which mean far more to me than any poem that William Logan will ever write: "I believe that stars are the headlights of angels / driving from heaven, to save us, to save us. / Look at the skies. / They're driving from heaven into our eyes. / Though final words are so hard to devise / I promise that I'll always remember your pretty eyes, your pretty eyes." In a class on poetry and songwriting and the relationship between the two, it was a no-brainer to use Berman's book and some of his lyrics. See David Berman, *Actual Air* (New York, NY: Open City Books, 1999).

8 I selected this book because of the way it juxtaposes high culture allusions (literature, history, art) with pop culture (music and television). It sparked some good conversations, but if I were to teach the class again, I would

teach the work of another poet/songwriter, maybe Leonard Cohen or Kim Addonizio.

9 I tried to do all of the in-class writing exercises along with my students, especially the songwriting exercises, as I am still an eager novice songwriter. I think my students appreciated seeing me sweat alongside them, modeling the messy, recursive nature of the writing process. I hope that my very rough early drafts allowed them to give themselves permission to write rough early drafts of their own. My student Derek Ellis (who is heading for greatness and the MFA program at University of Maryland) wrote, "I think what worked well was the fact that Dr. Tom launched into all the exercises along with his students. One, his attempts showed us that even the professor was willing to try new things and take part in what we were doing. Two, it gave us students (or at least myself) the courage to start writing. I'd been writing poetry for quite some time, but to try and tackle lyric writing was somewhat of a new beast."

10 Gerry was such a great visiting writer. The author of at least a dozen books including *Little Heretic* and *Vanishing Horizon*, he has po-biz credit to burn. He also played in a band, back in the 1980s, that opened for Suicidal Tendencies at CBGBs, so he brought street cred with him as well. Like David Berman, he proves that it is very possible to simultaneously be a successful poet and a successful songwriter. In addition to reading from his poetry and strumming on a Martin guitar that one of the students brought in, he offered the students the following prompt: "Since you are about to read *Actual Air* by David Berman, lead singer of Silver Jews, try writing a poem that quotes one of Berman's song lyrics OR try writing a song that quotes a line or two from *Actual Air*." See Gerry LaFemina, *Little Heretic* (Nacogdoches, TX: Stephen F. Austin State University Press, 2014). Also: *Vanishing Horizon* (Tallahassee, FL: Anhinga Press, 2011).

11 On March 3, I introduced a writing exercise from *The Poetry Gymnasium* called "I Remember Where I Was Heading the First Time I Heard Nirvana's 'Nevermind,' and I Remember Feeling Stupid and Contagious." The exercise's objective is to harness music's power to release memories and to create a new context for familiar song lyrics by placing them in juxtaposition with original lines of poetry. After reading and discussing model poems such as "My Story in a Late Style of Fire" by Larry Levis and "Mom Did Marilyn, Dad Did Fred" by Jack Myers, the students were directed to do the following as homework: "Listen to an old album, one that was either a chart-topper or a big personal favorite at a key time in your life, a time when you made a make-or-break life decision or when something foundationally transformational occurred in your life. (Or, if you prefer, put together a digital playlist of songs

you were listening to during a particular period of your life.) Freewrite as you listen, letting the music carry you back to those days, back into your younger self, into a specific memory. Write about that memory in vivid detail. Whenever you get stuck, quote a lyric from the song, whatever lyric you happen to be hearing as you write. Incorporate the lyrics into the memory. Let them give shape to the memory, and let the memory re-shape the way you experience the songs" (207–8). The assignment prompted my student Natalie Rickman to write this poem, "Grateful Morning."

Grateful Morning

The morning,
grateful and dead,
cold dewy mist falls
on my backpack.
I climb up high,
truck seat's wide,
and pat the clay dust off
before settling down.

Sweet sounds wind
in the tape deck
and I'm asleep.
The morning is new,
and the sun barely
creeps behind the
trailers and swing sets.

Black coffee
keeps you awake.
My protector, my driver,
earlier riser, take me
to knowledge,
tell me the truth.

My name escapes
your mouth,
you make a sound
and I'm awake.
The now rising sun
glares on the window.

"We're almost there"
is your quiet story
and "grandma will be back

to pick you up".
Climb out slow,
for sleepy eyes,
it's further than before.

Shoe laces, untied,
drag, as my feet do,
on the concrete entrance.
I love you rumbles,
in the beat of your heart,
in your truck, driving away.

Here's a process memo that Natalie turned in along with the poem: "For me, it wasn't a specific song that set off the memory I wrote on, but a band, The Grateful Dead. I started trying to jog my memory by listening to the band, which I heavily associate with my father and tried to freewrite on times that we had listened to that music together. I ended up expanding on a vivid memory I have of him taking me to school and playing cassette tapes of The Dead for me. From this prompt I delved into many poems of car rides in my childhood. So for me, the use of music as a 'memory jogger' was really helpful."

12 On March 24, the class reviewed what we had learned thus far about songwriting and collaboratively devised grading criteria for their first songwriting portfolios that they were to turn in two weeks later. The rubric for poetry portfolios, included in the syllabus, had been devised in similar fashion by one of my previous poetry writing classes.

13 This night was grand. Two wonderful Bowling Green-based singer/songwriters and one from Nashville played short live sets for my students, followed by mini-lectures and Q&A sessions about their songwriting processes. All semester long, I had it in my head to invite David Berman, giving that we used his book as a textbook and that he lives in Nashville, only an hour away from Bowling Green. But I love his work so much, I hold him so high, that I'm afraid I kept psyching myself out. Finally, a mere nine days before the guest panel on April 12, I worked up the nerve and fired off this email:

"Dear David Berman,

I meant to write to you about this a long time ago, but I kept talking myself out of it. I'm teaching a special topics course in writing poetry and song lyrics every Tuesday night this semester. *Actual Air* is one of the required textbooks, and I also introduced the students to your music. They wrote poems in which they quoted lines from your songs "Pretty Eyes" and "Tennessee," and they wrote songs in which they quoted lines from *Actual Air*. On 4/21 at 6 pm, a few songwriters will be visiting class and having a panel discussion on songwriting. One of the panelists will be Chris Rutledge of The Cartoons. You and Chris exchanged messages a year or so ago. He was on the moon about it. Chris and his band are sort of the indie kings of Bowling Green right now, the most original, sincere, alternative band in a scene that's crowded with Cage the Elephant/Sleeper Agent clone wannabes. The panel happens to fall on Chris's birthday. Silver Jews and Pavement are a couple of Chris's favorite bands. He talks about you all the time. I know that this is a shot in the dark, but I thought I'd ask if you'd be into making the trek up to BG, KY to be part of the panel and then maybe have a drink or something with Chris on his 27th birthday. I know that you're probably hella busy and not making a lot of public appearances, but I thought it couldn't hurt to ask. I'd love to meet you, I think my students would love to hear what you have to say about songwriting and poetry, and I know that meeting you would be a very big deal to my former student Chris, who is a great guy.

Yours faithfully,
Tom C. Hunley, PhD"

A few days after the guest panel on April 26, Berman graciously wrote back:

"Hi Tom,
Sorry i didnt get to this in time.

But seeing as I don't want to give the voice that talks you out of taking risks any kind of victory, let me just say that had i received your invite in time i very well might have joined the audience that night.

DCB"

All's well that ends well, according to the bard, and this story does have a happy postscript. On March 5, 2016, The Cartoons played a set of Silver Jews cover songs at The End in Nashville. Someone told David Berman about it, and he and Bob Nastanovitch, from the rock band Pavement, attended the show. Chris was like a kid in a candy store, and so was I (and it's been a long time since I was a kid in a candy store). Learning that Berman is a good guy with a generous spirit confirmed my decision to introduce his poetry and music to my class, none of whom had heard of him or his band before. I just wish they had been there for the show in Nashville. The takeaway for me as a teacher is that I should shoot for the moon when inviting guest speakers to class. The worst case scenario is that they say no; the best case scenario is an unforgettable learning experience.

14 Our end-of-semester celebration, hosted by Lost River Pizza, was a lot of fun. I kicked off the open mic with the world premiere of my song "Let's Get the Cops Called," which I hope will go down as a punk rock, house show classic.

Then each student either read two poems or sang one of the songs that they wrote during the semester. All of my poetry writing classes end with a live performance. This is designed to connect students to poetry's oral tradition, which predates Gutenberg. I believe that focusing entirely on the page provides students with only a partial introduction to the art, which is both written and oral. It likewise seemed logical to ask students to try their hand at musical performance at the end of this semester of songwriting.

7

Words With Borders, Projects Without: Screenwriting, Collaboration, and the Workshop

Joseph Rein and Kyle McGinn

In the spring semester of 2014, Assistant Professor Joseph Rein copiloted a three-course collaboration between the English and Film departments at the University of Wisconsin–River Falls. His course "Screenwriting" consisted of 24 students from both departments. At the midpoint of the semester, those students wrote and submitted original screenplays with criteria specific to the collaboration project.[1] The other two courses in the collaboration were "Acting for the Camera" and "Electronic Field Production." Rein and the two professors for these courses ultimately chose five scripts for production.

Kyle McGinn was a senior Creative Writing major enrolled in the course. His script—titled Authors. Letters.—was one of the five produced in the collaboration. He is currently pursuing an MFA at Hamline University in St. Paul.

The following is correspondence between Rein and McGinn discussing their perspectives on the project.

JR: Most screenwriting textbooks focus on writing "spec" scripts: scripts written on speculation, as of yet unsold to production companies. These scripts are driven by narrative and character, focusing less on production aspects and more on storytelling. But my own first venture into screenwriting was quite the opposite; a director friend had a story idea, and essentially wanted me to tell it. Working with a small budget, he had sets and characters and a rough idea of the main plot points laid out. The rest was up to me.

This experience led me to seek out the collaboration project. In writing that first script, I realized how anchored screenplays must be to the realities of film production. In the traditional genres of fiction, poetry, and creative nonfiction, the process is in many ways the product: the poem I begin, although likely to be revised and altered, is also the end result. With screenplays, however, a writer exists in an ambiguous space in which we have both utter control over the course of the narrative but, in the end, little to no control whatsoever over how that narrative will translate to the screen. Similar to playwriting, we must consider not only how we captivate, but also how we do so under constraints such as budget, resources, technical capability. We must accept the fact that we do not have total control.

In doing so, however, we often discover a strange creativity in the constraints. This follows art movements like Oulipo, which believes that creativity blossoms under guided, pointed constriction. Founder Raymond Queneau believes, for example, that "[t]he classic author who writes his tragedy in accordance with a number of rules that he knows is freer than the poet who writes whatever comes into his head and is the slave of other rules that he doesn't know."[2] In this regard, the liberating parts of screenplay writing come not from endless possibilities, but instead from the necessity in considering how each craft element fits into the larger whole. Since adding another character means another actor, for example, a writer must justify that character's existence with meaningful moments. The same can be said for sets or scenes, props, even down to the smallest lines of dialogue.

I wished in some part to recreate this experience for my students. Most of them—the English majors—came from writing the traditional genres, and were accustomed to the freedoms they afford. The film students who enrolled had the technical skills but wanted to learn how to craft an absorbing story. My hope was that, with the very real prospect of having their scripts produced that semester, these two worlds would meld. I hoped my students would find exciting venues for creativity within the confines of their production limitations. The end results varied, of course, but it did seem to me that, at the very least, many of my students found a new path to creative expression.

KM: Now that I'm two years removed from the course, I took the time to look over the screenwriting projects that I managed to produce over those few months in 2014. *Authors. Letters.* didn't strike me as a particularly strong piece of writing then, though the final product that I saw on screen stands out in my memory.

Working primarily as a poet, I might be at an advantage in screenwriting due to the constraints of form and structure that poets often place on their work and the inherent limitations of the screenwriting format. I saw many parallels between form poems and my early scripts from the course. As writers, it can be difficult to relinquish control to others. It's not unlike the workshop environment in that the need for trust is paramount. This is where the course was different than any writing class I'd taken to that point. I never met the production team or the actors who ultimately produced *Authors. Letters.* So, I never had an opportunity to establish any relationship with the people who were responsible for producing the final edit. At the final screening, I was seeing the finished product with totally fresh eyes. It was riveting and frightening; ultimately, I was afforded a rare opportunity to see my own work as an outsider.

The course held a valuable lesson in letting go. Part of the process—apart from learning the technical jargon of screenwriting, developing a plot, and getting down to the actual writing—was allowing the work to exist on its own without me, the overbearing parent, there to defend any bad dialogue or plot holes. If I remember correctly, the class turned in the final drafts of each script by the fifth or sixth week of the course. For a revisionist like me, this was a daunting deadline. I distinctly remember handing in my final edits at the beginning of class and then mentally revising scenes fifteen minutes later. At some point, I made the decision to let go of the script and leave it up to the other classes to decide if it were a story worth putting on the screen.

In considering the sometimes fraught relationship between creative writing and pedagogy, I think that screenwriting holds a valuable place in teaching young writers much about the "off the page" functions of writing. By working in the limited environment that is a screenplay, writers seem to be challenged to write through and around the obstacles that often appear in fiction and poetry by utilizing new and clever techniques. I felt many of the same creative muscles that are exercised by lessons in Peter Elbow's insistence on journaling or Donald Murray's acuity for developing voice were strengthened through writing screenplays. To my mind, the team approach to developing a film opens up a new dialogue for young writers, one in which the typically solitary act of writing is altered to include the considerations of practicality and realism—considerations that a writer would do well to apply to that of the reader as well.

JR: I find your comparison to the workshop model interesting. At its best, the workshop provides a collaborative environment in which writers mutually influence one another, as Phillip Gross states, a "species of play, in the sense that all creative art is ... It continues the developmental business begun in childhood where wide possibilities (some of them risky or absurd) get tested with thought and imagination."[3] Important to me in the ideal workshop is this sense of play, of testing, of collaborative feedback as opening avenues of possibility as opposed to narrowing choices. Some of the primary criticisms on the workshop model—the homogenization of writing styles and Donald Hall's conception of the "McPoem"[4]—never rang true to me, simply because every work, be it through a workshop reader or an editor or a publishing house, will become altered. To assume that a writer's unaltered intentions constitutes something more valuable than a work that has been critically analyzed, scrutinized, and reedited, seems to me ludicrous.

But on the other end, I often find workshops lacking in this very area. I have attacked the workshop model in the past for not following through on its promise of collaboration. Through the years, I've become less and less convinced that a workshop is the best way for writers to learn, or, in some cases, even a good way, particularly for beginning writers. I find the conversations meaningful, the critiques astute, the classroom experience enjoyable, but ultimately I find a majority of the work itself nearly unaltered. No matter how valuable the in-class workshop seems, no matter how pointed and insightful both my and their classmates' critiques are, no matter how many drafts I require, no matter how much weight I place on revision, graded or otherwise, I simply haven't seen improvement like I have in almost every other course. Those who thrive in a workshop tend to enter with an open mind; few seem to acquire it there. It seems to me writers value their own creative impulses and the critiques of others on a sliding scale, and when most beginning writers sit down to revise, they slide to the former.

To bring it back to the screenwriting project: one thing I appreciate, from a pedagogical standpoint, is the overt nature of its collaboration. Essentially, the end project—an eight-to-twelve-minute short film—will not, and cannot, be made alone. The idea of one's vision as a primary driver for creativity acquiesces to a larger idea that the blending of unique talents—for example, a writer knows good dialogue, but a director knows good shots—can lead to products otherwise unattained in a general creative writing curriculum. This perhaps speaks to your idea of the need to relinquish control to others. This project forces it, whereas the workshop, at best, merely suggests it.

My views on the workshop, as I look at them now, seem rather jaded. It has been some years since I participated in my last workshop as a student. I honestly cannot remember my first. I do, however, remember entering them and not being interested in how I could collaborate with others. Like so many others, I had stories and wanted to tell them. I wanted an outlet for the things that seemed more important to me than pretty much anything else. I wanted to affect someone the way my favorite stories and novels had affected me. I wanted to learn how to improve, sure, but I also didn't want that to involve others. I wanted something I could do all by myself.

KM: Workshops are a constant within an MFA program (both inside and outside of class), and I've found myself sharing some of your frustrations in response to my less involved peers. I think that the involvement (or lack thereof) of others is what can spawn those jaded feelings. The workshop, much like the screenwriting project, relies on an "all-in" mentality from each party. It's disheartening to get back a critique with a few lines marked or a simple "nice" in the margin of an otherwise critique-less page, and I think that therein is where the beneficial nature of a collaborative environment, like the one you've described, becomes evident.

Writers come into most creative writing classes with a "workshop ready" piece, which, in other words, means finished. Often, workshops settle into microanalysis of a certain character or a chunk of dialogue (in my case as a poet, a single word can exhaust ten minutes of valuable workshop time). Here is where that "letting go" can be so jarring and refreshing for the workshop-fatigued writers. I distinctly remember talking to some of the senior writers in that screenwriting class and discussing the strange feeling of uselessness and anxiety that came from submitting a work without the comfort of a workshop critique to follow. This feeling, I now know, was simply a precursor to the sensation I get when finally submitting poems for publication consideration. It's exhilarating in a particular fashion, as the work is finally allowed to exist on its own without the defensiveness or pride that sometimes appears in the workshop setting.

In thinking about this class, revisiting my notes, and rereading the screenplays I wrote for various assignments, it dawned on me that I haven't written a screenplay since. The striking aspect of that revelation was that—after seeing a final project fully produced as *Authors. Letters.* was—I've adopted a mode of writing that considers the back end work of others (editors, publishers, slush pile readers) similar to the considerations made for a director, actor, and cinematographer. I've wondered about that mindset since then. Why did I never think that way when submitting work before taking the screenwriting class? Why did it never occur to me that I should consider the editors and readers of my work? How is so much attention paid in creative writing programs to producing work but not to negotiating an editorial process with a publisher?

I've come to the conclusion that this is due to the insular culture of creative writing programs. Sure, students establish relationships and personal workshops with their peers, but, in my undergraduate experience, it was never a requirement that writers collaborate. On more than a few occasions, the standout writers in a given workshop would turn out to be the most antisocial, the least open to criticism. Those same standout student writers and that same insular culture are severely tested once involved in a project like screenwriting. That's not to say that the creative writing students suddenly became social butterflies making fast friends with the production and acting classes; rather, the creative writers suddenly have to consider how their work might be analyzed, interpreted, and ultimately produced in living color.

I have the benefit of having taken another workshop of yours too. Although I learned much in the lecture portion of that course, my revisions were only somewhat influenced by peer critique; I worked more off of your comments. I think that the sliding scale that you mentioned develops more often than not in a workshop environment, which is startling to me because for so long I believed that I was collaborating with my peers in improving my work.

A part of me wants to see the collaborative nature of the screenwriting project somehow applied to a workshop setting, but I don't see it working without being invasive to the writing process. That inability to see how it fits tells me that you're probably right about the limitations of the workshop model. I think the obvious question to ask is: how can the successes of the screenwriting project be applied to a creative writing education in broader terms?

JR: There's the question I've been looking for! The very act of collaboratively writing this essay has produced the kind of creativity I champion—variance over assurance, possibility over probability. You've asked of me the very question that has been unconsciously sticking with me since that first screenwriting course.

It seems important to note that there is more than one way to work in groups. In looking at collaboration, I find Donna Lee Brien and Tess Brady's breakdown of the different types of collaborative work useful. The screenwriting collaboration project falls under what they classify as a "secondary collaboration model,"[5] in which one party begins a project and then hands it over to others for completion. Though many films, particularly short ones, involve a single person in many important capacities (writer/directors, director/actors, etc.), a majority of screenwriters often engage in this "handing off" of their material, and the less input they have afterwards (or, as I have heard said, the less they interfere with the filmmaking process) the more likely their script becomes a movie.

But of course secondary collaboration is only one of many kinds. Another common approach would be the "synchronous collaboration model," in which all parties contribute equally to each aspect of the writing process. (This model is also what we most commonly think of when we hear the term "cowrite"). Since that first class, I have adopted quite a few exercises and freewrites implementing this model, where two or more students create a script from conception to completion. In a way, it's the purest form of collaboration, because each party has the same opportunity and (ideally) provides equal input. The ways in which writers bounce ideas off one another creates an atmosphere that's pregnant with potential. And as a bonus, students generally love it.

I find, on the other hand, that I feel the exact opposite. It's not that I dislike the process, the lessons learned, or the final products when using the synchronous collaboration model, but that students for some reason instinctively turn to comedy. At its worst, these projects become a contest in whose creation can become the most preposterous. In other words, they enjoy the collaboration, but rarely do they treat it with the sincerity and care of their individual projects.

For workshop, another common collaboration type is what Brien and Brady would call the "cooperative collaboration model," in which one person begins a project and then circulates it through the larger group, for example having the class form a literary journal of sorts. In these workshops, the class acts as its own editorial team, selecting pieces on the condition that the writer revise based on the editorial board's recommendations. Though less "collaborative" in an overall sense, this type of project does closely mimic both sides of the publishing process and provides students practical experience in gearing their work for specific audiences.

But this is what has been done, as opposed to what *could* be done, and your question is asking me to consider that potential. How might the workshop adapt itself to better bridge that gap? I have some vague notions about class size—how smaller may be better, not just in total number of students per class (which is, in our political climate, sacrilege) but in dividing for portions into smaller collaborative groups. I have ideas on incorporating what Brien and Brady term the "contribution collaboration model," in which each writer would write a portion of a piece and then bring it together to try to make a coherent whole. But I'd like to pose your own question back to you. As a graduate student right now, as someone at the outset of his teaching career, you have perhaps a better vantage point from which to gauge the effectiveness and limitations of collaboration. Do you believe that, in the future of creative writing, collaborative work can, or will, or should, become common practice? Or is the lure of singular authorship, of creative genius, too strong to penetrate? Should we even want to penetrate it? Or, like you and me and so many budding creative writers, do we need that allure of sole creativity to enter the field in the first place?

KM: I think the singular authorship vs. collaboration question is very interesting and layered. But, before I address that and the broader implementation of collaborative projects in creative writing programs, I think it's important to consider the distinctive cultures of undergraduate and graduate writing. One significant way in which the workshop might let down young writers is through disconnect between receiving critiques and recognizing how a work is interacting with the reader. I admit to being a young writer who used the phrase "they just don't get it" far too often after a workshop session. The truth was that even I as the writer often did not "get it" either, but the kernel of the particular perspective I was hoping to share was still embedded within the piece. So, being young and amateurish, I didn't know how to listen to what my classmates were sharing with me as a means of learning how to cultivate that perspective. Perhaps addressing this problem is the first step for the collaborative workshop.

I'm envisioning an introductory workshop in an undergraduate program where the critiques are focused on developing an ability to open a dialogue with the writer on the page. In my undergraduate workshops, we employed a version of this through requiring a full page write-up to accompany the line edits (a practice I've been sorely missing in my graduate program, though I still do it in critiques more so for my sake than for my peers). Often, the most involved students produced write-ups that contained more questions and philosophical considerations than practical suggestions. This phenomenon, although not collaborative in the screenwriting project sense, was often more beneficial to improving the quality of my work—and more importantly my approach to my own work—than moving toward a finished story or poem. I believe that if this kind of organic development could be refined for use in an introductory workshop, it would serve well as a catalyst for seamlessly moving toward more overtly collaborative projects.

My opinion that collaborative writing should become a common practice is probably obvious by this point, but I'll offer you a direct response since I believe that you've raised a good question, one that has actually bothered me since starting my graduate studies. I think that addressing the lure of singular creative genius is a worthwhile endeavor. First, it would save many young writers the growing pains and humbling experiences that you and I have certainly experienced. Beyond that, I think that it creates space within the writing community of any given college or university for those who don't share that desire for individual recognition but still value writing and working on their craft. Students who strive for creative genius status can certainly pursue that goal within a collaborative environment, and I'd like to think that it actually benefits them in honing their singular craft by learning to recognize the shortfalls of their work through working with others.

The Information Age has afforded writing a bounty of topics and perspectives to consider. Collaboration between those of near or differing viewpoints seems to be not only the natural course of things, but a positive one. Of course, an argument could be made that collaborative work invites a potential for homogeneity, but, given the scope and varied experiences of the writing world, I don't think that's a valid fear. To my mind, the writing craft only stands to benefit from cultivating a generation of new writers who are willing to share with open eyes and hearts. After all, writing, at its core, is an act of sharing.

An important distinction to make is that I'm still beginning my career as a writer, and, though I have some publications to my name, I'm not as established as you or others who are educating the next generation of authors. Since I've offered the young, idealistic writer's opinion to the collaborative argument, my question for you is: as you've found success and frustration in your career, has the allure of singular authorship continued to hold any priority for you? And do you think that you would have seen any differences in the trajectory of your career had you come up in a collaborative environment?

JR: The answer to both of your questions is, paradoxically, yes. Of the various forms of accomplishments related to writing, I still get the most joy from a published story, which ultimately holds only my name. No matter how many people read it and give me feedback—which is often many for any given piece—there's still something unique about the ability to see a project from germination to final publication that stands as a singular, exciting experience. And that is something I would never want to take away from creative writing, least of all from my students.

However, more and more I find that for my most successful work—not my favorite, but my best—the stories arrive at me, not the other way around. Things I hear, read, research, become the basis for what I'm writing. In that way, I tend to claim less "ownership" over the story itself, and focus instead of doing the story justice: on telling it as well as I can tell it. There's something incredibly liberating, and I feel essential, in this shift, because it allows for constant adaptability with every new piece of writing. This mindset implies that success cannot be reached like a level on a videogame; rather, it lets us reinvent ourselves every time we write.

And to your second question, I do believe that I would have arrived at this understanding much sooner with a stronger undergraduate education. My coursework—which was heavily literature-based and, for creative writing, highly traditional—lacked for opportunity. If I hadn't pursued a graduate degree, it's hard to say if I would have continued to write, if I would have had the (modest) success I've had.

I see now I'm caught in the no-man's land; I don't want to squash the latent enthusiasm in creative writing's promotion of self-expression. In many ways, we offer something that few—or even no—other programs do. But as we've expressed here, the very thing that brings them in might be the thing that keeps them from advancing to a place where they truly understand the professionalism, and the collaborative nature, of creativity. Especially for the majority with undergraduate diplomas who pursue no further education, the notion that they may enter and leave essentially the same sincerely troubles me. The publishing world itself thrives upon the myth of the creative genius; a certain author is the only one who can do what she does, and thus gains a fan base, and thus makes more money. So if this change is to occur, it must be in creative writing programs, and, I think we would agree, at the undergraduate level.

KM: You're absolutely right that a creative writing pedagogy should avoid any inhibiting of a young writer's enthusiasm or self-expression—I think that it's important to have an honest conversation with those undergraduates (and perhaps ourselves).

The more I've thought on this, the more I've realized that somewhere in considering the effects and implications of a collaborative environment there is a sweet spot. That sweet spot differs from student to student, I'm sure, but perhaps the larger obligation of the creative writing program is to build an understanding among students that, as difficult as writing is, it is much less difficult with an open and active collaborative option among fellow writers.

Here is where I've come to a significant conclusion. Like you, I feel my most successful efforts have had the most hands on deck, from editors to professors to friends, but I don't think that compromised my voice as a writer. In fact, I'd like to think that it actually made it stronger. The people that I entrust with my work are often the people that know me and the ultimate goals I have for my writing most intimately. The poems and stories that arrive on the page of a finished draft are a product of that intimacy and they're that much better for it.

The problem with applying an individual experience like yours or mine to the broad field of creative writing pedagogy is that the intimacy I've described can't be manufactured within a workshop exercise or a specific project. But that's not to say that those endeavors won't foster the roots of those relationships, which is really the best we can hope for. I firmly believe that through some gentle coaxing and a bit of structure, many undergraduate writers will find the value of seizing the rare opportunity of embracing the community that the university experience offers. In other words, we can only show these young writers the map. It's up to the individual to determine how they might forge ahead, whether that's cutting a new path or sharing the road. But, either way, they're never totally alone.

Appendix: Screenplay Assignment

Midterm Screenplay

Assignment

For your Midterm Screenplay, you will write a screenplay that adheres to the following criteria:

- Must be between eight and twelve pages
- Must be realistic drama or comedy/drama
- Must have two to four primary (speaking) characters*
- Speaking characters' roles must be fairly evenly distributed
- Must have minimal to no minor characters
- Must have between two and four sets, all within the vicinity of UWRF, all accessible for shooting.

Screenplays must also be written in standard screenplay format, and submitted to D2L as a PDF file.

*Note: Roles in which the gender of characters might be easily changed (without affecting the nature of the story) might be given preference for actual production.

Film Production

I will collaborate with the instructors of DFT 351 (Acting for the Camera), and DFT 260 (Electronic Field Production), to choose *five screenplays* for production. The authors of these five screenplays will have a chance to make *minor* adjustments to their screenplays after Spring Break.

In addition to the above criteria, your screenplay will be graded on the following:

- Story
  - Screenplay tells a unique and compelling story
  - Screenplay has a clear beginning, middle, and end
- Scene
  - Scenes are detailed, thorough, and clearly delineated
- Character
  - Characters are dynamic and active agents in the story
  - Dialogue is realistic and reflective of character
- Conflict
  - Screenplay involves central/primary (and perhaps peripheral/ secondary) conflicts that reach some form of resolution
  - Each character has investment in the outcome of the narrative
- Screenplay format
  - Story follows proper screenplay format for shots, transitions, characters, dialogue, etc.

Notes

1 See Appendix for assignment sheet.

2 Quoted in Jacques Roubaud, "La Mathématique dans la méthode de Raymond Queneau," in *Oulipo, Atlas de literature potentielle* (Paris: Gallimard, 1981), 42–72, 57.

3 Phillip Gross, "Small Worlds: What Works in Workshops if and When They Do?" in *Does the Writing Workshop Still Work?*, ed. Dianne Donnelly (Bristol, UK: Multilingual Matters, 2010), 61.

4 From Donald Hall's "Poetry and Ambition": "To produce the McPoem, institutions must enforce patterns, institutions within institutions, all subject to the same glorious dominance of unconscious economic determinism,

template and formula of consumerism. The McPoem is the product of the workshops of Hamburger University." *Poetry and Ambition: Essays 1982–88*(Ann Arbor: Michigan UP, 1988).

5 Donna Lee Brien and Tess Brady, "Collaborative Practice: Categorizing Forms of Collaboration for Practitioners," *TEXT* 7.2 (Oct. 2003), web, April 12, 2016. <http://www.textjournal.com.au/oct03/brienbrady.htm>

8

Sequential Experiences: Course Design as Resistance in Creative Nonfiction

Michael Dean Clark

One of the most compelling elements of literary creative nonfiction is the way in which it constantly seeks to challenge the rules of whatever forms it inhabits. Where academic essays demand expository transitions, lyrical compositions leave transitions submerged in their language. Where lyrical essays eschew technical writing modes, writers construct the lyrical as a user's manual or legal brief. Creative nonfiction, by nature, is a form responding to itself. But teaching this resistance-as-aesthetic posture is often confounding as less experienced writers are apt to default to tropes and safer essay constructions when called upon to challenge expectations. And just as often, these safer choices are assessed as lacking student experience or engagement with the process or, less charitably, lacking skill. But what if the course is not designed to foster the resistance and experimentation we think it is? What if students can't challenge forms because they don't have a clear sense of what they actually know about them? And how might what they know be made more central to their exploration of new expressions?

The response to all three of these questions is found in the ways instructors plan and sequence writing experiences that elicit ways for students to interrogate their own expectations while exploring new modes of expression. To accomplish this, I'd argue that the work needs to be extremely process oriented, final essays are viewed as experiments rather than products, and the combination of all course elements must leverage new ideas about how memory and process intersect to form nonfictional resistance. Finding the proper balance of these three elements offers the best opportunity to help expand writers' understanding of creative nonfiction while encouraging them to resist the very rules they are learning.

Challenging expectations within a given form to find new and creative expressions is, of course, by no means a new approach. It's as old as human history and the arts themselves. The relatively recent emergence of creative nonfiction as a field of study and as a set of genres contains ample evidence of this. The broad strokes of New Journalism's well theorized path offers a specific example of this as it was born out of pushing back against the limitations of its unmodified namesake. In his definitive essay on the form, Tom Wolfe wrote the hope was that "All I meant to say when I started out was that the New Journalism can no longer be ignored in an artistic sense. The rest I take back ... The hell with it ... Let chaos reign ... out of such glorious chaos may come, from the most unexpected source, in the most unexpected form. ..."[1] And it did, driving genre-resistant forms like Capote's "nonfiction novel" *In Cold Blood*, the split-personalitied fiction–nonfiction Mailer hybrid *The Armies of the Night: History as a Novel, The Novel as History*, the embedded narrative claims of Herr's *Dispatches*, Thompson's nascent "gonzo journalism" in *Hell's Angels*, and Wolfe's own combustible blend of exhaustive reporting and literary style in, among others, *The Electric Kool-Aid Acid Test*. All these works, and the myriad others included in discussions of this particular moment in literary nonfiction, relied heavily on pushing back against the overlapping yet segregated expectations of print journalism (both newspaper and magazine), fiction, and historical texts to name just a few.

Predictably, the moment Wolfe codified his elements of New Journalism in somewhat genre-based terms, he started the clock on an inevitable resistance to those very elements. This came in the form of Robert S. Boynton's "New New Journalism," which sought to swing back toward a more conservative form of representation in favor of a more radical focus on reportage. "The days in which nonfiction writers test the limits of language and form have largely passed ... Contrary to the New Journalists, this new generation experiments more with the way one gets the story."[2] This mode of resistance has since given way to the current catchall category of "long form" which, in big tent fashion, creates boundaries and transgressions of those boundaries in the sheer divergence of expectations from piece to piece and context to context. This brief history of one facet of creative nonfiction illustrates a very important point for educators: resistance breeds creativity. And that resistance, I would argue, requires serious consideration of what one is resisting in the early stages of experimenting with creative nonfiction, both in the work of student writers and instructors' design aims.

The first challenge, then, is to define that resistance. A really solid collective look at this urge to resist categorical imperatives comes in the 2014 collection, *Bending Genre*. According to editors Margot Singer and Nicole Walker, the essays are curated to "serve as a guide and inspiration"[3] for further work in the burgeoning field of Creative Nonfiction studies. Further, they describe the collection as a "useful companion to traditional textbooks and anthologies" with perspectives on everything from creating a "poetics of creative nonfiction" to exploring the challenges of writing between and against genre conventions to philosophical notions of whether the field can be defined in any substantive way without gutting it of the very freedom that makes creative nonfiction compelling to write and read.[4] In the end, the majority of the book explores these ideas in compelling and, in many cases, embodied forms that lead to deeper thinking on a range of issues. However, there is little explicit concentration on the rudiments of pedagogies connected to these ideas, even as the essayists open a number of compelling doors.

Viewed from a course design perspective, one of the most compelling themes laced through a majority of *Bending Genre* is the need for disruption in both the practice and study of creative nonfiction. In summary, the message underlying the various perspectives included in the collection was this: the DNA of creative nonfiction is more than its refusal to operate via expectations and constraints—of genre, style, gender, class, language, and audience to name a few—but its outright attempt to blur and transgress those expectations in search of the most useful construction for each situation. As Michael Martone puts it, art is best "... in its natural habitat, in the wild. Or if it's in journals, acting like a bug, a germ, resistant to the antibiotic. Art that doesn't know its place. Art out of place. Art that disrupts convention, corrupts expectations."[5] This definition aligns neatly with Wolfe's notion of the expansive freedom of nonfiction that pushed past the limitations of a single form or expression. As such, resistance to expectation is the soul of creative nonfiction, not a facet of it.

If this reliance on resistance is the core of what students must explore, it opens a number of intersections of pushback regarding traditional forms.

Ander Monson articulates the overarching idea of this in the tension between reader response and authorial control, citing forms like hypertexts and videogames to illustrate his thoughts. "The reading experience is an experience of exploration of a created world. The question is how closely do you want to control your reader? … We like focused work, when the writer's made a thing to interact with. …"[6] T Clutch Fleischmann extends this idea by centering the notion of the "bent essay" as an act of resistance available to writers. As Fleischmann puts it, the "… resistance of the permeable essay to explain itself, to define its terms in a way that holds the audience's hand." This resists the "authoritative essay's" attempt to explain in informative terms.[7] In this way, "the role of knowledge is not so much to inform, but to encourage exploration … further into the places we call the margins."[8]

Taken for granted here is that the author is familiar with the rules, structures, and expectations between said margins as they push into them. This, however, is not an expectation instructors can treat as a given in their students' understanding of the work they are doing. It requires a pedagogy of intervention to help students develop a language for the boundaries within they worked. Colloquially, I refer to this as a "vocabulary of self" with my students because I want them to understand, from the outset, that they have internalized sets of expectations about what they can and cannot say and do when writing nonfiction. The key then is to use course experiences to expand that vocabulary.

Eula Biss explores the dual potential for power and problems in giving names to particular approaches to writing nonfiction in her essay "It Is What It Is." On the one hand, "Naming something is a way of giving it permission to exist. And this is why the term *lyric essay* was so important to me when I first learned it."[9] This sense of empowerment leads to consideration of the lyric essay in contrast to other forms, allowing authors to employ what they have seen in other examples of the form while issuing their own challenge to expectations they have encountered that might limit their expression. However, the moment a form is defined is the same moment it can become concretized. Biss addresses this hardening of expectations. "I suspect genre, like gender, with which it shares its root, is mostly a lie we have agreed to believe … Genre is not at all useful as an evaluative tool, but we seem tempted to try to use it that way. And we seem to be tempted to rely on just about anything but our own reading of a text to determine its value."[10]

This is a critical point. The resistance of a compositional process can easily become the constraint of genre. As such, one of the aims of the creative nonfiction course must be a consistent interrogation of the expectations of various forms and the demands created by what the writer is trying to communicate. This leads to a slightly different mode of goal-setting in terms of what writers want readers to take away from their experience with the text, allowing space for meaning to come in impressions a work creates, unexpected divergences from textual expectations, and meaning as accumulation rather than explicit efforts of the author to explain. In short, creative nonfiction must engage the reader in a conversation they feel a part of without resorting to the hand-holding Fleischmann refers to.

Inspiring disruption via course design that avoids feeling contrived or distracting, however, is not easy. In the first place, there are two ways students confront the very limitations a form seeks to resist without realizing this is the work they must do. The first is through introduction to formal expectations they do not know exist. This is the point of the readings instructors select; they must be discomforting in terms of a student's reading experience. The response, "I didn't think that was something you could do in nonfiction" is absolutely necessary in terms of opening dialogue about different forms of creative nonfiction and the expectations they carry. And the more a reading grates against students' ease of categorizing and "getting" what it means, the better it is for generating those useful conversations. This irritation serves as an introduction to the potentials of creative nonfiction that writers may not be aware of at the beginning of the course.

At the same time, these types of readings—coupled with a developed sequence of writing situations—open a second way by which students must assess their internalized and often transparent understanding of nonfiction. These expectations range from the way essays "should" be written to the types of language and devices they can or should employ, according to Margot Singer. "We tend to talk about these elements of craft as givens—laws of nature, almost—but they're not ... But realistic narrative has a way of naturalizing the operation of its conventions so that we forget they're there."[11] In much the same way, the elements of genre and form that students have picked up via their experiences with writing are what they cling to when trying to figure out how to engage the array of options creative nonfiction presents. And,

In many cases, what they have experienced as acceptable in terms of nonfictional forms and craft is very limited. In terms of compulsory education, the de facto priory position of explanatory and binary argumentation forms are what most students have internalized as the breadth of nonfiction via their overrepresentation in K-12 classrooms. Further, the limited variety of writing styles readers encounter in their daily interface with online text based on taste-based selections and algorithm-curated suggestions can also have a narrowing effect on the implicit definitions of nonfiction that students carry with them into the creative nonfiction class. Even higher education's posture toward forms of knowledge can play into constraining these expectations, according to Martone, who writes that colleges and universities "... seem to be diabolical engines for sorting, categorizing, defining."[12]

The creative tension of this categorization and division is the setting for Mihaly Csikszentmihalyi's work on understanding how creativity works. In his essay, "A Systems Perspective on Creativity," he situates creative production at the intersection of three separate forces: the Domain (knowledge, tools, values, practices), the Field (community, practice, gatekeepers), and the Person or individual practitioner.[13] All three are necessary and exert influence on the other. The job of the educator, then, is to help this individual practitioner cultivate two key responses to the systematic notion of creativity. First, Csikszentmihalyi contends a person must have access to the domain and desire to learn its rules (read: directed self-motivation) to understand where opportunities for creativity lie. And second, those most likely to innovate tend to want to break the rules they learned to gain access to the domain.[14] Applied to course design, this perspective demands a sequence of writing situations balancing rule following and breaking in the same spaces.

Another element of Csikszentmihalyi's perspective becomes important in the service of helping writers expand their understanding of the possibilities of creative nonfiction. In his book, *Creativity: Flow and the Psychology of Discovery and Invention*, he discusses the influence of gatekeepers in the field that an individual works within. These gatekeepers—editors, teachers, other influential practitioners—shape implicit and explicit understandings of what is appropriate and inappropriate for various writing situations before writers have even begun to compose.[15] For example, when assigned a formal academic essay, students are beholden to the assignment's requirements, the course's writing context or rules, the expectations of the professor and the field of study, and formalized stylistic concerns. If that paper is going to be made public, either in terms of a class reading or via publication, the dual pressures of editorial and audience expectations further exert pressure on the way the student must write. Or, as he put it in "A Systems Perspective on Creativity," "In order to function well within the creative system, one must internalize the rules of the domain and the opinions of the field, so that one can choose the most promising ideas to work on, and do so in a way that will be acceptable to one's peers."[16] In practical terms, this view makes creativity the expression of an individual practitioner's knowing resistance within their creative domain and field.

The particular challenges, then, are not the explicit gatekeeper expectations. These, by virtue of their external nature, are prescriptions that can be arrested and considered via typical means of study. Rather, the difficulty of this type of work is identifying and making visible the ways in which literal gatekeepers have passed through the permeable membrane of the human psyche and become transparent influences or, in many cases, limitations on writers' creative expression. The exploitation of studying the very boundaries that instructors are encouraging students to break is, then, an opportunity and a necessity. "Boundaries & the thrill of violating them would not exist if it were not for each tidy box of genre, complete with the rules for the performance of each."[17] Or, as Kevin Haworth puts it, "every breaking of genre is also an embrace of genre; we recognize the platform, even as the train rushes by."[18] Taken together, these two ideas add up to call for an active course construction that lays out the rules of creative expression in a given environment even as it deconstructs those same ideas.

The question in all of this for instructors, of course, is how does one help writers bend or break the constraints they carry into any writing situation? It's not nearly as easy as a well-wrought lecture, exemplary reading selections, and a robust course discussion. All of these act as forms of confirmation and reinscription minus an increased awareness of those expectations experienced in real time and through work that challenges the mental scaffolding regarding "proper" nonfiction that writers have encountered and then submerged. This is especially true of the rule-oriented forms of nonfiction students are most familiar with before taking a course in creative or literary nonfiction.

In the past, I have employed a very handy metaphor from neuropsychology and computer programming research to help shape my attempts to disrupt and illuminate these implicit expectations: the notion of scripts. If the brain operates like a computer, as theorists ranging from linguists to artificial intelligence designers have conceived it, then humans have stored operational programming running in our subconscious. These are known as scripts and are most commonly defined as "a program or sequence of instructions interpreted or carried out by another program outside the computer processor" or "a list of operating system commands that are pre-stored and performed sequentially by the operating system's command interpreter."[19] In this way, changing behavior has been compared to interrupting particular scripts and recoding them in the programming language of the script itself or in repositioning it within the larger network of programming languages and scripts it is supposed to operate.

However, compelling current research challenges the notion the brain stores information in this way, or even at all. In "The Empty Brain," Robert Epstein argues that not only do human brains not work like computers, but also the pervasiveness of the metaphor actually hinders discussing how it does work. Rather, "As we navigate through the world, we are changed by a variety of experiences. Of special note are experiences of three types: (1) we *observe* what is happening around us . . . ; (2) we are exposed to the *pairing* of unimportant stimuli (such as sirens) with important stimuli (such as the appearance of police cars); (3) we are *punished or rewarded* for behaving in certain ways."[20] This experiential way of "remembering" then is a more interactive notion of constructing the processes we will replicate, such as shooting a basketball or greeting someone we do not trust, or, in the case of the writing class, learn the expectations of a writing situation and then to challenge those very rules. One of the challenges of this new formulation, and one of its most exciting posits, is that it operates in response to the complete uniqueness of each person. "Because neither 'memory banks' nor 'representations' of stimuli exist in the brain, and because all that is required for us to function in the world is for the brain to change in an orderly way as a result of our experiences, *there is no reason to believe that any two of us are changed the same way by the same experience.*"[21]

As such, it makes the most sense to build courses that regularly places writers in the position of responding to the demands of experience. This activates the responsive nature of memory. Coupling this with creative obstructions and restrictions in a carefully laid out sequence of assignments allows for multiple forms of development. In this regard, I propose a four-step approach to course and assignment design that is progressive, effectively deconstructive of the silent expectations of form and genre, and dialogically reflective.

1. Divorce course work, as much as possible, from product-based thinking. Essays are of the Montaigne variety—tests, not products. They can become products, but usually in parts and later.
2. Other than portfolio contents, assignments run no longer than 300 words and employ restrictions and obstructions highlighting both a skill set and the tension of evoking rather than explaining.
3. Acknowledge and embrace discussion of rules and genre expectations as intertwined with craft concepts rather than as ornamentation or flourish. All work feeds discussion of practice, framing both writer's experience with the work at hand and ways in which experimentation enhances all forms.
4. Design assignment sequences culminating in the longer nonfictional attempts described earlier. Sequences should build awareness of both craft emphases and resistance modes.

In this way, students are provided the strongest possibility of employing the type of divergent thinking Csikszentmihalyi describes as "indexed by fluency, flexibility, and originality of mental operations,"[22] and opportunities for the associative experience Epstein describes as the functional core of building memory.

The reality of helping less experienced writers who have internalized via rote repetition the mechanical drudgery of the didactically meme-like five-paragraph argumentative essay as the soul of nonfiction is not something that can be explained. To use a sports analogy, I can't merely roll the basketballs out at the beginning of practice and expect my team to teach themselves the offense I want them to run, let alone why I want them to play that way in the first place. Similarly, to help students move beyond mere awareness of their notions regarding the limits and possibilities of nonfiction to actively working against them, the way my course is designed and—most importantly—sequenced has to do more than encourage them to read good examples and practice in their own work. It must make them productively uncomfortable through useful confusion, ragged edges, and ignorance of final product until the end of the term.

In terms of sequenced disruption, my course culminates in three final essays that students collect in a portfolio along with an aesthetic exploration allowing them to demonstrate lessons they've taken away in the, hopefully, expanded vocabulary of self the work has helped them develop. One of the most productive forms in terms of accomplishing the course goals is the pastiche or collage essay. In very short form, students choose a topic and create the impression of it via the way they collect and sequence their research rather than a position or message about it via their expository imposition. "Collage starts getting us there, with the reader's nontrivial effort required to make connections, to elide white space and fragment."[23] The key to this assignment is in a combination of it being left open to any form of source material and the requirement that students construct it in a self-selected digital format supporting that openness to sources. This allows students to use music, images, gifs, text, video clips, spatial relationships (the use of Prezi has been extremely helpful in this regard for students with limited or no design experience), and a number of other forms of information. The hope is to achieve a level of discomfort in the expansiveness of the writer's options while also exploring the reader's responsibility and control in making meaning.

But the pastiche is the end result of the sequence that leads to it. The first session of the process consists of a full class discussion regarding what a collage is including some history of the form linked to the Dadaist movement[24] and a class-sourced experiment in collaging a group childhood story. To facilitate the collage, each student provides details from a common memory (getting hurt while playing, a specific birthday, etc.). Once collected, the class creates a pastiche that employs one detail from each student and gives the impression of the general topic. The discussion, then, focuses on the way in which the collection of such disparate elements can serve a single aim.

At the end of the session, students are assigned readings for the next meeting. Two specific pieces that generally find their way into the discussion of the pastiche are Ann Carson's "The Glass Essay" and a section of David Shields' *Reality Hunger*. While Carson's piece is generally considered lyrically poetic, the way she overlays its elements—a personal narrative of loss, a domestic discussion of returning to her mother's home, a sense of connection to Emily Brontë's life, and vivid dreams—illustrates the potentials of disregarding more mechanical means of transitioning between ideas in a piece. Shields' work shows the scope of what collage can be in its attempt to wrestle with art's connection to the real in the age of replication. Both of these readings form the backdrop for a discussion of the implications and opportunities of collage as an approach to creative nonfiction.

The subsequent assignment sequence is relatively short at three activities, each completed in less than 300 words and leading to class discussions of what might be taken from them in terms of writing other forms of nonfiction as well as the pastiche. The first is an assignment called "Redefinitions" in which students select an explanatory word like angry or sad or happy and four synonyms for the word before finding the dictionary definition for all five terms. Then, their task is to represent the meanings of all five words using source material and without explanation. When they are done, classmates read their passages and try to determine what is being represented. The goal of this is to consider the representative qualities of the details nonfiction writers have to select from when writing a story and explore how much can be explained without explanation.

The "Redefinitions" exercise allows writers to ease into the basic premise of the final pastiche project: the eventual collage-form essay must present readers with an implicit sense of its topic via the selection of source material and the organizational structure they employ. The next activity, "@ Me," builds on this in a public forum by requiring students to create a series of five to seven tweets on Twitter conveying their emotion regarding a trending topic without labeling it or resorting to emoticons. The goal is to find other modes of eliciting their bias without didactic exposition to push the reader toward an interpretation. Like "Redefinitions," classmates read their tweets once posted and decide what emotion the writer is conveying and why, pointing to the evidence in the tweets guiding their interpretations.

The final assignment of the sequence is stolen from my fiction class called "Senses for the Senseless." Students select one of five sensory details I provide them without context. After making their selection, they must describe that detail to a person who lacks the correlative sense. For example, they must convey the smell of popcorn to a person who cannot smell or the taste of aluminum foil to someone who cannot taste. They can use any details to do this, but they need to bring the specific sense to the person via the other four senses. This underscores the work of all three assignments in that it leans on using details and order to explain rather than exposition. At the end of the session, students who wrote about the same details form and compare their attempts, discussing the decisions they made in light of what they see in each other's work.

Once through this final assignment, the class has a general discussion regarding the three activities and then transitions into a drawdown of the final pastiche project. At this point, I have the opportunity to guide students to thinking about how the work of nonfictional collage challenges their notions of what essays are and are supposed to do, and then extend into how they might use some of what they've learned in other forms. This is also a very effective point to step out of the work of the class and discuss the notion of their personal aesthetic and where it comes from before moving on to the next sequence and form.

The pastiche sequence is generally representative of how the other two forms built out in their portion of the semester, though I do want to gloss another really effective form in terms of learning to challenge expectations. The longest essay of the term is a narrative that runs eight to ten pages operating only in scene and dialogue. Again, this sequence begins with a class discussion and full group exercise before turning to readings like "Frank Sinatra Has a Cold" where we are looking specifically at Talese's insertions of himself into the narrative[25] and the opening of Jeff Sharlet's GQ piece "The Invisible Man: The End of a Black Life that Mattered"[26] to examine how it resists the expectations of expository journalism. The student activities in the sequence, in a nod to the New Journalists, rely heavily on finding ways to employ fictional techniques like dialogue, setting, characterization, and mood via research and nonfictional rules.

All three of the sequences leading to final projects come early in the term and leave students the rest of the term to draft, conference, small group workshop, and refine their final pieces. As they do, class sessions cover other elements of nonfiction such as research, form, structure, drafting, and professional concerns. However, setting the foundation of the course design in the experience of resistance allows that notion to carry through into more traditional discussions of craft. And this is the point of designing the course this way. For 15 weeks, it holds students in a consistent conversation between what they think nonfiction is when they show up and what they, hopefully, see that it can be by the end. Philip Gerard tells students, "[d]on't write too soon—before you write, ask the last question you need to ask."[27] He's discussing research, but his point is even more accurate in terms of resistance to form. And not all questions are analytical. In the work of creative nonfiction, they come in attempts to drop the restraints of form if they get in the way of what the writer wants to say.

Those attempts to bend and break the rules, however, must take into account the rules writers carry with them in the first place. A great metaphor for this comes in Epstein's attempt to illustrate the change in how readers conceptualize the operation of memory. He describes a classroom assignment in which a student draws a dollar bill from memory. The result is a clear but rudimentary depiction with only a few of the bill's elements included. The student is then shown a dollar before they turn away to draw it and the resulting picture is much more accurate. Comparing the two, Epstein is able to construct a way of differentiating how he sees memory working in opposition to the dominant computational understanding. In the same way, the first dollar can be seen as representing fuzzy notions of nonfiction that students are responding to when asked to write creative nonfiction and the second the challenging models of writing that instructors can and should present them with. The work required by the sequences that lead to those forms then is where students find the language to differentiate between the two and grow as writers.

Notes

1 Tom Wolfe, *The New Journalism*, ed. Tom Wolfe and E. W. Johnson (New York: New York: Picador, 1996), 51.
2 Robert S. Boynton, *The New New Journalism* (New York: Vintage, 2006).
3 Margot Singer and Nicole Walker, *Bending Genre* (London: Bloomsbury, 2014), 6.
4 Singer and Walker, *Bending Genre*, 5.
5 Michael Martone, "Hermes Goes to College,"' in *Bending Genre*, ed. Margot Singer and Nicole Walker (London: Bloomsbury, 2014), 54.
6 Ander Monson, "Text Adventure," in *Bending Genre*, ed. Margot Singer and Nicole Walker (London: Bloomsbury, 2014), 85.
7 T Clutch Fleischmann, "Ill-Fit the World," in *Bending Genre*, ed. Margot Singer and Nicole Walker (London: Bloomsbury, 2014), 47.

8 Fleischmann "Ill-Fit the World," 48.
9 Eula Biss, "It Is What It Is," in *Bending Genre*, ed. Margot Singer and Nicole Walker (London: Bloomsbury, 2014), 196.
10 Biss, "It Is What It Is,"' 196, 198.
11 Margot Singer, "On Convention,"' in *Bending Genre*, ed. Margot Singer and Nicole Walker (London: Bloomsbury, 2014), 142.
12 Martone, "Hermes Goes to College," in *Bending Genre*, 54.
13 Mihaly Csikszentmihalyi, "A Systems Perspective on Creativity,"' in *Creative Management and Development*, ed. Jane Henry (London: Sage Publications, 2006), 4.
14 Csikszentmihalyi, "A Systems Perspective on Creativity," 15.
15 Mihaly Csikszentmihalyi, *Creativity: Flow and the Psychology of Discovery and Invention* (New York: Harper Collins, 1996).
16 Csikszentmihalyi, "A Systems Perspective on Creativity," 15.
17 Karen Brennan, "Headiness," in *Bending Genre*, ed. Margot Singer and Nicole Walker (London: Bloomsbury, 2014), 59.
18 Kevin Haworth, "Adventures in the Reference Section," in *Bending Genre*, ed. Margot Singer and Nicole Walker (London: Bloomsbury, 2014), 94.
19 Margaret Rouse, "Script" on *Search Enterprise Linux* (San Francisco: TechTarget, August 2005, June 22, 2016), <http://searchenterpriselinux.techtarget.com/>
20 Robert Epstein, "The Empty Brain," in *Aeon* (London: Aeon Media, May 18, 2016, web. June 22, 2016), <https://aeon.co/>
21 Epstein, "The Empty Brain," in *Aeon.*
22 Csikszentmihalyi, "A Systems Perspective on Creativity," 14.
23 Monson, "Text Adventure," 89–90.
24 The best source for this that I've found for a combination of accessible history and specific content is David Hopkins' *A Companion to Dada and Surrealism* (Oxford and Chichester: Wiley-Blackwell, 2016).
25 For this essay, we read an annotated version found here: http://niemanstoryboard.org/stories/annotation-tuesday-gay-talese-and-frank-sinatra-has-a-cold/
26 Sharlet's piece can be found here: http://www.gq.com/story/skid-row-police-shooting-charly-keunang
27 Philip Gerard, *Creative Nonfiction: Researching and Crafting the Stories of Real Life* (Long Grove, IL: Waveland Press, Inc., 2004), 52.

Part Three

Creative Collaborations

9

Collaborative Story Writing and the Question of Influence

Mary Ann Cain

It is necessary to somehow keep both faces of [collaboration] in play, as collaborationism and as cooperation, and to discern how we can move from emphasizing one to emphasizing the other.

Holly A. Laird, *Women Coauthors*[1]

Every semester I teach the advanced course in writing fiction, I suck in my breath and prepare for struggle—mine, but more importantly, the students'. We try to remodel, as Nancy Welch says with regards to revision, many previously held assumptions about writing fiction.[2] Why do I keep doing it? It would be easy enough to scrap the collaborative project that I added over fifteen years ago and teach this 400-level course as I do the 300-level: a course portfolio with two or three revised stories and a final reflection. Much less struggle. None of us have to work as hard. After all, it's already hard enough to engage us in revision, in critical thinking, in peer reviews that go beyond a "thumbs up, thumbs down" mentality, and to go beyond the conventional workshop model so prevalent in MFA programs. These are undergraduates, with a few Masters students in the crosslisted mix. They don't know what to expect; they wouldn't know the difference. So why do I keep up the struggle?

* * *

In my doctoral program many years ago, I was taking a course on myth and language. The instructor, a senior professor who was also a fiction writer, offered serious, critical and, at times, searing critiques of students' class presentations.

At least one student thought the instructor was going too far. "We're still learning; go easy on us," seemed to be a shared sentiment.

Later, some of us talked about it in the Writing Center, where we often met to rehash our classroom experiences. The Writing Center director, a professor of rhetoric and composition, listened in as well. I don't remember who brought us to this conclusion, but at least some of us argued that the senior professor was taking us seriously, and that that was a good thing.

What we didn't talk about was how absolutely frightening a thing it was to be taken so seriously. To be listened to. To be held accountable. To be seen, fully.

* * *

Who among us really wants to be seen, fully? In fiction writing exists the conceit of the omniscient narrator, the voice of the all-knowing that speaks without error, without challenge. We trust this voice because it's a pervasive convention that we enter willingly, knowing the marvelous stories it can produce. We can enter the realm of imagination, fully, with that delicious sense that we are in charge, that what we imagine is ours and ours alone, and whatever we want to happen, can happen. We are the gods of our fictive universes.

* * *

I had chosen to go on for a doctoral degree rather than an MFA, partly because I already had an MA in creative writing, partly because I didn't think I'd learn anything new from going back into a workshop-driven degree program. I didn't know what I expected to learn except that I wanted to keep writing and learning. And if some school was willing to pay me for the privilege, even better.

I hadn't been introduced to critical theory besides more than passing references during my undergraduate and Masters' years. I heard sniping from some of the student writers in the MA program about theory and how it ruined "real" writing. I heard attacks from one professor, my thesis advisor, toward postmodern writers like William Gass, who wrote so far removed from human feeling, characterization, plots—all the things that one expects in a story.

I learned to mistrust such writers. Theory, I believed, was suspect. I couldn't make heads or tails of writers like Gass, mostly male, mostly white, and apparently only read by professors who liked to assign them to graduate students.

* * *

The real killjoy for some of my students has been Foucault, who seems to reduce the author to a social cipher, the "author function," and thus drains the delight of the omniscient conceit, the power of the individual authorial voice, the agency necessary to write against the grain, to be original, unique, and well, creative, right out of the classroom. Who cares about this theory sh–? they complain. We just want to write.

And indeed, I agree that it is hard enough to write fiction without some French theorist telling you that authorship is a social construction, and that the conventions that construct the author function are socially and historically driven and thus subject to change, influenced by the ebb and flow of power in a given society.

Of course, excerpts from Foucault's "What is an Author?" are the first readings in my advanced fiction class.[3] And this puts us on a course of struggle that threads throughout any given semester. We are not deities in control of a vast fictive universe. We are granted those conceits, those illusions of control by a collaborator, language. And this is a collaborator who, as Holly Laird has observed, is as likely to collude against us as it is to cooperate with us.[4]

So, in the act of being seen, we, too, are implicated in this complex web of language, power, and control. We as language users are as apt to collude against ourselves as well as others as we are to cooperate. There is no neutral ground to retreat to. The struggle is always present.

As I said, a bit of a killjoy, that Foucault.

* * *

To begin to answer the initial question I've posed—Why enter this struggle?—I start by saying how I want students to encounter language as if something real is at stake. What that means is that what happens in the classroom must be understood not only as entering a familiar terrain, as conventions brought to light and practiced for refinement, but also as an experience of the unfamiliar, of the never-before-known. Of strangeness and the possibility of being overtaken. As Toni Morrison has said, it's about control and surrender.[5]

In my class, it's about control of and surrender to language—yours, mine, and the Other's. It's about learning that my control depends upon yours that depends upon the Other's. We don't operate in a vacuum. We are seen, fully, and we are both colluders and cooperators in the acts of using language. There is no neutral space here. We're all implicated. The stakes are high.

But I also see opportunities for great bursts of play, swinging from one word to another, one discourse to another, without fear of getting lost or hurt, knowing that we are all taking the same risks, together, and so if we all crash we can look around and ask, What happened here? This is where my work really begins, at the crash sites, but also at peak moments of liberatory joy. My struggle is in being the one who, if not omniscient (I like omniscience as much as anyone, but it's not a conceit I find very useful in the classroom, at least not very often), provides perspectives on what such lows and highs might mean in terms of their relationship to conventions of fiction and fictional techniques. My struggle is to see what is not what I already expect to see but what else is happening that I haven't seen before. Of course, I start with what I already know has happened countless times—students straying into the first assignment, what I call an intertext draft (Appendix One), and feeling that they have lost themselves and their "voice" in the process of collaborating with a canonical writer like Sherwood Anderson or Ernest Hemingway and can't find themselves in those texts, such texts being so completely Other that they either resist collaborating or get swallowed up by it, but in either case can't find engagement vis-à-vis collaboration.

My work, as I understand it, is to pay attention to how they have either resisted or been overtaken by the Other, and tell them what I see is going on, or in other words, tell them a different story than they are telling themselves about what has happened, is happening, to their "voices" and their sense of the familiar. When students observe that they are "ruining" the works of these "great" writers by collaborating with them through the intertext, I focus on what exactly is being "ruined" and what that makes visible about the "great" writer's text as well as their own writing habits and conventions that they hadn't noticed before. My role, then, is to work at helping them see what they are uncovering in this collaboration that they would not have previously seen about their own work, as well as in the Other's. Sometimes it is as simple as, I write mostly in internal monologue, and Hemingway does not. Sometimes it is about the lack of active verbs and imagery in their own work. My work is to help them see themselves in the eyes of this Other and help them reimagine what they thought was possible to do and say as a writer. I can affirm, Yes, you are intertexting mostly with internal monologue, but I also question, And how does that add to and/or take away from the text? I do this by way of helping them see the problems as well as possibilities of a given convention. Similarly, in their observation about the "lack" of active verbs and imagery in their work, we can pose the question of how does it matter to include or not include such conventions in their work?

Another theory that informs this practice of collaboration as both cooperation and collusion with language, self, and Other is that of "remodeling." Nancy Welch's very important and useful book, *Getting Restless: Rethinking Revision in Writing Instruction*, explores how writing classrooms typically present revision as a means to find greater conformity with the teacher's Ideal Text, and thus toward a greater conformity to collectively held assumptions about what "good" writing is and does. Welch juxtaposes "remodeling" as a way of understanding revision not as a binary opposition, as either the writer conforms to conventions or rejects them, but instead as a way to reconceive conventions, and thus an Ideal Text, as presenting multiple identifications beyond the binaries that shape classroom interactions and determine how power is distributed. Welch accomplishes this by using what feminist philosopher Michelle Le Doeuff calls a "third factor." According to Welch, "[T]he introduction of a third factor to relationships we tend to think of in twos—student and teacher, apprentice and master, scholar and discipline—places particular systems and particular philosophers, mentors, or teachers in historically *interdependent* relationships with others. Third factors ask new questions, reveal unexamined assumptions, and work to deconstruct that myth of the complete and stable model."[6] By using a third factor, this binary, with its attendant power structure of the teacher's Ideal Text dominating the student's text, is disrupted, opening up a multiplicity of identifications for the student writer to draw upon, beyond the teacher's Ideal Text.

In the case of the intertext assignment, I urge students to "mess up" the canonical author's text by way of including whatever they see is missing, whether it sounds "good" or not. This leads to a discussion of the conventions employed by the canonical text and how they limit, for better or worse, what the story says and does. The discussion also includes observations about students' own uses of conventions and the limits those impose, for better or worse. Then students write another draft, moving away from the scaffolding of the canonical text and generating their own story that both draws from the original and at the same time goes beyond it. Unlike fan fiction, which simply seeks to extend the original by way of imitation, intertext work sets up a dialogue between author, text, and reader through the students' written responses to it. Rather than being overtaken by a text or trying to overtake it, I coax students into reimagining their relationship to language as one in which they not only receive it, but say something back. Their agency comes not in acts of compliance or rebellion but in inquiry and critical practice. It is about staying responsive.

The intertext assignment sets up the collaborative story writing project that runs through most of the semester. Admittedly, I introduce an approach to composing that few, if any, of them, anticipate. I, too, can function as a kind of killjoy to students who, by and large enter my classroom with expectations that they will be able to write "freely" and with "inspiration," unlike their other academic classes where the writing is constrained and the expression of self is often discouraged. Pairing critical practice with creative expression can feel constraining, and in feeling constrained, students can feel stifled in their "free" expression.

But feeling and recognizing what constrains their writing is the point. Nothing in writing comes "free," in this sense. There is always something that constrains the work. As Judith and Geoffrey Summerfield have written in their marvelous pedagogical text, *Texts and Contexts*, constraints can be enabling or disabling, depending upon the contexts that give rise to them. Their classroom is not a peaceable kingdom as much as it is one of engagement: "[T]he air is experimental, tonic, collaborative, athletic, genial, sometimes urgent, always productive. It's not without tension, but if things go well, the tension is not destructive but generative. Utterance is dialogical rather than monological."[7] Sometimes that engagement leads to questioning and resistance, complaints but also breakthroughs. It is not a neutral ground. Risks abound. Something real is at stake.

So learning that writing is not free, that risk taking is inevitable, that language is as much about collusion as it is about cooperation with a writer's ideas is not what they are expecting to learn. This puts me in the position of a rhetorician. I can't simply say, Now do this, and expect unquestioning compliance. The whole point is to get them to question, and sometimes to question me, my methods, even my teaching philosophy. Sometimes I fail to be persuasive or even clear, to them, about what I'm leading them into and why, let alone how to do the tasks I lay out. Sometimes it doesn't matter if I succeed as a rhetor because the work of collaboration takes over, first in the intertext assignment, and then with the collaborative project they must write in conjunction with peers. They can safely ignore my attempts to persuade them because they are persuading themselves and each other. Collaboration depends upon peer-to-peer dialogue and instruction. Without it, the class would collapse. I as one writer among many cannot carry the weight of being the sole collaborator for a class with 15 or so students. But I am, I tell them periodically, one of their many collaborators. I am not simply a judge; I am a cocomposer.

***

The collaborative story assignment has evolved over the decade or so that I have used it in the advanced fiction course. What has stayed the same is that each student is responsible for producing one story for their final course portfolio that has been written and revised in response to a collectively generated prompt, as well as the stories of their peers. So, for instance, in some semesters, students have developed a common character. In other semesters, they have produced a common setting. The entire class writes a first draft, then reads everyone else's and comments. They must negotiate what is a "fact" of the character or setting that they can agree upon. However, I also urge them to explore the possibilities of meaning derived from *not* adhering to an agreed-upon backstory or profile. I say, what if there are differences or contradictions? How might that serve the collection as a whole? So they must "remodel" their assumptions about either complying with the group's direction or throwing out the constraints that have been presented. More recently, I have limited the scope of their collaboration to small groups who work on their own, small-group collaborations. They also have the option of also composing stories jointly, that is, one long story that they all contribute to.

Successful groups tend to share more of their thought processes and ideas with each other, both inside and outside class. I have learned to provide ample time for such conversations, as well as to require written peer reviews of the group's drafts. I also scaffold some metadiscourse—talking about how they are talking to each other about collaboration—as part of teaching them how to remodel the concepts they have internalized and that currently constrain them when faced with a "forced" collaboration in the classroom. And again, I place myself as a rhetorician, charged with persuading them that yes, on one hand, they are being "forced" to do something that they think is at best a voluntary task, and no, in another sense, they are always required, if not forced, to collaborate with that Other we call language, with its attendant "rules" and conventions.

Whether they agree with me or adopt my theoretical and political stance on composition in their final written reflections for their course portfolios, they more often than not demonstrate some of my positions in their writing, which gives us rich material for our exit conference discussions. By this point, I hope they have learned that disagreement or agreement with me in and of itself isn't the point; it's about engaging the ideas and assignments, and bringing themselves into them. I am, in a sense, just another writer. But I am also one with experience. I also hold the power of the grade. It's a complicated relationship. But rather than shy from the complications, I try to meet them head on. I enjoy the privilege, as well as the burden, of being their collaborator and judge.

* * *

In closing, I hope I do not come across as a hero or a villain in this narrative about collaborative writing. I do not see myself as having the luxury of "choice" as to whether I should risk introducing engaging but at times very challenging, and even frustrating work and expectations into the classroom. I am not a hero for entering the struggle. It is going to be there whether I bring it or not.

I am also not a villain in forcing my will upon students, thwarting their expectations of "free" expression and an unconstrained classroom unlike many of their others. They are already constrained. They are already risking their "free" expressions by remaining unconscious of what constrains them.

I keep learning because I don't really have a choice. I listen, adapt, "remodel" as needed. I struggle to stay responsive.

And I learn, like my students, how to fail. Perhaps that is the best lesson of all. When we fail together, we can share the multiple ways failure hurts but also helps, even heals. We can find joy again in the collective enterprise that is language, that is writing.

Appendix one: Intertext assignment sheet

Write: A complete first draft of a story based on an intertext of a literary work of your choosing.

Some potential "collaborators" for your intertext include:

- a literary work (of any genre) you particularly like or admire, that you might even consider (consciously) influential on your writing;
- a literary work you have negatives feelings for and do not want to influence your writing;
- a random literary work you've never read before but will now;
- yourself, using a previous story that you've written to generate an intertext.

Again, an intertext comes from writing "in between the lines" of another text, so to speak. This means identifying what the original text leaves unsaid and creating a new story based on the "left out" material. Your goal here is to create a new story that stands on its own (i.e., a reader would still understand it without having to read the original). Remember, you're not trying to "fit" the original but "engage" it. That means you can (and perhaps should) make it quite different from the original.

Step one: Requirements for the intertext

You must take at least 300 words from an original source and add at least 600 words to it (more is better and probably necessary to create a complete draft). Please use different font styles (or bold face, italics, or color) to show what is the original text and what is your intertext addition.

For this assignment, rest assured that it's perfectly ok to use parts of someone else's text in your story. Don't worry about copyright laws or plagiarism at this stage of the process.

Step two: Requirements for the story draft

Using the intertext as your jumping off point, draft a complete story of no less than 1360 words (four pages double-spaced) that uses the "left out" materials of your chosen text as your prompt and inspiration.
Keep in mind:

- You will need at least one revised story (plus the collaborative project) for your final portfolio. So aim for a complete draft here.
- I will expect SUBSTANTIAL revisions ("re-visions") from first to final drafts. We'll talk more in class about what I mean by revision.

Turn in:

- Intertext
- Story draft

Appendix two: Collaboration models

Types of collaboration

- Single authored—collaboration hidden. Scribner Editor Maxwell Perkins had a big role in H's work, however. (His letters w/ Hemingway and F. Scott Fitzgerald are published in *The Sons of Maxwell Perkins*.[8])
- Couple: Call and response. Dorris and Erdrich wrote everything together, even those things with single author. Publishing/marketing/review/ libraries all set up for solo author. See more on their process. *Crown of Columbus* something that comes out of VERY close proximity.
- Group: asynchronous writing. One person acts as lead writer/editor. Others write their chapter as assigned. *Finbar's Hotel* written this way; each writer chose a room in the hotel. Writers don't really have much contact except through editor.
- Group: synchronous writing. Kesey's class literally sat in the same room for three semesters and wrote together over coffee and wine, in his house off campus.
- Group: semi-synchronous. W401/C611 class. Develop location together. Each person writes a story about that location through some feature of the location.

- Pairs/Groups: Creating links between individually authored stories. W401 this semester.

Appendix three: Collaborative project assignment sheets (two examples)

1. Small group or pair collaborations

Collaborative project assignment #1

Write: Using the menu we developed in class on ways to link stories, write a complete story draft that includes a full narrative arc. Also, keep in mind the various models for collaboration that we discussed in class. These can help you decide what direction you and your partner will go in your collaboration. For instance, you can choose to write two separate, but linked, stories or one jointly written one. Write at least four pages (eight total if you are writing one joint story), typed, double-spaced; more is better. (The final length must be 8–10 pages separate/16–20 joint.)

- Post your draft on your peer group's thread on Blackboard. Bring a hard copy to class.
- Another, longer draft will be due November 23. We'll be doing some smaller assignments in the meantime to help you move forward.

Second draft assignment

Write: A second draft of your collaborative story. Using the evaluation criteria that we developed in class as a guide, write another draft.

Make sure this story has a complete arc, that is, beginning, middle, and end. It should stand alone as an independent piece. But it should also clearly reflect your peer collaboration.

Also, if you haven't already, make an effort to borrow stylistic and other technical elements from your peer's draft. You can afford to "overdo" this quite a bit, since you will need to do a third and final draft for the portfolio. Hint: You may be surprised at how difficult it is to "overdo" it but also how easy it is to "underdo" this approach. Remember that it's easier to scale back than to add more when it comes to final editing. So add LOTS more now and subtract later if need be.

Evaluation Criteria for Portfolio Stories—Individual and Collaborative

Plot

- Use of a narrative arc or an alternative dramatic shape that provides a sense of "completeness," including that of a resolution.
- Clear and balanced use of some of the seven archetypes.
- Endings should reflect the fulfillment of questions, problems, suspense, and so forth introduced in the beginning of the story.

Characterization

- Main characters should have a reason for being there that helps further the plot.
- Minor characters should help portray other feelings or meanings that show contrasting and/or supporting perspectives than the main character's.
- Characters should read as consistent but (as appropriate) also round.

Style

- Use of imagery and patterns of imagery that contribute to the overall meaning of the story, for example, setting a mood, following a theme, creating an emotional landscape.
- Transformation of clichéd or stereotypical language, characterization, plot lines, etc. into something more vivid and powerful.
- Unique use of language to express complex emotions, characterization, and events

Overall techniques

- Consistency in use of technique—in other words, striking a good balance between using the same throughout and contrasting techniques that provide emphasis. (For instance, narrative perspectives might rotate between two or more characters consistently, but if the perspective changes once and only once, that might provide an important emphasis OR it might create an imbalance in the narrative arc.)

- Dialogue that is realistic to the story world that is constructed.
- Connections are drawn between all story elements. All elements are used consistently and with purpose. (For instance, if you introduce a character, make sure they are used to some effect that connects to the story overall.)

Process

- Demonstrable and purposeful use of influence by peers, instructor, and other sources

Evaluation criteria for portfolio stories—collaborative only

Overall use of techniques

- Shared worlds or settings.
- Shared stylistic and other technical elements (point of view, plot lines, dialogue, etc.).
- Overlapping narrative voices that echo but don't simply imitate each other.
- Thematic sharing.
- Point of view techniques that echo or complement each other.

Process

- Overall sense that both stories belong in the same collection.
- Balance struck between individual and collective expression.

2. Collaborative project assignment using a collaboratively composed and shared setting

Collaborative project assignment #1

Write: Using a specific aspect of our collaborative location (you may want to draw from our in-class exercise), write a complete draft that includes a full narrative arc. Write at least four pages, typed, double-spaced; more is better. (The final length must be 8–10 pages.)

To ground your narration, I want you to imagine your main character(s) as metaphorically linked to this location.

- Think of this location as exerting itself upon your character. For instance, you might think of a "powder room" as a potentially explosive location centered on female vanity; perhaps your character engages in an explosive interaction, or witnesses one, or escapes one, or just imagines the potential.

- Use specific imagery and action to bring across this location as a character in its own right. For this draft, it's better to exaggerate this feature. You can cut back on the revision.
- Post your draft on the discussion thread, Collaborative Project, on Blackboard.
- Another, longer draft will be due November 17. We'll be doing some smaller assignments in the meantime.

Notes

1 Holly A. Laird, *Women Coauthors* (Champaign-Urbana: University of Illinois Press, 2000).

2 Nancy Welch, *Getting Restless: Rethinking Revision in Writing Instruction* (Portsmouth, NH: Heinemann, 1997).

3 Michel Foucault, "What is an Author?"1969, web, www.movementresearch.org.

4 Laird, *Women Coauthors.*

5 Toni Morrison, Fiction Writing workshop, State University of New York, spring 1988.

6 Welch, *Getting Restless*, 62.

7 Judith Summerfield and Geoffrey Summerfield, *Texts and Contexts: A Contribution to the Theory and Practice of Teaching* (New York: McGraw-Hill College, 1986), 2.

8 Perkins, Maxwell E, Matthew Joseph Bruccoli, and Judith Baughman, *The Sons of Maxwell Perkins: Letters of F. Scott Fitzgerald, Ernest Hemingway, Thomas Wolfe, and Their Editor* (Columbia, SC: University of South Carolina Press, 2004).

10

Steampunk Rochester: An Interdisciplinary, Location-Based, Collaborative World Building Project

Trent Hergenrader

For the past five years I've been experimenting with an alternate approach to teaching creative writing that I call *collaborative world building*. This pedagogy has a number of different learning objectives, only one of which (and perhaps one of the least important) is learning about the craft of fiction writing. The others include learning to use digital writing tools that involve wikis and online mapping software, gaining experience working on a nonlinear collaborative narrative, and, above all, thinking critically about representations of people, places, and things—both in fictional worlds and the actual world we inhabit. One of my students termed collaborative world building as "critical theory meets creative writing" and I couldn't have described it any better myself. Collaborative world building courses are messy, sprawling, chaotic, confusing, difficult to manage, challenging to assess, and absolutely worth doing.

This approach grew out of my frustration with students writing plot-driven fiction at the expense of other aspects of craft, most notably character and setting. Basing my work in scholarship in literacy studies and game-based learning, I designed a fiction writing course using the role-playing game as a model for creating flexible, character-driven stories.[1] The course adopted the science fiction genre of post-apocalyptic fiction and was structured in three roughly equal parts: examining narrative across media, world building, and role-playing sessions. In the first unit, we read short stories from the post-apocalyptic short story anthology *Wastelands*, watched the films *The Road* and *Mad Max: Beyond Thunderdome*, and played the videogame *Fallout 3*. For each story we discussed the nature of each post-apocalyptic world, the attributes and personalities of the protagonist and other main characters, and how plot was the result of characters attempting to overcome obstacles presented by their specific environment. In the second unit, students populated a wiki with details of their own fictional world—a post-apocalyptic version of Milwaukee—that included adding entries for numerous people, places, and things and pinning those entries to a Google map of the city.[2] They also each created a character for the role-playing sessions who would serve as the protagonist in the short fiction they would write based on the sessions. The third unit split students into five groups that engaged in role-playing sessions where students played the parts of their characters. Together, they explored the fictional space they'd created, drawing details and plot twists from the information in the wiki entries and map. The players had to make choices based on their characters' personality traits and motivations, and the outcomes of those actions were resolved by the game rules. For example, players might need to reference their character's stats sheet and roll dice to determine whether their bluffing attempt worked, if their character scaled a drainpipe successfully, or if they hit their intended target when throwing a punch. After each role-playing session, students wrote a vignette of roughly 1,000 words and critiqued each other's fiction in ways similar to more traditional fiction workshops.

The course turned out to be a profound experience for my students and myself alike. Something happened in that class that went far beyond learning a body of craft tips or improved technique. Of their own volition, a group of students took a weekend field trip to parts of the city they'd never visited before to get a better sense of the environment their characters had explored; one student fell seriously ill but wrote to me from her hospital bed to check on her group's role-playing campaign; and two groups felt they didn't get the closure they wanted from their narratives and thus threw a barbeque party to finish their campaign, three weeks after the last day of school and long after grades had been posted. Now, over five years later, I still get emails and notes on social media from these students recollecting that semester. I was so inspired by the class that I used the world the class created as the setting for my dissertation, a hypertext fiction, and I thanked each student by name in my acknowledgments.

If I thought I'd developed the perfect course design, the second iteration of the course, taught two years later, brought me back to earth. I used a near-identical approach but did not replicate the previous near-magical experience. For starters, the second group of students completed less of their work by the due dates, which wreaked havoc with the course schedule and delayed the role-playing sessions. Second, I had fewer students who could serve as competent game masters, making the role-playing sessions uneven experiences for different groups. The sessions themselves were compromised by barren areas of the map that students failed to populate with interesting characters or locations. The completion rate for their fiction writing and critiques was spotty as well. All told, the results of the work were similar to other classes I had taught, albeit with the benefits of lower absenteeism and more enthusiastic class participation. Despite my frustrations, students' evaluations still rated the course very highly, with most noting the usefulness of the collaborative world building unit as well as experiencing an unpredictable narrative through role-playing sessions. Even if the class failed to meet my expectations, their thoughtful post-course evaluations strongly suggested that it had been impactful in other important ways.

These two experiences taught me a number of things. First, I needed to be more deliberate in my course design to leverage portions of the course that worked well and to minimize aspects that caused problems. Second, students unanimously responded positively to collaborative world building and role-playing in a fictional world. And third, the process of world building and telling stories from a highly subjective viewpoint required students to *think critically* about fictional worlds and a given person's place in it, but allowed them to *respond creatively* when reflecting on what they had learned. While I'd originally designed the course to emphasize craft lessons, I now turned my attention to investigating why certain aspects of this methodology seemed to work consistently, and how I might adapt this approach for other learning objectives.

Learning theory and collaborative world building

Collaborative world building has two phases: the first is the writing of a metanarrative or an overarching story about the fictional world; the second is the creation of a catalog of wiki entries that describe the people, places, and things that populate this world. When writing the metanarrative, the students have to work out in detail how different aspects of the world operate and interrelate, including different aspects of governance, economics, social relations, and cultural values. When the group reaches a general consensus about the broad narrative that describes the world, each student then begins writing their own unique wiki entries for specific people, places, and things. Each wiki entry functions as a discrete writing exercise that showcases the writer's individuality but it must also be consistent with the collaboratively written metanarrative. The growing body of wiki entries expands their understanding of the world they've made, and they continue to refine it by adding small details and revising the metanarrative and individual entries as the world continually evolves.

This act of assembling a world from lots of disparate bits has much in common with *constructivist* and *constructionist* learning theory. Piaget's theory of constructivism posits that people construct internal models of how the world works, and these models are derived from many different types of learning experiences a person has, both with different forms of media (books, television, films, games) as well as in their personal relationships (interactions with parents, peers, teachers, coworkers, etc.); Papert's constructionism extends Piaget's theory, arguing that our constructed knowledge of the world is always developing through the making of things, and thus our creations provide a point of conversation with others about how we see and then represent the world.[3] In short, people construct models of how the world works (metanarrative) based on a series of experiences, each of which functions as an individual unit of meaning (wiki entry); in essence, these units of meaning are the building blocks upon which the person formulates his or her understanding of the world.

Thus the process of collaborative world building is both *dialogical* as well as *dialectical*. This means students must carry on an extended dialogue about the fictional world to iron out details and resolve inconsistencies while also continually rethinking and readjusting their viewpoints and opinions based on the feedback of their peers. In practice, students naturally move between making statements about how the reality of our actual world "works" to make a case about how the reality of the shared fictional world ought to "work." This in turn allows for provocative discussions of whether all people who inhabit a world would agree on how reality works, bringing to the fore questions of objective and subjective aspects of worldviews. As philosopher Richard Paul[4] explains:

> Dialogical and dialectical thinking involve dialogue or extended exchange between different points of view or frames of reference. Both are multilogical (involving *many* logics) rather than monological (involving *one* logic) because in both cases there is more than one line of reasoning to consider, more than one "logic" being formulated. Dialogue becomes dialectical when ideas or reasonings come into conflict with each other and we need to assess their various strengths and weaknesses. (310)

Students move between critical thinking and creative production, back and forth and back again, where the two become so intertwined that it's difficult to distinguish one from the other. Thinking and making are not separate activities but part of a whole. A majority of the classroom time is spent hosting these debates and discussions, so students can witness how their peers work through these questions, and so the instructor can ask provocative questions and encourage students to complicate their thinking even further.

The digital nature of the world building project encourages a different view of writing more broadly conceived than print on paper. Along with the descriptive text for their wiki entries and stories, students must include a representative image. This can be something that they find on the Internet or a work they produce themselves. This move acknowledges the visual element of webpages and opens up space to talk about the rhetorical strategies for pairing appropriate images with their narrative. This allows creative writing instructors to contribute to the development of students' "multiliteracies" beyond just text, as the New London Group urged instructors to incorporate it in their teaching.[5] All of the wiki entries and vignettes feature several links to other people, places, and things as well, reinforcing the notion that the world and the stories in it are part of a larger collaborative effort as well as urging students to consider their writing as a single node in a much wider network of connections.[6]

Thus this type of large-scale collaborative project begins as a blank canvas that students gradually fill in as the semester goes on. Students usually begin hesitantly, not sure if they're doing things "right" and not wishing to step on anyone else's toes with their creations. With guidance and support and structured small assignments, the world takes rough shape and they soon begin making connections between the people, places, and things coming into being. Soon enough the project reaches a critical mass and the students take over—it's *their* world now, and the instructor's job shifts from encouraging participation to ensuring that new contributions are consistent with the established narrative, and that students continue to apply their critical faculties throughout the creative process.

The Steampunk Rochester project

Collaborative world building is an approach rather than a methodology; in other words, rather than following a step-by-step process of how to complete the project, the general principles and theories can be applied by different instructors for different purposes.[7] The remainder of this chapter will be spent describing Steampunk Rochester, an ongoing project that brings together students from creative writing, visual culture, and game design and has included the participation of faculty from history and digital humanities. In the future the team hopes to add faculty and students from 3D digital design, graphic design, and students interested in improvisational acting to add a performance aspect to the project.

Steampunk is a subgenre of science fiction that imagines a society primarily run by steam-powered machinery. The best examples of the genre deal with the relationship between technologies and societies, and how each influences the other. While some steampunk enthusiasts revel in steampunk's Victorian-era aesthetics, as a literary genre, it can also function as cutting social criticism along the lines of race, class, gender, and sexual orientation, giving voice to characters who were marginalized or completely written out of the history of the nineteenth century. Steampunk owes much to the vivid imaginations of Jules Verne and H.G. Wells and their fascination with flying machines, clockwork, and computing devices, often built by DIY tinkerers dedicated to transforming society through some improbable invention.

Steampunk Rochester, then, takes these technological fever dreams and roots them in the local history of my university. Early-twentieth-century Rochester was a nexus for competing social forces, including booming industry along with a rapidly growing immigrant population, which fueled conflicts between workers' unions, management, and millionaire philanthropists such as George Eastman of

Kodak. Other national and global issues mixed with the experience of Rochester daily life, such as the prohibition of alcohol, racial and nationalist tensions in the wake of the First World War, the 1918 flu pandemic, and a strong connection with the women's suffrage movement. Much of this history can still be seen downtown through plaques, street names, and murals, though much of the city from that era has been torn down and built over. The rich history of the city in this era serves as a stage for students' fiction, at which point they are encouraged to engage with the underlying social conditions of the city where they attend school.

The fall semester combined twenty fiction writing students with twenty students enrolled in a course on visual culture. For the first month, the classes operated independently, laying groundwork for the project. My creative writing students studied the genre of steampunk, reading a combination of critical work and short stories that highlighted social and political critique; the visual studies students engaged with spatial theory and reading cities as texts. At the end of week four, the classes met in a single space to attend a guest lecture by Michael Brown, a professor specializing in local history, who showed photographs that captured the architecture of the time, and he shared stories of the lived experiences of those who inhabited Rochester from 1915 to 1925. This lecture concluded the first unit of the course.

The second unit began with the writing of the Steampunk Rochester metanarrative, where the forty students formed small groups to begin researching aspects of Rochester in this era that they found most compelling. This ran a wide range of interests that included women's suffrage, prohibition and bootlegging, the immigrant experience, unions, the Progressives and other political parties, transportation, machinery and manufacturing, and more. The classes visited the university archives to learn about the history of the school and the experiences of students who attended school there, training for professions in everything from engineering and mechanics to service work and healthcare. Our students leafed through the course bulletins, yearbooks, diaries, and classroom photographs that depicted campus life in the early part of the twentieth century. This helped ground the broad history in the narratives of students who attended the same school almost a century before.

To the historical record they added speculative elements such as incredible steam-powered inventions and an aggressive government program aimed at attracting European engineers who were seeking brighter futures in America after the devastation of the Great War. With the steampunk element wedded to Rochester history, students began adding their wiki entries to populate the world of Steampunk Rochester with people, places, and things. Using online mapping software, students added markers to a 1915 map of Rochester and linked the markers to their corresponding wiki entry. To make the map visually informative, fictional location markers had a white icon and dark background, while historically accurate markers featured a dark icon on a white background (Figure 10.1).

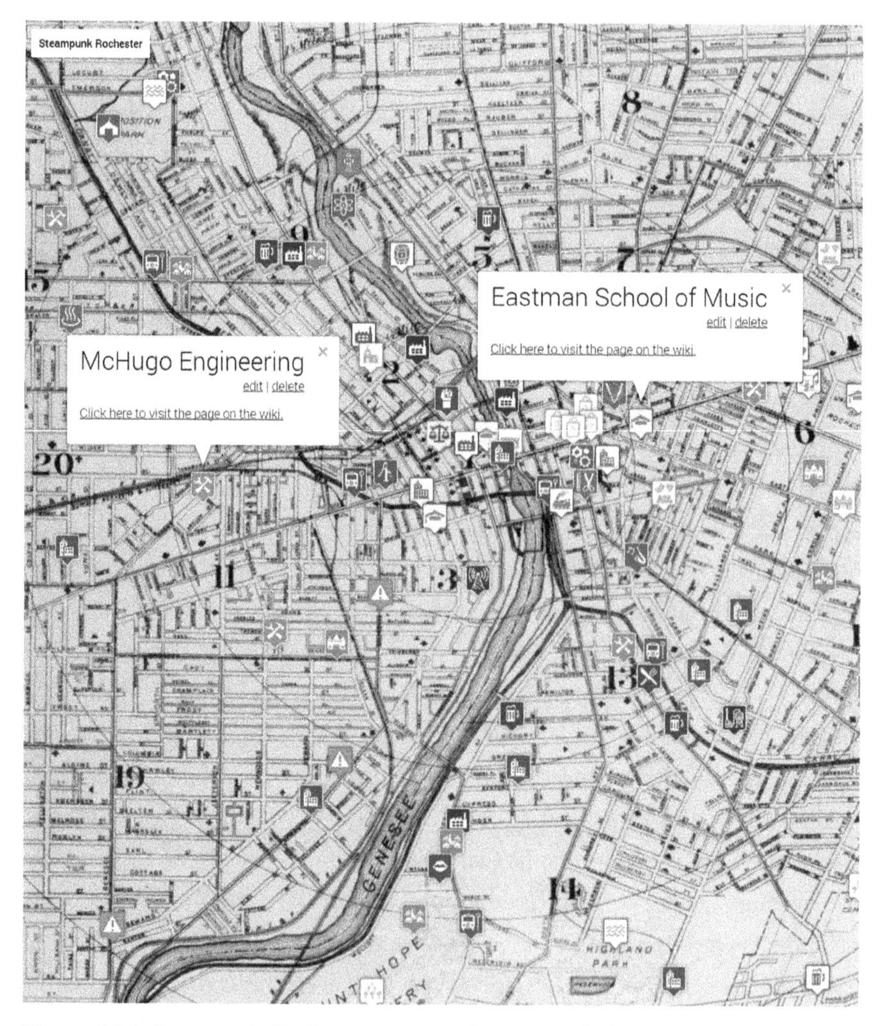

Figure 10.1 Steampunk Rochester map markers with dark and light backgrounds, indicating fictional and historical locations

By the tenth week, the students created a deep, dense world that featured 141 characters, 129 locations, and 115 items that blended fact with fiction, with all of it grounded in the actual historical, political, economic, and social realities of the time. At this point the classes split, with the visual culture students moving on to another project, while my creative writing students transitioned to the role-playing portion of the course.

In the final six weeks of the course, my students participated in a role-playing game campaign where their respective characters had to navigate the world of Steampunk Rochester and write vignette-length scenes based on their characters' experiences. Many chose to be steampunk tinkerers seeking funding for their inventions, while others bootlegged whiskey via steam dirigibles; an undercover detective hunted down a murderer; and competing aristocrats tried to outdo each other by procuring the most elaborate or exotic steam-powered artifact. We met twice each week, once for role-playing sessions where the players found their characters in precarious situations, and once to read and critique the fiction the students wrote from their characters' perspectives.

Reflections on Steampunk Rochester

Since the course crossed several disciplines—there were significant aspects of history, digital humanities, and game design—I invited faculty members to participate in the project on an informal basis. After the conclusion of the course, I asked these faculty members to comment on the interdisciplinary aspects of the course, and what values or challenges they thought accompanied working with a creative writing class.

History professor Michael Brown saw particular value in how the project was rooted in humanistic concerns and related through the eyes of characters. He says:

> Historians have long struggled with the inaccessibility of historical agents' thought processes—how did people think about what they were doing, feeling, and seeing? The further back in time and the further from elite groups we go, the more we face a paucity of sources for addressing such questions. Collaborating with creative writers, particularly those entirely invested

in developing a character and then operating within a decision matrix in accordance with that character's traits and background, offers a salutary reminder of the complexity of human motivation.

English and Digital Humanities professor Lisa Hermsen rearranged her syllabus for her course entitled "Maps, Places, Spaces" to let her students participate. Of her experience participating in the role-playing sessions, she wrote:

> Students had to think critically about various ethical questions, like human–computer interaction, animal testing and experimentation, health care availability for the wealthy or for all, capitalism and high risk investments, women's place in the economic class structure … and so on. I asked complicated questions and it took thoughtful replies from students who were in character to keep the plot moving forward … After seeing how the students engaged each other and the various narratives through interaction with ethical questions, I decided to get my own students in on the game … The experience challenged my students to think about how space is populated and to describe how narratives turn empty map space into historically-situated place.

Professor Jessica Lieberman, whose visual culture students helped build the world of Steampunk Rochester, identified one unexpected drawback: her students became more interested in the creative work than in the course for which they were enrolled.

> A side-effect of this deeper collaboration was that many of the Visual Culture (VC) students wanted to do the work assigned to the creative writing students as well, creating their own fictional characters and deploying them in the game space. As the faculty was not fully prepared for this, and credit was not clearly allocated for such work, student interest could only be encouraged, but not followed through with. Visual Culture students were interested in authoring characters and playing the game, but were not prepared to engage with actual creative writing and character development. Therefore, it was not entirely clear how to support their engagement with the next phases of the project. How best can the VC students participate in later stages of the collaboration when those stages are carefully integrated with curriculum that the VC students are not enrolled in?

From its inception, Steampunk Rochester had been conceived as a year-long project where writers would build the world in the fall semester, and game design students would use that world as inspiration. Using the setting and selected characters and locations, the students chose to make a point-and-click adventure game, where the player assumed the role of an investigative reporter. Steve Jacobs, a professor in Interactive Games and Media, said this about the project:

> The Steampunk Rochester effort allows for the kind of process one finds in what Geoffrey Long has called "Hard Transmedia" i.e. the creation of a piece of IP meant to cover multiple narratives and media deployments. In the Liberal Arts class, students participate in world building first and narrative creation second. This is a process few undergraduate students have an opportunity to do, whether in literature, media, or games development courses. By creating a corpus of people, places and things, as well as a collection of fiction built around it, Professor Hergenrader's students build a narrative platform for other creators to build from.

Jacobs also noted that he had several students who had taken the creative writing course in the fall, followed by the game design course in the spring. This caused a unique tension in the class as those students resisted suggested alterations from the source material they'd helped to create. Despite it being a large-scale collaborative project, these students maintained a sense of ownership over the world when newcomers suggested making changes.

Conclusions and future plans

What did we learn from Steampunk Rochester? The project presented a number of logistical challenges and often felt like an enormous Rube Goldberg machine that needed constant attention and tweaking to keep it working. The amount of faculty effort required is a significant drawback, though the second iteration of the project taught during the 2015–16 academic year went much more smoothly as we better understood the rhythms of the project. Despite those challenges, the project has struck a chord with faculty both within our institution as well as within the wider academic community. The project was highlighted in the "Interfaces" section of the MLA publication *Digital Pedagogy in the Humanities*[8] and received special mention in a *Chronicle* article recapping standouts of the Games+Learning+Society Conference.[9] The Steampunk Rochester project has been used in marketing our college's new degree in Digital Humanities and Social Sciences, and several faculty members have expressed interest in having their classes contribute to the project in the future, from everything from 3D digital design to spontaneous theater, where student actors would assume the roles of the characters at performances during our school's homecoming events and other local festivals for the arts.

Steampunk Rochester is an idiosyncratic, amorphous beast shambling into an indeterminate future and, as one of its primary inventors, I wouldn't have it any other way. What I find most encouraging from my colleagues' reactions to the project is how core concepts of creative writing craft—particularly the interplay between characters and their setting—provide a useful handle for their students to better understand their own disciplines. An area I am interested in exploring in the future would be to co-teach the classes, where the disciplinary boundaries were even more porous. How might we teach other subjects, such as history or game design, where creative writing is integrated into those content areas? How might role-playing through different scenarios and having students write stories through their characters' unique perspectives shed new light on other areas of humanistic inquiry, such as political science, public policy, criminal justice, philosophy, psychology, and even the natural sciences eager to the tell story of their discoveries? The first step in answering this question is knocking on our colleagues' doors and seeing if they'd be interested in trying something new.

Guidelines for starting an interdisciplinary creative writing project

Institutional cultures vary widely, so the steps listed below are intended as a broad guideline rather than strict step-by-step instructions. It's best to find faculty members who seem open to experimentation, possibly in well-established programs who feel comfortable taking some curricular risks. They must be flexible, open to changes on-the-fly, and willing to let the students lead the project where they may; they must also tolerate messiness, uncertainty, and ideally possess a fair amount of humor.

1. Find a Local Connection
   For starters, pick a setting sufficiently different from our own, so students have to bridge the gap between our consensus reality and the world they're

building. This could be an earlier historical time period, an alternate history, or a dystopian, cyberpunk, post-apocalyptic future. Think about physical landmarks, geographical features, or historical sites that lend themselves to investigation, both in terms of research as well as getting off campus and exploring the local community.

2. Contact Colleagues across Departments and Disciplines
   The key to finding a good connection is to be flexible in what you want to accomplish in your class and to be open to a variety of possibilities. Graphic designers could provide concept art, and history students can add a historically accurate perspective; students studying policy, political science, or economics could use the world building activity and action within it as a thought experiment. Geographic Information Systems (GIS) could add narrative layers to an interactive map. The more your colleagues see that this project will fulfill their traditional course objectives, the more invested they will be with the project.
3. Focus on Narrative Craft, Not Technology
   Creative writers excel in the meticulous use of language and understanding the architecture of strong storytelling. Think about any news story, any scientific experiment, or any historical event in terms of narrative pieces, of how a story emerges from complex characters making choices based on their specific motivations and their environment. Isolating characters and details about the setting are useful craft exercises, even for students not focusing on creative writing, as it highlights that the world we have is largely shaped by people making decisions for differing, and often opposing, reasons. The societal power structures in play help determine whether certain people's decisions carry more weight than others, and thus who has more influence in terms of how events unfold.
4. Talk, Write, Repeat
   A good rule of thumb is for the instructor to speak as little as possible and give only enough direction so students can move forward. This means using the opening weeks of a course to frame the project and its goals broadly by bringing up the big picture questions: What's at stake in this world? Who are the major players? What do they want and why? Where are the most obvious lines of tension in his society? This should be a wide-ranging discussion where students are encouraged to try out different viewpoints and ideas supported by primary sources. Put students from different disciplines in contact with each other as much as possible so that

they can share their different perspectives, and make sure they capture these ideas in writing. Every week or so hold group meetings to guarantee everyone is on the same page and critique the work that's been done. The metanarrative can always use detail, and characters and locations usually can use more nuance. The work of revision is a necessary part in improving the entire narrative, and students tend to respond better when they see it improves the group project.

5. Adjust Assessment Accordingly, but Don't Drive Yourself Crazy
   Project-based learning challenges traditional assessment in a number of ways in that learning happens over a longer period of time and makes certain learning outcomes difficult to quantify. I use a very basic rubric that values getting work done on time and providing evidence of more than minimal effort. In years of doing this, I can say with confidence that usually a full third of the class becomes deeply engaged with the material and really makes it their own. Another third keeps up and participates but not with the same kind of overriding enthusiasm. That leaves a final third that tends to lag behind. These students often have other time-intensive classes, desire explicit instructions rather than self-directed prompts, or are simply lazy. The first two-thirds largely take care of themselves and only need the periodic check-ins mentioned above; the last third require more time and attention, and often with a little support they can contribute meaningfully to the project. The key to success with assessment is to not burden yourself with what I call "bean counting," or grading every little bit as the world grows very large very quickly; rather I keep an eye on participation and ask students to occasionally submit a list of what they've added. I also have experimented with anonymous peer-assessment and self-grading. What I discovered through trial and error is that a majority of students do exceptional work and deserve their high grades, though a few struggle to get things in on time and settle for mediocre grades, and others check out completely and don't pass the class. This remains true whether I grade every last thing or take a more laissez-faire attitude and use a more holistic grading approach. I save the time I would have spent bean counting to become more involved with students' work in other ways, most notably in smaller comments and especially in discussion. My office hours tend to fill quickly when I'm teaching these courses, and that's a very positive sign.

6. Have Fun and If At First You Don't Succeed, Try Again
Perhaps what I enjoy most about these world building courses is that they become semester-long creative works of art. It's taken me years of experimentation and course revision to get this method to a point where I can share it with others, and I can no more explain how to run a course like this than I can explain how to write a good short story. Sure, there are some tips and best practices, but ultimately you just have to roll up your sleeves and give it a go, accepting that you will make mistakes you can learn from and be better off for it the next time. I get deeper levels of engagement and pride of ownership from my students in these classes than any others, which makes the work and the uncertainty more than worthwhile.

Notes

1 The evolution of this role-playing game methodology can be tracked in a series of published conference proceedings from the Games+Learning+Society Conference that I've included here: Trent Hergenrader, "Dense Worlds, Deep Characters: Role-Playing Games, World Building, and Creative Writing," in GLS 10 Conference Proceedings (Madison, WI: ETC press, 2014), 118–24; Hergenrader, "Gaming, World Building, and Narrative: Using Role-Playing Games to Teach Fiction Writing," in GLS 7 Conference Proceedings (Madison, WI: ETC press, 2011), 103–8; Hergenrader, "The Narrative Potential of Tabletop Role-Playing Games," in GLS 9 Conference Proceedings (Madison, WI: ETC press, 2013), 168–74; Hergenrader, "When You Play the Game of Thrones ... Everyone One Wins! Role-Playing Games and Fanfiction for Fiction Writers," in GLS 7 Conference Proceedings (Madison, WI: ETC press, 2017); Trent Hergenrader and Steve Jacobs. "Steampunk Rochester," in GLS 11 Conference Proceedings (Madison, WI: ETC press, 2015), 398–402.

2 The course site, "Rivertown Chronicles," can be viewed at http://rivertown.wikispaces.com.

3 Edith Ackerman, "Piaget's Constructivism, Papert's Constructionism: What's the Difference?" Accessed March 1, 2016.http://learning.media.mit.edu/content/publications/EA.Piaget%20_%20Papert.pdf.

4 Richard Paul, "Dialogical and Dialectical Thinking," in *Richard Paul Anthology*, 309–19. Accessed March 8, 2016. http://www.criticalthinking.org/pages/richard-paul-anthology/1139.

5 New London Group, National Languages & Literacy Institute of Australia, and Centre for Workplace Communication and Culture. *A Pedagogy of Multiliteracies*

(Haymarket, NSW: NLLIA Centre for Workplace Communication and Culture, 1995).

6 Graeme Harper, "Creative Writing in the Age of Synapses," in *Creative Writing in the Digital Age: Theory, Practice, and Pedagogy*, ed. Michael Dean Clark, Trent Hergenrader, and Joseph Rein (London and New York: Bloomsbury, 2015), 7–14.

7 Jack Richards, "Difference between an Approach and a Method?" *The Official Website of Applied Linguist Dr. Jack C Richards*, June 4, 2013. http://www.professorjackrichards.com/difference-between-an-approach-and-a-method/.

8 Kathi Berens, "Interfaces," in *Digital Pedagogy in the Humanities*, MLA, 2015. https://digitalpedagogy.commons.mla.org/keywords/interface/.

9 Anastasia Salter, "Report on Games and Learning from GLS11," *The Chronicle of Higher Education Blogs: ProfHacker*, July 17, 2015. http://chronicle.com/blogs/profhacker/report-on-games-and-learning-from-gls11/60473.

11

Place-Based Pedagogy and Creative Writing as a Fieldwork Course

Janelle Adsit

Given that any work is located in, and shaped by, its time and space of creation, there is reason to consider *where*—not just *how*—creative writing is taught. Our global and local situations prompt us to ask: What is the relationship between pedagogy and place? Place-based pedagogy has seen growing interest in recent decades as this mode of instruction has been linked to increased retention and hands-on learning.[1] What does place-based pedagogy offer the field of creative writing specifically?

The outdoors, for instance, may best support our students' engagement with what Mark Doty calls the "art of description."[2] Out of the classroom, students can make inferences. How does the texture of the rock tell us what it has been through? How does the robin perceive the space? Out of the classroom, it may be easier to shift scales—to perform macro and micro descriptions, to methodically attend to the singular object and then identify how each object is imbricated in larger systems. Out of the classroom, we may find new ways of teaching the core principle that to look outward is to also see inward—to realize that, in Robert Yagelski's words, "no split exists between an inner and outer world"[3]—countering the figure of the writer constructed in the popular imaginary as an eminently interior being, probing the recesses of the psyche in a featureless garret.

The creative writing class that takes a fieldwork approach provides an environment where the common conceptions of the writing process can be tested, where divisions and categories proffered in craft texts can be interrogated. As David Abram suggests, "imagination is not a separate mental faculty (as we so often assume)." Rather, "Imagination is from the first an attribute of the senses themselves."[4]

We tell our students about the importance of image, we give them the history of the imagist poets, and we say *show, don't tell.* But do we teach them how to perceive what we want them to show? Observation is its own art and entails a complex process and technique. To observe is to listen in on the silent conversation between body and the larger physical world. It is to ask how we name such encounters in an alphabetic language. Abram suggests that writers have the task of "carefully writing language back into the land," writing in contact with the more-than-human world and the sensing body, as Wallace Stevens did in "The Idea of Order at Key West": putting the sound of the sea on the tongue of readers with the poem's sibilance and rolling rhythm—not to substitute for the physical presence of the sea but to change the geometry of our attention through defamiliarization.[5] Given these possibilities, creative writing should revisit the question of educational environment, which is too often cordoned off from pedagogical discussions that tend to focus on content and method without considering how one's surroundings influence everything that happens in a course—both what is taught and how it is taught.

Risks and possibilities of place-based creative writing

Yet there are risks here: An emphasis on the out-of-doors experience can swiftly become an ableist ode to the inspirational power of walking. "Reading with one's feet" and reading with one's eyes—as Rebecca Solnit puts it in her book *Wanderlust: A History of Walking*—cannot be the only ways of reading the world.[6] Accessibility must be central to decisions about educational environment. Among the other risks: The *place-based* and *environmental* may be inherently exclusionary frames. When a place-based pedagogy valorizes the local setting over other sites, it risks alienating students who transfer into our universities far from where they call home. Moreover, a place-based pedagogy cannot neglect the violent histories that are everywhere present in the spaces where we teach. The "moss, rivers, trees, dirt, caves, dogs, fields" are, as Camille Dungy notes, "elements of an environment steeped in a legacy of violence, forced labor, torture, and death."[7] What was here and what is here now are inseparable. This is the argument of Lauret Edith Savoy's biogeography *Trace: Memory, History, Race, and the American Landscape*. A place-based pedagogy must be a history-based pedagogy. It is an opportunity to interrogate how storied places are represented in the literary texts that students produce.

Using the environmental as a frame carries some of these same risks. Accounts of environmental literatures sometimes rely on a genealogy that has neglected the experiences of many indigenous and diasporic cultures. To respond to this tendency, we can offer an integrated curriculum that centers the experiences of students who do not identify with the history of environmentalism in the United States—which is specifically not to say that students who disaffiliate with environmentalism are without ecological interests or values. On the contrary, Priscilla Solis Ybarra articulates why Mexican American and Chicana/o writers may eschew the term *environmentalism*: "[w]hile the American project of environmentalism denotes an explicit quest to find alternatives to exploitative approaches to nature … Mexican American and Chicana/o culture enacts values and practices that include nature all along" and thus, in Ybarra's view, peoples of these cultures "never became environmentalists in the first place" because they were thinking in such terms from the start.[8] No matter our pedagogical orientation, we must be vigilant in pursuing the literatures that our field has systematically underrepresented and a push toward better integrating the curriculum is equally important in an ecological approach to literary writing.

Interrogating our assumptions

Teaching creative writing in the field requires thorough consideration of inclusivity, accessibility, and educational environment, as it also requires that students and teachers think critically about the presumptions and expectations of the environment they bring to bear on their experience of composing-with-world. We must remember, following Yagelski, that writing is ontological. Each rendering on the page makes or remakes our experiences of the world. He argues that "writing is a way of being in the world" and that creative composing processes "enact a sense of ourselves as beings in the world."[9] That enactment always comes with inherited preconceptions about the self's and communities' relationship to environment.

To open up conversations about our inherited preconceptions, I ask students what they expect from the experience of leaving the four-walled classroom. From this discussion, we can collaboratively identify common narratives that undergird and shape our expectations. Students will articulate assumptions such as the idea that to leave the classroom is to explore a new frontier, to experience an individualized and transcendent relationship with "nature," to find peace and harmony in the non-human. We probe these narratives and expectations. Why do we expect an epiphany from the natural world? What (human-centric, Eurocentric, capitalist, class-based, gendered, etc.) assumptions lurk beneath that expectation? How do these assumptions affect how you will see, hear, smell, touch, and taste when outside of the classroom space?

If literature is the overturning of presumptions, if it is the insistent sharing of the overlooked, we can understand careful sensory inspection, so often elided in the college curricula,[10] to be a tool for destabilizing clichéd representations of the human and nonhuman. That is not to say that sensory observation will automatically subvert stereotypes and distortions; there is additional work to be done to identify how literature is shaped by cultural inheritance even as it also reciprocally shapes that inheritance as a form of cultural production. Creative writing is uniquely equipped to undertake this examination because, as geographer Yi-Fu Tuan notes in *Topophilia*, "Literature rather than social science provides us with the detailed and finely shaded information on how human individuals perceive their worlds."[11] It is crucial that creative writing classes, where students engage their own cultural productions with a critical eye, provide opportunities to recognize the preconceptions and ideologies that are embedded in the texts that they produce.

The goal is to put up for examination the stories that have framed our understanding of the world. Our realities are narrative constructions, and we produce those narratives in the creative writing class. To write with accuracy and precision is to attempt to connect the reader to the world via the page—not to make the page a transparent window, but to connect the page in its materiality and its rootedness to flora with other roots—to the reader's own emplacedness. This is part of an ecopoetic project that responds to the belief, articulated by Dan Beachy-Quick, that "we hurt the world because it isn't real to us."[12] The sensory world has become inaccessible to many of us, flooded as we are with commoditized and cleansed representations of nature—edited calendar photographs, for instance, that obscure history, death, sickness, decay, dirt, and so on—and by the literatures that make some of the same obfuscating and distancing gestures in their representations of setting.[13] To counter this tendency, and attend to the ethics of representation as well as the contingencies of culturally informed views of place-in-history, is to, in Abram's words, write "phrases that place us in contact with the trembling neck-muscles of a deer holding its antlers high."[14] And it is to remember that "we are always part of the natural world, even when we feel most alienated from it," as Camille Dungy elucidates in her introduction to *Black Nature*. It is, Dungy continues, to recognize that "treatments of the natural world ... are historicized or politicized."[15]

To take up the literary task that Abram and Dungy describe is to radically alter writing pedagogy. What Yagelski describes of composition pedagogy is true of creative writing pedagogy as well: "the basic lesson of mainstream writing instruction (and of formal schools in general) is disconnection, and it is this sense of disconnection that is at the root of the crisis of sustainability."[16] The disconnection he identifies as endemic to writing instruction may be endemic to much cultural production and knowledge making in the academy: "The word *science*, of course, is derived from the Latin *scire*, 'to know.' What is rarely, if ever, pointed out is that the semantic development of the verb *scire* shows that it originally meant 'to separate one thing from another.'"[17] As a counter to scientism, creative writing has an important place in the academy and an important role in world shaping. But perhaps it can go farther. Approaching the art of creative writing with a fundamental acknowledgment of the limitations of anthropocentrism and a curiosity about the interconnected nature of our ecological world can transform some of creative writing's established pedagogical tropes. For example, as James Engelhardt and Jeremy Schraffenberger note, an ecological approach to creative writing reevaluates the common workshop mantra "write what you know" as it challenges "what it means to 'know' at all" or what it means to be a knowing subject who is also an animal within an evolutionary history and deep membership in complex ecological systems.[18] This sense of ecological interconnectedness, as advocates of the fieldwork course model have noted, is difficult to teach and for students to experience with the barriers of a four-walled classroom on all sides. The question, then, for creative writing becomes not "can it be taught?" but "*where* can it be taught?"

Revision and responsibility

A reorientation toward a fieldwork model changes where and how we talk about texts in creative writing. The writer is never separate or apart—a fact that foregrounds the writer's responsibility to the ecosocial world. This responsibility was always already part of the writing life. Nadine Gordimer argues in "The Essential Gesture," that "The creative act is not pure. History evidences it. Ideology demands it. Society exacts it. The writer … comes to realize that he is answerable. The writer is *held responsible*."[19] To revise is to think in terms of responsibility—to an audience, ecologies, and earthly futures. Because writing is an act that affects others, ethics are inherently at stake. That is not to say that stories and poems should be overtly moralizing. Rather, we should be mindful that our texts produce meanings that have the potential to shape thought and action. To create a fictional world is to offer a theory of being on earth, an understanding of inhabitation, and this theory is evinced in every rhetorical choice a story makes. Given this, a discussion of the values a text perpetuates can be an important part of the creative writing workshop.

For instance, to have a poem or story that makes no reference to place is to say that there exists something that is not place-bound. If a story we value does not require the environment, the logic might go, then perhaps we need not consider the environment at all. The story with a setting that is in essence a backdrop—or a two-dimensional, passive platform—can also forward practices that overlook the environment. A backdrop setting does nothing more than provide a stage for character-driven (human-centered) action, as opposed to representing humans as part of a system—and this sense of humans in relation to place has political and social implications. Scott Russell Sanders' argues in "Speaking a Word for Nature" that contemporary fiction is "barren" when it "pretends that nothing lies beyond its timid boundaries. … What is missing in much recent fiction … is a sense of nature, any acknowledgement of a nonhuman context."[20] Literature has a long history of activism. The creative writing course provides spaces to discuss how constructing a sense of place in language may be linked to sustaining what composes that place in its materiality.

What this means is that content in creative writing "will not necessarily take care of itself and ... cannot simply be subsumed under discussions of craft," as Lynn Domina acknowledges in her contribution to *Colors of a Different Horse*.[21] To point students to the ecologies they are part of and ask them to attend more thoughtfully to what happens in the spaces that make up their days is to increase the visibility and rigor surrounding questions of content in the creative writing.

Ecological literacy, a term brought into popularity by the work of David Orr, becomes a generative tool for the creative writer. Indeed, scientific terms have provided poets such as Linda Bierds with rich metaphors and allusions: abyssal plain, oxbow lake, permaculture. To see and sense unaided by a knowledge-base can take a writer only so far. Indoor libraries of course have something to offer the ecowriter too. Reports on scientific discoveries, dictionaries of ecological terms, identification handbooks allow one to see what one couldn't see before. As has been noted by Donald Murray and Janet Burroway and others, writer's block often is the result of a lack of information,[22] and research is one way of pushing through this daunting experience of the blank page. The vagaries and unpredictability of research and fieldwork together can lead to the necessary surprises of the literary writing process. "[I]n outdoor settings it is impossible to predict what students will find," Hal Crimmel writes, and this is part of the fieldwork course's value.[23]

The things we couldn't expect, the things we stumble upon and don't know how to identify, our information gaps, too, can be generative. Karen K. Lewis suggests asking students to create their own myth or legend from the questions they don't have answers to: "Why are poppies orange? How did the skunk get its stink? Why are fawns spotted?"[24] She prepares for this activity by assigning readings in folklore and by examining the cultural forces associated with folklore as a genre and tradition.

Along similar lines, I sometimes facilitate an assignment in my creative writing courses that I call the "Investigating Muse." Drawing from the postmodern impulse to take one area of inquiry or methodology and apply it to what it was never intended for, the assignment asks students to investigate the idea that intersections are always possible, that any subject can meet with any other. To begin the exercise, I tell my students the assignment involves a type of misuse, or repurposing. It's a type of misuse to place in a collection of poetry a data chart that presents the contaminants in a local water supply, but such a chart is included in Mark Spitzer's *Age of the Demon Tools.* A list of endangered, threatened, or extinct species appears in Eleni Sikelianos's *The California Poem.* Examining these texts and other examples, we discuss what it means to count environmental data as poetry or to count graphs as fiction.

For the "Investigating Muse" exercise, I ask students to bring two texts to class that they feel do not belong in creative writing. They might bring a lab report, a scholarly article from a peer-reviewed journal, an infographic, a pie chart, a greeting card, a shopping list, and the like. To ensure a diversity of texts, I bring a wide range of texts to share as well. We then shuffle and redistribute these texts. If they wish, students can tear pages in half before they send the materials on to another classmate. Students receive three texts different from those they brought to class. Their goal then is to invent these texts' intersections, to discover how each text relates and speaks back to the other, to discover a worldly interconnectedness through three apparently disparate texts.

After taking some class time to write and research, we then discuss the experience of completing this exercise. In the discussion, I introduce the principle from Barbara Herrnstein Smith's *Contingencies of Value* that "our survival, both as individuals and species, continues to be enhanced by our ability and inclination to reclassify objects and to 'realize' and 'appreciate' novel and alternate functions for them—which is to 'misuse' them and to fail to respect their presumed purpose and conventional generic classifications."[25] We discuss how uses have been created and sustained through narrative, and I move the conversation toward a consideration of how all subject matter, across the disciplines and the range of human experience, intersects with ecology and environmental studies. Because "nothing happens nowhere" and everything is conditioned by place, ecology becomes a useful frame for thinking and writing about, in, and with the surround.

Classroom application

While a focus on ecological issues in creative writing can stand to reorient a curriculum, it is possible to integrate types of environmentally aware assignments into a traditional workshop class in fiction, creative nonfiction, or poetry. An assignment I call "Repeat Photography, Repeat Words" asks students to make repeat visits to one place and to take a word picture of the place, describing it with writing that is precise and detailed so that an image is rendered in the reader's mind. Taking these textual snapshots, accompanied by camera snapshots as well, students notice how a place changes over time, as they practice and discover how point-of-view influences the art of description.

Another assignment asks students to transform the personal essay into an "autobiogeography." The autobiogeography assignment builds from the research orientation of autoethnography, which has been influential in the teaching of creative nonfiction. Extending autoethnography's focus on studying the self within the structures of power and dynamics of culture, autobiogeography questions what it means to be human in an ecologically and socially diverse world, within an ecosocial justice framework. The genre, as defined by Gillian Whitlock, is exceedingly capacious and includes "scenes of auto/biographical expression that may seem bizarre: animalographies, bioart, narratives of chronic pain . . . It embraces creatures, critters, produsers, and avatars . . . [and theories] not traditionally associated with studies of life narrative."[26] Engaging this genre, students profile a living, nonliving, or fictional persona in geographical terms. What sense of place, topographies, toxicities, economies, migrations, weathers, technologies, resources, water sources, and companion species have shaped this human life? How can this genre challenge traditional conceptions of the "natural" by recasting the mechanical and organic, metals and flesh, in different terms? How could this human life be written in such a way that decenters the human and moves beyond an anthropocentric worldview? What is at stake in representing multiple interconnected subjectivities in memoir or autobiography? What can be lost in the decentering of the human—particularly human experiences of inequity and oppression? What social and ecological forces have shaped the human and nonhuman lives constellated in the locality the writer calls home? What is the relationship between land and power in these lives?

In these ecological assignments, I invite students to engage the work of Stephen Collis, Rusty Morrison, Cecily Nicholson, and others—artists who have enacted collaborations with the nonhuman world. Nicholson's *From the Poplars*, for example, is a documentary poem about an uninhabited island located on the Fraser River, the traditional territory of the Qayqayt First Nation that was declared to be the property of New Westminster and Brownsville Indians and transformed into British Columbia's first "Indian Reserves" where indigenous smallpox victims from the south coast were forced into quarantine. Nicholson's poetic and archival investigation of this complex ecosocial past—a history that includes clear-cutting and pollution—is a good example of intersectional and interdisciplinary creative writing fieldwork research.

A final example of a creative writing assignment that engages an ecological perspective is one I call "Ecological Ekphrasis." This exercise can be a useful way of further investigating the extent to which it is possible and/or valuable to escape a human-centric worldview in art. To introduce this assignment, I invite students to view a documentary film of Andy Goldsworthy's work. We follow this film with a discussion of Doug Harvey who has exhibited a selection of moldy slides he describes as a type of collaboration with the environment. As the mold grows on each slide, it recreates the slide, selecting what parts of an image will be distorted or eradicated, creating haloes and new shapes on the image. With these two artists in mind, we consider how words work in and with the world. As writers, what opportunities do we have to cocreate with other species and forces, to find languages that are outside of the classroom, and to add language to spaces in ways that are less predefined than a bound book? We discuss what is meant by the term "artistic space" and how our conceptions of the studio have been limited and are limiting of art making. We read a part of Meskimmon's "Practice as Thinking" to consider what it means to think "of spaces as aesthetic in the fullest use of that term. That is, constructing spaces which admit of productive desire (rather than unfulfilled lack), coextensive difference (rather than assimilation) and becoming (rather than being)"[27]

Central to these assignments is an acknowledgment of how established academic ways of thinking and disciplinary divisions are outmoded. Many of us feel compelled to take part in ecosocial justice advocacy that entails multiple, interstitial examinations of the forces at work upon us. It means promoting cultural and biological diversity. It means combating colonial eradication of languages and ways of knowing. It means recognizing the forms of privilege that are embedded in representations of environmental engagement. It means critiquing legacies inherited from the pastoral tradition and moving beyond a false division between human and nature, between subject and object.

Creative writing and environmental studies are not separate; they face some of the same problems, wanting to understand and transform the world in all of its complexity. In creative writing we teach students to become cultural producers. Every story and poem that is put to page is world shaping. What our students put to the page reflects and shapes the cultures they are part of, and thus their words have the potential to change social and ecological spheres. We teach a practice that *matters*, in both senses of the word. To truly grapple with this fact is to seek new directions for creative writing as it continues to find its place in—and out(doors) of—the academy.[28]

Notes

1 As Hal Crimmel notes in introducing the collection *Teaching in the Field*, "In 1991 [a year prior to the founding of ASLE and subsequent establishment of the journal *ISLE*] there was little written about teaching arts and humanities outdoors, especially literature and writing courses."See Hal Crimmel, ed., *Teaching in the Field: Working with Students in the Outdoor Classroom* (Salt Lake City: University of Utah Press, 2003), 4.

2 Mark Doty, *Art of Description* (Minneapolis: Graywolf Press, 2010).

3 Robert Yagelski, *Writing As a Way of Being: Writing Instruction, Nonduality, and the Crisis of Sustainability* (New York: Hampton Press, 2011), 62. Tina Welling puts this idea in other words: She writes, "The act of writing weaves our inner and outer environments together. It makes us conscious of our bodies and of the earth and brings the whole experience into physical form—words on paper." See Tina Welling, *Writing Wild: Forming a Creative Partnership with Nature* (Novato: New World Library, 2014), 12.

4 David Abram, *Spell of the Sensuous: Perception and Language in a More-than-Human World* (New York: Vintage Books, 1996), 58.

5 Ibid., 273.

6 Rebecca Solnit, *Wanderlust: A History of Walking* (New York: Penguin, 2000), 70.

7 Camille Dungy, ed., *Black Nature: Four Centuries of African American Nature Poetry* (Athens: University of Georgia Press, 2009), xxi.

8 Priscilla Solis Ybarra, *Writing the Goodlife: Mexican American Literature and the Environment* (Tucson: University of Arizona Press, 2016), 273.

9 Yagelski, *Writing as a Way of Being*, 3.

10 Susan Zwinger and Ann Zwinger argue that "college curricula attempts to obscure our evolutionary dependence on our immediate senses." See "Learning Nature Through the Senses" in ed. Laird Christensen and Hal Crimmel, *Teaching About Place: Learning from the Land* (Las Vegas: University of Nevada Press, 2008), 21.
11 Yi-Fu Tuan, *Topophilia* (Englewood Cliffs: Prentice-Hall, 1974), 49. Quoted in Corey Lewis, *Reading the Trail: Exploring the Literature and Natural History of the California Crest* (Las Vegas: University of Nevada Press, 2005), 40.
12 Dan Beachy-Quick, "Poetry and the Environment," AWP 2008 Conference, New York, New York: Jan. 31, 2008.
13 Rebecca Solnit, "Uplift and Separate: The Aesthetics of Nature Calendars," in *As Eve Said to the Serpent: On Landscape, Gender, and Art* (Athens: University of Georgia Press, 2001), 200–5.
14 Abram, *Spell of the Sensuous*, 274.
15 Dungy, *Black Nature*, xxvii, xxix.
16 Robert Yagelski, *Writing as a Way of Being*, 4.
17 Julia Penelope Stanley and Susan J. Wolfe (Robbins), "Toward a Feminist Aesthetic," *Chrysalis* 6 (1978), 60.
18 James Engelhardt and Jeremy Schraffenberger, "Ecological Creative Writing" in *Creative Writing Pedagogies in the Twenty-First Century*, ed. Alexandria Peary and Tom C. Hunley (Carbondale: Southern Illinois University Press, 2015), 271.
19 Nadine Gordimer, "The Essential Gesture: Writers and Responsibility," *Granta* 15 (1985):137.
20 Scott Russell Sanders, "Speaking a Word for Nature," *Michigan Quarterly Review* 24.4(1987):649. Quoted in Engelhardt and Schraffenberger, "Ecological Creative Writing," 272.
21 Lynn Domina, "The Body of My Work Is Not Just a Metaphor," in *Colors of a Different Horse: Rethinking Creative Writing Theory and Pedagogy*, ed. Wendy Bishop and Hans Ostrom (Urbana, IL: NCTE, 1994), 34. Katherine Coles echoes this perspective, interrogating a central assumption in creative writing that "Content, we [creative writing teachers] secretly believe, just *happens*, as if by magic." See Katharine Coles, "Short Fiction," in *Teaching Creative Writing*, ed. Graeme Harper (New York: Continuum, 2006), 13.
22 Donald Murray, "The Essential Delay: When Writer's Block Isn't," in *Norton Book of Composition Studies*, ed. Susan Miller (New York: Norton, 2010), 715–20; Janet Burroway and Susan Weinberg, *Writing Fiction*, 6th edition (New York: Longman, 2003), 17.
23 Crimmel, *Teaching in the Field*, 7.

24 Karen K. Lewis, "Sacred Nature Workshops." Online posting. Feb. 15, 2009. Teachers & Writers Discussion Group, June 11, 2009.

25 Barbara Herrnstein Smith, *Contingencies of Value: Alternative Perspectives for Critical Theory* (Cambridge: Harvard University Press, 1988), 33.

26 Gillian Whitlock, "Post-in Lives," in *Biography* (35.1, Winter 2012), v–xvi.

27 Marsha Meskimmon, "Practice as Thinking: Toward Feminist Aesthetics,"' in *Breaking the Disciplines: Reconceptions in Culture, Knowledge and Art*, ed. Martin L. Davies and Marsha Meskimmon (London: IB Tauris, 2003), 241.

28 The author would like to thank Matthew Cooperman, Michael Masinter, and Corey Lewis for providing ideas, models, and insights that contributed to this chapter.

12

Our Town: Teaching Creative Writing Students to Love Research and Collaboration

Cathy Day

According to the Association of Writers and Writing Programs, one of the hallmarks of a successful undergraduate creative writing program is that students produce a senior portfolio, an undergraduate thesis manuscript of original creative work that's been thoroughly edited and revised. My first book began as my undergraduate thesis, and over my 20-year teaching career, I've relished the opportunity to help my students start their own "big things" in senior seminars for creative writers structured much like the one I took in college.

But since 2010, I've taught in a department that does not have discipline-specific senior seminars for each of its major concentrations (Creative Writing, English Education, Literature, Rhetoric and Writing, and English Studies), but rather a single capstone class (ENG 444 Senior Seminar) comprised of students from all five concentrations who produce a major, student-driven *research* project. At a time when the disciplines housed within English Studies seem to have less and less in common with each other, it's incredibly interesting to teach in a department that wants to accentuate what its faculty and students have in common rather than how they differ.

In Spring 2015, I was assigned to teach a section of ENG 444, the first creative writing faculty member to do so. I decided to modify a creative writing course I've taught several times over the years, which I call "The Town Class." After reading several books written in the form of "linked stories," students create a fictional town, the cast of characters who live there, and write interrelated stories. At the end of the semester, they collaborate—editing and assembling their anthology. But I decided to take it one step further; this time, their collaborative fictional town would be based on a particular real town, the town where they attend college—Muncie, Indiana—and students would be required to do research as part of their creative process.

Adding a research element to the course was born of curricular necessity, but it also caused me to rethink some of my pedagogical assumptions. If I could make the title of this essay even longer, it would be "Our Town: Teaching Creative Writing Students to Love Research and Collaboration as Much as They Already Love Expressing Themselves in Isolation." What follows is an explanation of not only how other creative writing instructors can teach such a class, but also why they might want to.

Teaching my students to love Middletown

Ball State University, where I currently teach, is in Muncie, Indiana, and (lucky for me) Muncie is one of the most thoroughly studied cities in the country; sociologists Robert and Helen Lynd arrived in the early part of the twentieth century in search of a "typical" American city, which they called "Middletown," and to conduct longitudinal studies of cultural continuity and change in America. They published two books, *Middletown: A Study of Modern American Culture* (1929) and *Middletown in Transition: A Study in Cultural Conflicts* (1937). Ever since, whenever researchers or journalists want to take the temperature of America, they come to Muncie because it's considered the most average small city in the country (which made my students chortle), a community that's seen as the barometer of social trends in the United States.

I've taught my Town Class three other times (at state universities in Alabama, Minnesota, and New Jersey), but the stories students wrote for those anthologies were set in contemporary times in fictional towns that were amalgams of several real towns they all knew well. This anthology, on the other hand, was set in a "real" place: Muncie's alter ego. Two of my students were from Muncie, but to the rest of the class, Muncie was just "where they went to college." The class required that my students learn about the town surrounding their campus by venturing out on field trips (that required no busses) and by making use of the city's vast historical archive (conveniently located in their university library).

At the beginning of the term, we acquainted ourselves with the Middletown study by reading portions of the first Middletown book, by watching searchable portions of the *Middletown* documentaries on YouTube (the six-part, landmark series from the 1980s), and by touring the Middletown archives (thanks to some very helpful archivists). The Middletown study was famously divided into six "spheres":

1. getting a living
2. making a home
3. training the young
4. using leisure
5. engaging in religious practices
6. engaging in community activities

The students were required to set their story in Middletown in a year in which they were not alive. This would force them outside the comfort zone of their own time and do historical research. We also decided at the outset that our Middletown would not be as white nor as straight as the Lynds' had been.

Teaching my students to love research

These were the essential questions of my course that we returned to again and again throughout the semester and upon which the students reflected at semester's end.

- What does "research" mean in the making of art?
- How do we conduct research fiction writers? What is our methodology? What questions inform our process of inquiry?
- When should we research? At what part of the writing process? How do we avoid over-researching?
- What are the rewards and dangers of using Google and online databases vs. doing "hands-on" research in a library or in the real world?
- What kind of "data" do we need? How can we conduct qualitative research (such as focus groups, individual interviews, participant/observation,

review of literature and artifacts) and quantitative research (surveys, longitudinal studies)?
- How do we incorporate this research? How do we determine what material is relevant to our fiction and what's not?

As a writer of researched fiction, I wanted to demonstrate to my students and to my colleagues that "a researched story" and "a research paper" aren't all that different. More broadly, I believe the product of a creative writing education, like that of a literary or composition studies education, is the result of a thinking process involving student-centered questioning and inquiry. In other words, I believe that creative writing is the result of research, that the creative process and the scientific process aren't all that different. As Jennifer Blackmer, a professor of playwriting, puts it:

> The process [that artists] undergo is remarkably similar to scientific research. The artist has an idea that she wishes to explore, and asks a question: "How can I evoke a visceral response to the horrors of war?" or "How can I visually represent the ethical gray spaces of genetic engineering?" The artist works with tools such as text, space, and bodies on stage to test hypotheses: "How would the audience respond if I made this choice?" The artist revisits her choices as the process evolves, and just as the scientific process culminates in publication, the artistic process culminates when the work is presented for a different group of collaborators, the audience.[1]

Typically, the publications of faculty creative writers are referred to as "creative activity" rather than "research," and I've always felt ambivalent about this. I've taught in four different English departments, and in each case, promotion and tenure documents, yearly reports, and internal grants and awards made a distinction between the work of scholars and the work of artists. However, the Council on Undergraduate Research (CUR) defines research at the undergraduate level in broad enough terms to include both creative activity and research. They define it as "an inquiry or investigation conducted by an undergraduate that makes an original, intellectual, or creative contribution to the field." In their introduction to *Undergraduate Research in English Studies*, Laurie Grobman and Joyce Kinkead are quick to point out that such research is "distinct from the ubiquitous research paper" and that students should gain an understanding of field-specific debates, develop relevant skills and insights for future careers and graduate study, and most importantly, contribute their voices to "fill a gap" in the knowledge base through their research.[2]

At the beginning of the semester, my students didn't see a relationship between research and creative activity, and so I found it helpful to assign articles and essays in which fiction writers (other than myself) discussed how research informed their creative process, and how the product of that synthesis—literary historical fiction—could be viewed as filling gaps in our knowledge base. The most thorough discussion was found in "Raiding the Larder: Research in Fact-Based Fiction" by Debra Spark.[3] She begins with a quotation from author Lorrie Moore: "For the writer, the facts of life are like ingredients in a kitchen cupboard. The cake you make is the fiction. That's how life and art are related." Spark says that many writers raid their own larders, engaging with characters and places that are familiar to them, using "the spoon of the imagination" to stir the ingredients together. (This is the type of story most of my students were used to writing.) "But," Spark says, "what I want to examine here is a very different sort of writer. I want to look at writers who don't seem to use their kitchen cupboards, who, if anything, raid other people's larders. I want to consider writers who go looking for something different, find it, explore it, then come back to report." She quotes from interviews with Colum McCann, author of works of literary historical fiction such as *Let the Great World Spin*, who says "I feel that I go to university each time I write a new book." While many see creative writing as "inward-looking" and therapeutic, McCann says, "I revel in getting away from myself."

McCann's research produces three kinds of results: (1) historical verisimilitude and avoidance of anachronism, (2) actual characters and plot points inspired by real people and events, and (3) imaginative access to the material. This last result is difficult to explain, but for me, it's similar to the way actors describe "getting into character," whether they are playing a real person (alive or dead) or a fictitious character. For example, to portray a prostitute circa 1974, McCann went through boxes of rap sheets from that time period, searching for someone he might interview. Unfortunately, most were dead, but he found that the rap sheets themselves had allowed him to travel into the past, into a way of life, and eventually, into the voice of his character. Spark compares his method to the "immersion journalism" practiced by nonfiction writers such as Ken Kesey and Katherine Boo: such writers spend so much time in a community and among people that they know what their "characters" are thinking. This research technique bears some resemblance to participant observation and ethnographic methods of data collection. As Spark says, "McCann's fiction doesn't showcase his research … but in every case his research makes his books possible, the research allows McCann to imagine in a convincing way."

Teaching a research methodology

For me, the first phase of the research process is about discovery, so I created an assignment for students called an exploratory research report. I asked them to pick one of the six Middletown spheres, whichever one interested them the most. They read the corresponding section in the Lynd book (1929) and watched the corresponding documentary (1982). They were instructed to make note (by hand) of possible "takeaways," anything that hit them emotionally or intellectually, and then to type those notes into their report, but only if the item seemed to have "traction." This two-step process helps students learn how to pay attention to their instincts by concretizing the abstract concept of traction: if something interests you enough to record it twice —once by hand, another via typing—then that item resonates for you for some reason. Students were also instructed to think about what *wasn't* on the page or on the screen, to find holes in the story the way a journalist or detective might. They turned in both their handwritten notes and their typed reports, the last section of which required that they ask themselves critical questions about *why* a takeaway interested them, sketch out two possible story ideas, and consider what they might have to research next in order to write those stories.

These reports were posted to our Google Drive folder, and students read each other's reports, sharing their research within the group, wiki style. In many cases, students found even more takeaways discovered by others to use for their own stories, and they responded to each other's story ideas with affirmation, support, and advice.

Now that they had some story ideas, they were ready to begin researching more purposefully. Over the next few weeks, I required them to turn in ten annotations of sources, briefly summarizing the methods, critical approach, interpretive conclusions, and the possible relevance to their story. The hard part was convincing them that a photograph, a movie, a 1978 high school yearbook, an interview with their grandfather, or a personal research trip could all be sources that might provide imaginative access to their material. Another tricky part was getting them to stop Googling.

I had to schedule a second trip to the library and show them how to find and make use of newspapers and magazines (both bound and on microfilm) and other non-scholarly sources. I also did a sample annotation of one of my own writerly field trips. Once students realized that they could go for a walk to research the real-life setting of their stories (a bridge, a house where a murder occurred, a high-school field house, a restaurant, a historic neighborhood) and have this trip "count" as one of their ten annotations, they finally shut their laptops and started exploring the city they call home nine months of the year. In "Raiding the Larder," Sparks asks how writers become someone else? How do we travel through time? "We imagine," she says, "and we do our homework." So that's what I endeavored to do: show students how to do that homework.

But they were also learning how much the setting of a story (including the year) influenced everything else. One student in the course wanted to write a story about a female undertaker living in Middletown in the 1960s. She learned that female morticians were in no way common at that time. Rather than change the sex of her character, she worked through the difficulties her character would have faced—and why those difficulties existed in the first place. And since a pivotal plot point of her story was an actual embalming, she needed to learn about mortuary science appropriate to that time period. The student interviewed a local mortician and obtained hard-to-find details about tools, instruments, and practices, details that gave her story a great deal of authority and verisimilitude.

Most creative writers, presented with a similar subject matter, would do exactly what my student did—but they wouldn't include a bibliography page at the end. And that's what I asked my students to do—in a nutshell: to write a story, and then write about researching and writing the story, to "show their work," via first an exploratory research report, then a series of annotations, and finally a bibliographic essay that synthesized their process. This bibliographic essay closely resembles the "critical introduction" that master's students in creative writing include with their graduate thesis in creative writing, a document that asks writers to locate their work in its literary or historical contexts.

A key component of research is disseminating the results. We "published" the anthology available digitally on Issuu and also submitted it to the Center for Middletown Studies archive, where it will remain and be available to future Middletown scholars.

Teaching my students to love collaboration

In *The Triggering Town*, poet Richard Hugo advised his writing students to distance themselves from their real hometowns by creating a fictionalized place to call their own, a "triggering town." This practice has a long-standing tradition in American literature: Edgar Lee Masters' Spoon River, Sherwood Anderson's Winesburg, Faulkner's Yoknapatawpha County.

We began the semester by reading three books written in the "linked stories" or "novel-in-stories" form: *Winesburg, Ohio* by Sherwood Anderson, *The Sweet Hereafter* by Russell Banks, and *A Visit from the Goon Squad* by Jennifer Egan. Other books that work well for this course include Louise Erdrich's *Love Medicine*, Annie Proulx's *Close Range: Wyoming Stories*, Elizabeth Strout's *Olive Kitteridge*, Edwidge Danticat's *The Dewbreaker*, Tim O'Brien's *The Things They Carried*, Susan Minot's *Monkeys*, Donald Ray Pollock's *Knockemstiff*, and Stuart Dybek's *The Coast of Chicago*, to name a few. Our class discussions revolved less around *what* the books meant, but rather *how* they meant—how the structure informed the content, and vice versa. A particular helpful class activity asks students to "reshuffle" a book in order to see the difference story order makes. I do this by writing the title of each story on a 8 ½ by 11 piece of paper, taping them to the board, asking each group to find another plausible order for the stories, and to explain how the book would read differently.

It's also very important to get students thinking about how authors create deliberate linkages between stories (via theme, historical era, place, family, characters, events), because soon enough, my sixteen students embarked on sixteen different stories that had to be deliberately linked together. I highly recommend David Jauss' essay "Stacking Stones: Building a Unified Short Story Collection," first published in *AWP Writer's Chronicle* in 2005 and reprinted gorgeously in *Alone with All That Could Happen: Rethinking Conventional Wisdom about the Craft of Fiction.*[4]

Initially, I wanted to organize our class into six groups and our anthology into six sections—all for six spheres. But I decided it might be best to let students write whatever story interested them the most, in whatever time period interested them the most, and in whatever sphere interested them the most. What emerged were stories that were set from the 1920s to the 1980s. They dealt with race and class and gender, politics, war on the home front, unsolved mysteries, and friendship. At first, there wasn't much linking the stories except for the fact that they all took place in Middletown. So I decided to group the students into four groups of four:

- Group A's stories were about Muncie's (and Indiana's) troubled racial past.
- Group B's stories were about WWII.
- Group C's stories took place in the 1960s and 70s and dealt with cultural changes.
- Group D's stories took place in the 1980s and were about characters trying to leave Middletown.

Instead of trying to get all sixteen stories to link, they only needed to find ways for the four stories in each group to do so. They created what I call "nodes of conjunction" between their stories. For example:

- Two of the four students in Group A wrote stories loosely based on the famous lynching in nearby Marion, IN, of Thomas Shipp and Abram Smith that took place in 1930 (a tragedy that inspired the Billie Holliday song "Strange Fruit"). This event had a Muncie connection: an African-American minister and mortician in Muncie retrieved the bodies and brought them back to his church so they could be prepared for burial.
- Another student in Group A wrote a story set in the 1950s about a murder that was staged to look like that lynching.
- And the fourth student wrote about Muncie's connection to another important event in American race relations: Robert F. Kennedy visited Ball State on April 4, 1968. Shortly after his speech, Kennedy learned about Martin Luther King Jr.'s assassination and penned a short, soon-to-be-famous speech about his own brother's assassination that he delivered that night in Indianapolis. In my student's story, the main character's grandmother tells him about the 1930 lynching, at which she'd been present.

Each group linked its stories in a similar fashion. These linkages were discussed and agreed upon by the students, and negotiations that required them to compromise for the sake of editorial continuity were held; for example, changing a character's name or age, combining characters, adding scenes, altering the sequence of events, and in a few cases rethinking their original vision of their story so that it would "fit" into the larger whole.

Just as we'd reshuffled the three published books we studied, at the end of the semester, we reshuffled the students' stories, taping each title page on the board. We discussed how to best begin and end the book, whether to use chronological order or thematic order. They offered up possible titles, found appropriate epigraphs, decided on the story order, created a table of contents, wrote their "about the author" paragraphs. One student designed the book's cover, and another used InDesign to format the manuscript. Thus, my students became the editors of their book and gained valuable knowledge about the necessity of collaboration in the editorial process.

Grading

I should mention that my students *were not* graded on their short stories, but rather on the bibliographic essay they wrote about the writing and research process that produced the story. Why didn't I grade their fiction? For one, this wasn't technically a creative writing class. Most of my students were *not* creative writing majors, although everyone had taken at least one introductory course. Another reason why I elected not to grade their stories is because the stories were not workshopped by the entire class—a rigorous but time-consuming process that would have taken up a great deal of the semester. Instead, they each got feedback from their small group and from me.

In most creative writing courses, student writing undergoes many revisions and the final product receives a grade. In ENG 444, however, the point of the course wasn't to write a "publishable" product, but rather to go through a process as evidenced by the bibliographic essay (which was graded). For me, the point of the course was the research/thinking/writing *process*, not the creative product. Rather than devoting weeks of class time to big-group workshops, I devoted only one week to small-group workshops so that we would have more time to devote to the research process. In the end, what some students lacked in craft proficiency, they made up for in research/thinking/writing proficiency, which was the point, after all, and a much more fair way to grade students from different major concentrations.

Learning outcomes

In the final bibliographic essays, students reflected on the considerable lessons they'd learned through the process. One student, an English Education major, wrote:

> I found that even one sentence, or the premise of a story, takes research. I didn't realize that every single part of the story is dictated by the time period … Growing up in academia, we are told to always look for "valid, credible sources" such as academic journals. However, those sources would not have been as helpful as photos of clothing or the map of Ball State's campus in 1968. This process has changed my opinions on what is research and what its overall purpose is in writing and life.

I was gratified that a Literature major said, "In a literary analysis paper … you shine a light on your research. In researched fiction, though, the research needs to be invisible." I love this insight, especially because the student articulated it herself. If I teach this class again, this is an analogy I'll be sure to use. Another student who was double majoring in Creative Writing and Telecommunications wrote:

> The research process … became much more of an unstructured process of exploration than the strict, orderly thing that I've always thought research to be. This de-familiarization of the research process has been an encouraging experience, teaching me that doing research is nothing to be afraid of, and furthermore, that it can be fun.

An English Studies major drew directly from the Chicano Literature class she was taking that same semester:

> My professor asked the question, "Who are some famous Latinos/as from Indiana?" The whole class laughed … So I decided to write a character into

> history, one that would not have qualified for the Lynd studies, and one whose people had not been given a voice. After coming up with a story concept, I began asking questions. Why is a Latina girl in Muncie? How did she get there? How did people treat her? Why does this matter? What was Muncie like? What was Ball State like? And thus began the research process, filling in the gaps.

And one of our program's strongest creative writing majors (who was already publishing her work at the time) found the course to be extremely challenging. She admitted to being "a lazy researcher," a Googler, instead of someone willing to seek out "out-of-the-box" sources. Another creative writing major commented:

> I conducted interviews, analyzed photographs, watched videos, read magazines, watched documentaries, went to a house where a murder took place, read news articles, and looked at maps. Did everything appear in my story? No, but each source was rewarding in its own way because research, no matter how insignificant it seems, is still significant.

Why teach a class like this

This course challenged my students' perceptions about the importance of creative writing, research, and collaboration. They learned that creative writing is not simply about "expressing" oneself, writing what you want, when you want, how you want, but is also the result of rigorous critical thinking and necessary collaboration—important lessons, especially for students who wish to pursue literary lives themselves. I know that my students were often confused and anxious about "what I wanted" from them. This is understandable, considering that I was forcing them to undertake their own process of inquiry, their own independent research project—within a certain set of parameters. The creative writing majors weren't used to such parameters. The noncreative writing majors weren't used to writing something other than a research paper. None of them were used to doing this kind of research. As the Creative Writing/TCOM major said above, this kind of "de-familiarization" asks students to apply what they know (and know how to do) to new situations, new problems, which is what teaching students to be lifelong learners is really about.

My own capstone experience provided a clear bridge to my writing life; perhaps that's why giving my students a similar kind of meaningful experience matters so much to me. Most capstone courses for creative writing majors are structured as group independent studies, similar to a graduate workshop. Each student produces a portfolio of their work, and often times, the work in those undergraduate portfolios becomes the writing sample that students submit to Master of Fine Arts programs. Students in most advanced creative writing classes have free rein to choose their genre and subject matter. AWP clearly states, "an undergraduate creative writing major should culminate in a portfolio of substantial length, with faculty advisors mentoring students as they learn the skills of composing and revising in a given genre."[5]

But of course, I couldn't mentor students as they learned to compose and revise their fiction, because the learning goals of the course were different. And to be honest, I think this class failed a few of its students. Two or three of the creative writing majors might one day apply to MFA programs, and their writing sample will play a pivotal role in whether or not they are accepted. Perhaps these students will continue to work on their Middletown story. Perhaps I've helped them find their subject matter—if not Muncie, per se, their own postage stamp of Indiana soil. It's worth mentioning that I walked into my own senior seminar with absolutely no idea that I would write researched fiction about my hometown. I did so only because my professor thought my hometown sounded interesting, and then suddenly, amazingly, it was. But if my students don't stay interested in their Middletown story or find a way to use what they learned to write the stories they do want to tell, then they will submit to MFA programs a writing sample of work that I, their senior seminar instructor, did not mentor.

But teaching this course also forced me to think about whether *all* creative writing majors are best served by writing such a capstone portfolio. Perhaps they would be well served by one course in their curriculum (capstone or otherwise) in which "finding their voice" is less important than finding someone else's—a key skill for a technical writer, marketer, or communications specialist. I'm not suggesting that creative writers should be "trained" for the job market, but I am suggesting that creative writing students often don't know how to transfer their writing skills to professional contexts. Perhaps a course that purposefully de-emphasizes personal expression in favor of critical thinking and writing would demonstrate to students that research—whatever form it takes—is integral to their intellectual and professional growth.

I also think it's important to prove to students, faculty, and administrators that creative writing is a serious and rigorous discipline. I've worked in five English departments in my career, and in all but one case, creative writing majors vastly outnumbered majors in literature, composition, linguistics, and the like. (The only exception was a school where there was no creative writing *major*, only a minor.) Whether we like to admit it or not, students perceive that creative writing is "easier" than literary or composition studies. And to be frank, I think that's what many faculty members think, too. Perhaps the trick is to bring everyone to the middle of the creative vs. critical divide, to show those who are nervous or skeptical about creative writing that it requires critical thinking, and to show those who are nervous or skeptical about critical writing that it requires a good deal of creative thinking.

Notes

1 Jennifer Blackmer, "The Gesture of Thinking: Collaborative Models for Undergraduate Research in the Arts and Humanities," in *CUR Focus* 29: 2 (Winter 2008), 8–12.
2 Laurie Grobman and Joyce Kinkead, "Illuminating Undergraduate Research in English," in *Undergraduate Research in English Studies* (Urbana, IL: National Council of Teachers of English, 2010), ix–xxxii.
3 Debra Spark, "Raiding the Larder: Research in Fact-Based Fiction," *AWP Writer's Chronicle* (September 2014): 86–99.
4 David Jauss, "Stacking Stones: Building a Unified Story Collection," in *Alone with All That Could Happen: Rethinking Conventional Wisdom about the Craft of Fiction* (Cincinnati, OH: Writer's Digest Books, 2008), 149–82.
5 AWP Board of Trustees. "AWP Recommendations on the Teaching of Creative Writing to Undergraduates," in *AWP Director's Handbook*, 3rd revision (Fairfax, VA: Association of Writers & Writing Programs, 2012).

13

For WB: When Our Students Write Us

Katharine Haake

Recently, I was delighted to read Stephanie Vanderslice's tribute to Wendy Bishop, "'There's an Essay in That': Wendy Bishop and the Origins of Our Field,"[1] in the inaugural issue of the *Journal of Creative Writing Studies.* I read it within hours of its publication. I read it electrified and with mixed feelings—a deep and genuine gratitude for Wendy's recognition as having been the guiding force in the formation of this new, exciting field, even as it takes root and thrives; and an enduring feeling of enormous loss, both professional and personal.

Wendy Bishop was my closest friend, and if I'd had my way, she'd have ended up in Utah—with me—earning a PhD in Creative Writing, doubling down on the life of a poet, and none of this would have happened, or not the way it has. Believe me, I lobbied; I lobbied hard.

It's hard to imagine what this field would look like had Wendy done what I wanted, but while she would go on to earn a PhD in Rhetoric and Composition, by the time she rejected my entreaties and moved to Fairbanks instead (her base during her stint at IUP), I had already failed at teaching first-year writing. Although, in later life and under Wendy's influence, I, too, would go on to promote the rich connections between first-year and creative writing, I would never teach first-year writing again. First-year writing had proven far too difficult for me, so I was teaching technical writing instead, which had a textbook and rules.

And a half a lifetime later, I read Vanderslice's tribute and somehow was the first one to "like" it on Facebook. I'm not so good at Facebook—once I "liked" something there, saying something about how it takes a lot to get me on Facebook (it does), and someone wrote back: *what, you think you're too good for Facebook*? Naturally reticent, raised in a family that strongly instilled the feeling in me that the single worst thing a person can do is call attention to herself, basically I am *afraid* of Facebook. So when I "liked" Stephanie's article, writing something like, "Thank you for this beautiful tribute and essay. I can just hear Wendy saying there's an essay, there's a book . . . " I worried a lot about what I had written: why did I have to say that about me hearing Wendy, too? I worried about this for some time.

But Stephanie is right: Wendy was always encouraging the writing of others. She just had this almost preternatural ability to see it in ways we couldn't quite. But how can a "like" on Facebook begin to evince the resonance of Wendy's voice, the deep belly chortle of her laugh I can still sometimes hear rise up in and out of me?

In my case, it wasn't *essays*, but *books* she wanted me to write, lots and lots of books, which, as a slow and sentence-thinking writer, I can't help but find preposterous even now. Wendy wrote beautiful sentences, and she wrote them furious fast. We were all in awe, not just of her productivity, but also of her fearlessness, her brilliance, her mind and will of steel—if there was a book she thought needed writing, well, by George, she would write it. She wore out not one, but two keyboards on her early IBM Thinkpad. The people at IBM had never seen anything like it before.

But not me. I'm a slow and plodding writer. And even though I did want to change the creative writing world as much as Wendy did (for some reason, we thought we could), we found ourselves, by virtue of our different PhD approaching the issue from different sides of the divide between composition/rhetoric and creative writing, the both of us thinking that writing is writing, but in wildly different contexts. The senior poet at my school, for example, warned me against saying that thing about writing being writing where anyone else in the department might hear me, while Wendy, despite being top ranked (by virtue of her publications) in her department at her school, struggled for years to get a raise, since she was "only" a compositionist.

Bear in mind this was all happening in another century.

And we were women writing teachers who had not been taught writing by women—not one, between the two us.

In the end, I only managed to write one of the many books Wendy wanted me to write, along with a handful of assorted essays, among which is this one. There might have been more, but after she died, I couldn't even bring myself to think about all this for a long, long time. I was, in the most profound sense, *bereaved*. I do know that I'm not alone in this. But I also know that without Wendy to talk to all night about writing, what could possibly be the point?

Of the books I didn't write, the first was my idea, which had its roots both in our friendship and in my first sabbatical (Fall, 1993), when Wendy finally got me to try email, and when, after I managed to sort out the technology, we wrote to each other every single day throughout that fall, the both of us struggling in difficult marriages, and suddenly no longer quite so alone in them. Our words filled all those empty spaces of our lives, and I remember running from the dinner I was cooking or toddler I was tending, just to see what she had to say. These days, I resent the omnipresence of digital communication as much as anyone, but back then it was pretty much such a lifesaving miracle that I had this idea to invite five women from five different parts of the country who did not know each other to commit a single weekend to writing back and forth to each other, telling each other the stories of their lives, using the power of *writing* to become friends *online*.

Yes, yes, Wendy said. There's a book in that.

Once, long ago, this idea seemed radical.

The other book I didn't write (my kids were little; I had a 4/4 teaching load) was her idea, not mine. We were walking in the hills around her home one sultry summer evening (I suppose that summer evenings in Florida are always sultry), talking, talking, talking about writing and our classroom teaching. Or, I was. Wendy was listening; she was listening, as she always did, intently. She was the best listener I knew, and I think her gift in listening was the feeling she gave you that she was listening just and only to *you*—to the secret, inner, real *you*, whoever that might be. So of course it was always exciting when we got together, and, as ever, now, the ideas were coming on fast, especially with regard to how I was using theory to help students reframe their thinking and experience about what writing even was—how it happened, was made, worked, moved through, and took place in the world.

When I finally stopped to pause, she said, there's a book in that; you should write it.

Yeah, right, I said, not without some bitterness, with what time?

Oh, she said, that's easy. Just have your students write it. Make it part of the class. Each week, one person or group takes notes and writes minutes, and at the end of the semester, you have a book.

By George, I thought, *brilliant*—a book without labor, or even much writing. Just have your students write it for you! She was smart, Wendy was. What could be better? And indeed, the idea was hard to resist, but somehow I managed until, one day, that book wrote me. So, with all love and respect to Wendy, this one's for her.

In fact, it was a gift from a cohort of students who had worked together, and with me, for some time. This happens not infrequently in our program. We're a large, urban, public institution with nontraditional students who work and have families and sometimes stick around for years, taking both the BA and the MA before moving on. Having recently graduated my last such cohort, I can look back at the five or six others that preceded it and embrace my great good fortune as having worked with each of them. They have all been such wonderful students. Different cohorts have honored me in different ways, and I cherish all the memories, but this one made a book, or rather what they called "a compendium of the wit and wisdom of a brilliant writer, mentor, & teacher" (aka, "Haakisms"), which turned into a whole new education of my own, as reading through it, it's sometimes hard not wonder: huh, who said these things? Surely, not me.

Long ago, during my own Ph.D. years, one professor managed to reduce me, publicly, to red-faced and red clog stomping tears, not just once, but twice. This professor taught theory—*theory!*—and really, oh, the things he said, you can't imagine. Never before in my life had I encountered such brilliance. So of course, you can imagine my surprise when the time came for me to actually read a lot of theory in preparation for my exams, only to discover that none of the ideas I was entranced by had *originated* with him. He was just quoting the others, same as the rest of us. He was doing it a long time before David Shields,[2] but that's still what he was doing.

I've evolved into a big time quoter of my own—I like the *words* of others. But in class, I try to be more like Dorothy pulling back the curtain than the wizard behind it—that is, I cite my sources. Sometimes it's pretty hilarious—Derrida, Foucault, Ozick, Hugo, Barthes, Nochlin, Pratt, Brodkey, Forster, DeLillo, Stone, Gass—all jumbled together in a literal "tissue of quotations"

(Barthes). One sleepy-eyed boy looked up one night and incredulously said what may have been the only thing he ever said in class: *How many quote do you know, anyway?* But I want the seams to show, the connective tissues of the larger conversation. And I make a big deal of it, telling the story of my "brilliant" professor and his unveiling, never leaving out anybody's name. These days, we read Shields too.

But the first thing I notice when I open the little book of Haakisms is, astonishingly, *me*. Around each "witty" or "wise" thing I apparently said, the implacable imprimatur of quotation marks, without a single source or attribution. This is my first lesson from the little book my students wrote for me: it all comes back to me. No matter how many times I prefaced a remark with the words "(Author's name) says, … " I remain the absolute source of what happens in class, even if, on closer inspection, it bears little resemblance to what I may, or may not, have thought was happening.

Which is my second lesson from the book—that "closer inspection"—because it turns out that teaching really is like playing telephone: you say something, your students hear something else, they repeat it among themselves and it continues to evolve until a whole new lexicon has sprouted up around you. I suppose this is why teachers in other disciplines give tests, as if the ability to accurately repeat someone else's words proves anything at all about what anyone has learned.

In fact, I'm not all that attached to my words. They are out there in the classroom for students to do what they will with them. Wendy always said you can't control what students learn. She said it was your job to create the "structure within which learning can happen," as if teaching were an act of faith in which, if I did my part, my students would learn *something*. It might not be, she said, exactly what you want them to learn, but they would learn *something* and it would be of value.

Wendy was, above all things, a fierce advocate for students.

I was asked, in this project, to talk about practices related to gender. And while it may not seem that I have done so, it's possible to think of this flexible and open-ended, dialogic model of inclusion as one that can be said to proceed from feminist principles and in direct opposition to good-old phallogocentric discourse—that is to say, discourse that performs as monologic, domineering competition, that is, masculinist.

I really haven't addressed gender like this in a long time because, *ah la la*, gender remains so mystifyingly difficult to talk about. And how can that possibly be after so many years? It's certainly not that we don't have a language for it anymore—we are drowning in languages for it. But be careful of what you say—you might be construed as "anti-male." In the context of today's continuing and seemingly immutable inequalities (by which women continue to perform 40% more unpaid labor than men and earn 20% less than men for exactly the same work), never mind the current political climate (where it's not clear whether a substantial portion of the American populace hates women or African-Americans more), it's time to go back—and back, and back—to the stubborn persistence of gender. Not that it isn't easier—it *is* easier—to talk about gender as metaphor (for marginalization) or position (vis-à-vis dominant ideologies). Metaphor keeps us safely clear of all such sticky issues as biology and flat-out misogyny. But, at some point, a reckoning has to be made with the fact that we all had mothers, or are mothers ourselves, never mind that women are arguably more threatening—and potentially more powerful—than other marginalized groups because, at least as far as numbers go, we are not marginal at all.

Nonetheless, sometimes, at my most bored in my department meetings, I still find myself counting words. Even now, well in to the twenty-first century and in a department that has long achieved a basic gender balance, the vast majority of words—sometimes in the 80 and 90 percentiles—are still spoken by men, and most of them are predictable. As I count, I breathe—inhale, exhale. Yoga has taught me to breathe and to empty my mind, often simultaneously, both excellent skills at such times, and others.

And you know, it also turns out that inside your own classroom you can talk metaphor all you want—contact zones, and wild zones, and marginalization, and claiming authority for your own speech—as much as you want, and you're still standing there at the center: you're the man of the hour in the classroom, whether you like it or not. So, yet another lesson from the little book of Haakisms is that one possible pedagogical practice of value might be to introduce this paradox as a systematic course activity.

Or, like I say, this one's for Wendy. The book of Haakisms is not the book she wanted me to write so so long ago, but it is the book my students wrote using the things they heard in my class, and it is of value, even if it's not, quite, what I meant. Just imagine what your own students might write if they made one for you.

In fact, I don't know how a collaboration of this kind might work in actual practice, but it sounds promising. Wendy's idea was to have students keep and post minutes of class on a weekly basis. This could be constructed as an extended post-class dialogue in an online forum in which the professor writes back. Even as I try to think how, exactly, to frame this, I realize it wouldn't be the same, at least in part because my own book of Haakisms was a surprise, made for me by a close group of the highly motivated students, and not part of any classroom assignment. If you asked your students to make a book for you of you, would it become a chore? Would they pay more attention or listen differently? Would their listening be any more—or any less—authentic? If they knew you were going to read what they thought you had said, would it be like a test—would they worry, of all things, about being graded?

Nevertheless, I see potential in a classroom practice that proceeds from the professor looking at and responding to what the students are actually taking in from a class, constructed as an ongoing public dialogue that takes place without judgment, but only curiosity and engaged exchange. I have learned so much from my little book of Haakisms, but I do wish I'd have had a chance to write my students back. If I had, it might have looked a little bit like this:

From Marco Paolo De La Fuente, Ani Kachbalian, Sheryl Leonard, Jeannette Lindsay, Jennifer Lu, Kenneth Siewert, Darryl White, Omer Zalmanowitz—May 2009

The Work of Art

"A work of art is valuable only in so far as it is vibrated into the future."

I wonder what this means, but I love the idea. I know I do talk—a lot—about sustainability, what might make writing continue to be vital, even necessary, into a millennium already saturated with narrative. But vibrating into the future—what a provocative metaphor.

The Novel

"The novel is the heteroglossic text, the ever developing zone of contact with the open-ended present."

Well, hmm, that was Bakhtin, not me, who defines the novel as the only "ever developing genre that takes place in a zone of contact with the present, in all its open-endedness."[3] Important, yes, because that's where we find ourselves.

Don't forget Linda Nochlin: "Nothing is more interesting, more poignant, or more difficult to seize than the intersection between self and history."[4] That's our open-ended present, and the writing we do takes place just there, in that moment, in its own coming into being. I don't apologize for this—sometimes, I may exhort it.

"The novel can engage all things in the world."

Oh, good Lord, probably true. But I'm damned if I ever said anything like it.

What Is a Story

"Stories are a sequence of events; placement, displacement, replacement; equilibrium, disequilibrium, re-equilibrium."

Classic structuralism, taken from Cohen and Shires, *Telling Stories*.[5] Structuralism because we need to have a systematic way to talk about the things we are making.

"Literature is the recognition of the particular."

Cynthia Ozick, "What Literature Means"[6]

"Stories should not compete with their own conventions."

Interesting to frame this as a proscription. I know that I sometimes find myself concluding in workshop that here is a story that's "at odds with its own conventions." I suppose it's natural to draw a proscription from this—to think, don't do this. But it's always a surprise to me, when I discover in, how what may be failing to cohere in a story is simply the presence of incompatible conventions. But that doesn't mean that you can't bring things together in art that don't normally go together. In many ways, that's what art does.

"Things are made story-able."

I love that word—storyable. Thank you for giving it to me.

"A story does not expend itself, does not surrender to a moment, but lingers within it, fingering all the possibilities."

Hmm. Is "fingering" a typo?

"Narrative needs to be distinguished from its media."

As in prose-based narrative needs to tell stories in ways that cannot be filmed, a concept Saul Bellow presented to my class at Stanford and that remains a guiding principle in all of my classes. To do in language what cannot be done in any other media.

"Stories are part of a literary tradition—they don't take place in a vacuum."

Yes—a conversation, with all the other writing, all the other stories . . .

"Stories aren't about the world, they're about other stories."

Like signs are about other signs.

"We are engaging in a language based conversation between other texts."

See above.

"Fiction is slant; stories are never about what they are."

But it was Emily Dickinson who said, "Tell the truth but tell it slant,"[7] the other is—finally—me. I did say that. I say that all the time: stories are never about what they are about. Once a student had a t-shirt made with those words and the author photo from my first book to wear at his final presentation. He threatened to make them to sell.

"We have things to make. We are not interested in 'saying something.'"

Hmm, not so much that we don't have things to say—of course we do—but that whatever it is we have to "say" will never withstand the tremendous assault of our own most earnest intentions if we don't attend to the making first. Derived from Richard Hugo's distinction between one's "triggering subject" and one's own "idiosyncratic sense of language."

"Closure depends on the way the story manages the excess elements."

Taken from Cohan and Shires: successful closure depends on the "success with which the ending manages the excess of significations that are set into play along the narrative syntagm." I suppose "excess elements" is related to "excess significations,"[8] but they're not the same. Signification always takes place in excess; while excess elements will overload a story and sink it.

"Closure is the success with which the narrative excess is adequately resolved on the paradigmatic and syntagmatic axes."

Close; see above.

"The end of a story should make you want to go back to the beginning and read it all over again."

> Flannery O'Connor.

"Staying with a character to the end may provide clarity."

> No idea where this came from. And why clarity—why not mystery?

"Stories are over when they've taught you everything you need to know about them."

> But not so much about the story. And that's not to say they are over, either. What I meant was that it's important to know when to move on from a story—and that point comes when you are no longer learning as a writer from that story. Maybe you could keep fiddling with it, but it's better, at that point, to move on to whatever's coming next in your work.

"Write a sentence or two sentences between every sentence, and a paragraph between every paragraph."

> This is a strategy for developing work, or writing what Wendy Bishop used to call a "fat draft."

"All writing is about writing."

> Yes!

"If you are really writing, you ought to be able to recite your first page by memory."

> Well, by George, I really said that. And you know, I have always believed that. You should have run the first sentences through your head so many times you can't get them out of there. I've recently been experimenting with "memory" readings, where students present their work to the class from memory. These have been among the best readings I have ever heard from students.

"The process of writing is having a shimmering image and putting it into a drawer and then writing your way into it."

> ... from Joan Didion, "Why I Write."[9]

"Every time you rush where you are going you sell out where you are."

> Hmm. I'm pretty sure I never used the term "sell out," but it's true, if you're not working sentence by sentence, if you're rushing toward an end

or an idea, you will leave out all the connective tissue of the text, and it will collapse, a miserable failure.

"Move forward by doing what you don't know how to do."

Yes!

"Writing is the spontaneous coming into being of the structure of the moment, not the writing of an idea."

... from Trinh T. Minh-Ha, *Woman, Native Other.*[10]

"Writing (real writing) evolves out of the crisis of not being able to do what you've been doing anymore."

Well, yes, and also being willing to let go of what you already do know how to do in order to embrace what you don't.

"Writing is a process for being somewhere, not for getting somewhere."

I like this idea, although I'm not sure I ever put it that way, exactly.

"Every occasion for writing is an occasion for writing."

Yes!

"Writing proceeds from language, not from image."

Yes!

"Let go of meaning making."

... or the "thinking of thinking meaning," which, paradoxically, is the single most compelling way of making meaning that surprises and delights us.

"Ideas help us feel in control, but they cause anxiety and get in the way."

Now where could that possibly have come from? Although, I suppose it's good to be reminded that students do have anxiety in relation to the page, and I could be more sensitive to that.

"Write out loud."

Yes!

"Writing is not simply about mastery over form. It should be preoccupied with an explicit and self-conscious attempt to give voice to the wild zone."

See Elaine Showalter, "Feminist Criticism in the Wilderness."[11] And yes, that Wild Zone is, indeed, a wonderful place. Go there, play there, write there.

There is, of course, more of this, much more. But this is some of what they wrote and attributed to me. It is, more or less, how the project began, with little editing, as I wanted to show the kind of progressions and associations students were making, which remain something of a mystery to me.

Of course there were parts I hated to omit, what even I might refer to as a "Haakism": every sentence carries in it the imperative of its own next sentence; something about the "muscle memory" of sentencing; something about Derrida's "logic of supplementarity"[12] being the logic of writing (which it is); the part about using workshop to see what stories are doing and how they are made.

There is what they somehow left out: my frequent invocation, for example, of Derrida's, "coherence in contradiction expressed the force of a desire."[13]

There was good advice: start with a sentence; every story has to teach the reader how to read it; like a story, a sentence is first of all a sound (well, the second part is Frost, and I don't remember ever suggesting a story is a sound as well, but I think I will now).

There was this, which still makes me laugh every time: "compression is like a Japanese brush stroke statement—it can be half done and still be very beautiful." (No, no—not half done, but minimal, suggestive, resonant.)

There was this, which I never knew I knew: "To narrate is to give life. This is how we understand our own alienation within the dominant system," and "unconventional language and unconventional stories are a form of resistance."

There were plenty of misquotes and misattributions.

And finally, in the end, there was this: "If a story is to be pleasurable, it has to lead us into the belly of the beast."

I don't really know where this metaphor comes from, but sometimes, even now, I think about that belly. I'm pretty sure Wendy would like this book too. I wish it were more coherent, maybe, more systematic. I wish I recognized more of it. I wish I had a clearer sense of what holds it all together. And I wish it were more reliable. But as I tell my students, all narrators are unreliable (which is translated, in the book, as "your character can be unreliable"). Such a glimpse into the nature of my own lack of system, incoherence, and unreliability, coupled with such passion and conviction, is a rare gift indeed. So I want to say, to my students, thank you for all that. It may not be, like Wendy said, exactly what I'd hoped you'd learn, but it's yours now, and it's precisely for that reason that it has such value.

As for the rest of us, listen up. Ask your students what you're teaching them. It may not be what you want or think, but either way, and to borrow from Cynthia Ozick, it will be an "education that goes on and on and on."[14]

Notes

1 Stephanie Vanderslice, "There's an Essay in That: Wendy Bishop and the Origins of Our Field," *Journal of Creative Writing Studies* 1 (1) (2016), article 2. Available online at: http://scholarworks.rit.edu/jcws/vol1/iss1/2
2 David Shields, *Reality Hunger: A Manifesto* (New York: Alfred A. Knopf, 2010).
3 M. M. Bakhtin, "Epic and Novel," in *Essentials of the Theory of Fiction*, ed. M. Hoffman and P. Murphy (Durham, NC: Duke University Press), 48–69.
4 Linda Nochlin, "Of Self and History: Exchanges with Linda Nochlin," in Moira Roth (interviewer), *Art Journal* 59 (3): 18–33.
5 Steven Cohan and Linda Shires, *Telling Stories: A Theoretical Analysis of Narrative Fiction* (New York: Routledge, 1988).
6 Cynthia Ozick, *Portrait of the Artist as a Bad Character: And Other Essays on Writing* (London: Pimlico, 1996).
7 Emily Dickinson, in *The Poems of Emily Dickinson: Reading Edition*, ed. R. Franklin (Cambridge, MA: The Belknap Press of Harvard University Press, 1999).
8 Cohan and Shires, *Telling Stories.*
9 Joan Didion, "Why I Write," *New Yorker*, n.p.(Dec. 1976).
10 Trinh Minh-ha, *Woman, Native, Other: Writing, Postcoloniality, and Feminism*(Bloomington, IN: University of Indiana Press, 1989).
11 Elaine Showalter, "Feminist Criticism in the Wilderness," in *The New Feminist Criticism: Essays on Women, Literature, and Theory*, ed. E. Showalter (New York: Pantheon, 1985), 243–70.
12 Jacques Derrida, "Structure, Sign and Play in the Discourse of the Human Sciences," in *Modern Criticism and Theory: A Reader*, ed. D. Lodge (New York: Longman, 1988)107–23.
13 Ibid.
14 Ozick, *Portrait of the Artist.*

Part Four

Identity and the Creative Writing Classroom

14

Radical Imperfectionism

Tonya C. Hegamin

I walk into the stifling, windowless classroom, fingers crossed that the computer and projector work. This is the first day of class in the first of the three-tiered Fiction Writing sequence in an urban, predominantly black college. I've been teaching the class for almost seven years now; I have since reconfigured the entire program to reflect what my students need for their future as creative innovators. My syllabus is only posted on Blackboard because the department printer is chronically broken or out of paper, but also because I expect students to use this minimal form of virtual interaction. There are thirty students in this intro class; seventy percent are women. Most are first or second generation Caribbean or West African, and only a few consider themselves African-American and/or Hispanic.[1] One or two of them are under the age of twenty-one, but most are clutching at their late twenties, have children, and work full time. My syllabus is long and multimodal; I see the fear and boredom on their faces when I read it aloud and open multiple links and rubrics. I ask them to write in their journals for a while, to set an intention for their writing, to explore why they want to write creatively. There is a distinct tension—they don't want to set intentions, they just want me to make them better writers; I hear a few suck their teeth.

This chapter assesses the expressions of identity, authority, and privilege in a racial, cultural, language, and ability inclusive undergraduate CW classroom. Themes will address problems that arise and are conquered by rejecting the idea of "the perfect draft" in order to transcend basic writing and literacy levels. I will reflect on the use of flash fiction, high-level in-document editing, and Octavia Butler's stories, and specifically her essay "Positive Obsession" in the collection *Blood Child*, with nontraditional students in order to encourage writing with calculated risk as well as to amplify reading, writing, and editing/revision skills. Other tactics I discuss include establishing the reader-writer connection as a critical yet imperfect translation of the imagination and a vital part of the creative writing process using textual findings about code-switching, culture, and language translation.

When I first started teaching this class, I used texts I found interesting while I was writing my first novel, books I wished I had been shown in graduate school. So, my first syllabus proffered a craft and theory-heavy reading list that bored my students and I found they were clearly not reading the assignments. I would stand in front of the class and wonder why half of them were sleeping while I pontificated about the significance of what was being said behind the words. It bored me to teach those texts, too. Fiction writing class should be focused on the workshop, anyway. But the workshop part of those first classes was also difficult because students who had taken plenty of classes in literature and been taught literary terms were not able to utilize those devices in their writing.

I have always taught in urban settings, although I grew up in a very rural world. I lived isolated from a diverse community, so I had a lot to learn about urban education. I went through the gauntlet, from teaching sex education in high schools to poetry in women's prisons. Ten years, an MFA, and four books later, I feel like I am still making my way through the gauntlet, but there is value to find in every misstep. I have learned that perfection does not exist in teaching or writing, but mistakes make you a better teacher, even when you're an "expert" in your field. Adaptability and finding innovation in ambiguity are key foundations to creative writing and creative teaching. Some creative writing classes serve as emergency triage and rehabilitation for small, urban, or emerging English departments overflowing with students who have a variety of writing skills. How does the instructor navigate the complicated waters of diversity and practice inclusion without negating student needs beyond the construction of an effective yet beautiful sentence?

***

After about twenty minutes of journal writing in that first class, I open the book *Blood Child* by the groundbreaking science fiction novelist Octavia

Butler. "Positive Obsession" relays her experience as "a perennial out-kid" who wanted to be a writer in the homogenous male field of science fiction. The short stories vary from "hard" SF (aliens lording over humans) to not-so-straightforward taboo breakers. I chose this particular collection because Butler is in conversation with the reader throughout the text in that each story has an afterword where she explains her choices and process. After introducing other canonical and current African American SF, speculative, fantasy, and Afrofuturist writers like Samuel R. Delany, Ishmael Reed, and Tananarive Due to my students, one blurts with wonderment, "I didn't even know black people wrote Science Fiction!"

I read the preface of *Bloodchild* and then the students read paragraphs of "Positive Obsession" aloud from scanned pages I put on the projector; the essay is intensely honest, a bit sad, and because of the arc of Butler's career, ultimately triumphant:

> ... what good is Science Fiction to Black people?
>
> At its best, science fiction stimulates imagination and creativity. It gets reader and writer off the beaten track, off the narrow, narrow footpath of what "everyone" is saying, doing, thinking – whoever "everyone" happens to be this year ...
>
> And what good is all this to black people?[2]

Later, when I tell them the first story is about aliens impregnating humans, a student raises her hand and fearfully asks, "But you don't expect US to write ... this stuff ... do you?" I assure her I will not expect anyone to write about aliens or alternate universes. Instead, I ask her to use the stories as a challenge for her imagination—like reading Shakespeare. I ask why we would think we could or couldn't write or read in any genre or form that we want—are we limited by our imaginations? Or is it our lack of confidence that keeps us from daring to imagine? Or is it an unwitting acceptance of the dominant paradigm that says, "You can't do that"? Why do we have to believe that SF can't reflect on the current issues of people of color? Butler dared to write what she wanted to read, despite the roadblocks in her way.

That leads to a discussion about reading and writing outside of teacher prescriptions, outside of comfort zones in one way or another. In a survey

I conducted, only about 30 percent of my students regularly read outside of school assignments. A couple of students have read Butler's book *Kindred* in another class, perhaps one or two others discovered the book on their own. Some students are readers of comics or graphic novels, a handful read popular urban or church fiction, others don't read science fiction or fantasy, but like to watch it on TV or in movies.

I have begun to introduce the term "power reading" in all of my classes. Power reading is not only about comprehension, but also about being attuned to your reading habits and being honest about your reading abilities. I am easily distracted when reading nonfiction, but it tends to be what I read the most. Because of my borderline ADD, I use highlighters with pens and flags attached to focus my reading and for easy reference later on. Even when reading on a digital device I utilize all of the highlighting and note taking features and I encourage students to do the same, or to deepen and develop their own process. I also transcribe my notes if it's something I have to write about or fully comprehend. All of that takes a lot of time, and it's a process I developed over ten years of research for my historical novels, but since I am usually reading several books or articles in the same time frame, power reading helps to keep things in order, and keeps me from getting bored. I show students my personal copy of the text, how it is color coded with flags to identify sections of conflict, dialogue, symbolism, and so on, which correspond with what areas we will discuss in class. My students stare back at me with awe, disbelief, and perhaps with a twinge of horror and a drop of hatred.

"Ignorance is expensive,"[3] Butler reminds us and I am clear that I have had the privilege of a slightly above average education, a powerful cultural currency in my reading and writing. Students who have had a minimally average or below average education want to read deeper and faster, but there is so much to know when you have little or no cultural currency. I have been educated and encouraged into being a vigilant reader, writer, and researcher, yet I'm still learning and interpreting the codes of academic Standard Written English (SWE). After I explain my methods of power reading, a student murmurs something; that's when I start to hear muffled laughs and snorts from the class. When I pause to ask what was said, a student who I have had a few classes with says, "Professor, no disrespect, but you a mad nerd, yo."

I laugh, agreeing. "But here's the thing: If you don't geek out about the things you devote yourself to, what's the point? But I don't want you to write or even read like I do, or like Octavia Butler, or anyone else. I want you to find your own way, to be interested in how you read, how you write and to then apply that to your imagination. Be playful, experiment. Learning is an activity, no spectators allowed. That's how you write creatively. The best part of writing is that you can revise. You can't do that very often in life, and this is your chance. In this class, I encourage you to focus on the process of writing, not so much the product. You can't expect to master any craft after an introduction; I don't expect that from you. Obviously you're not going to finish writing a novel in this class. You might never get to the 'perfect' five-page draft, but you're going to learn a lot about how writers read and write. Writing creatively is essentially translating your imagination onto the page, and then you have to make sure that your reader is able to clearly translate what's on the page into their own imagination. That's a serious skill."

So how do I cram all of this power reading and a focus on grammatical skills into a semester when there are so many other issues to be addressed? When the students are often unable to afford books? When they have never been asked to take their self-expression seriously? Again, what about creativity? The basics of storytelling? Eventually I find myself saying that I can't be concerned with content—what they want to write is their business. For me as a teacher, their grade depends on how well a student can execute the craft and structure elements I have taught, how thoroughly they respond to their peers, how willing they are to revise, to take risks. For many of my students, the risk is simply sharing their work in an open discussion board for their peers to view. For some, the risk is merely writing in a different way, of thinking about writing as an enjoyable practice. Most of them struggle with the grey areas of writing, those moments when they don't know if what they're doing is "right" or "wrong."

So the answer is, we can't cram all of it into a semester. If we try, we end up disrespecting our field of study, our students, and ultimately ourselves as teachers. The only thing we can do is detach ourselves from any notion of perfectionism, not in a "devil may care" sort of way, but in the most caring way possible so that it allows our mistakes to become a fertile ground for creative growth.

* * *

My pedagogy has evolved to become an indirect hybrid of what Teresa M. Redd and Karen Schuster Webb would label as "culturally appropriate teaching (CAT)" and "the bridge approach" in their book *A Teacher's Introduction to African American English: What a Writing Teacher Should Know* (published by NCTE in 2005). They note that "... virtually the only AAE (African-American English)[4] speakers who learn to "edit out" SWE (Standard Written English) errors are those who intensively read and write SWE texts outside of school."[5] I began adopting these methods when I was teaching three sections of composition and a creative writing class in one semester. I saw that the same issues I was dealing with in basic writing classes were also present in 300 level writing classes. When I began teaching this class, I spent a lot of time trying to read around the grammatical mistakes, telling myself they didn't matter, only the creative content was at stake. Still, I didn't feel comfortable sending students off with a degree concentrating in creative writing without stronger writing and reading skills. I know how to write at a certain skill level because of my education and experience; however, that is not a skill automatically or easily translated into teaching. My composition class left little room for creativity and my creative class was in desperate need of composition skills. From there, I asked students what they thought they needed and they agreed that they wanted both. This in mind, I set out to really understand how to make that happen.

CAT pedagogy, "draws on the knowledge, strategies, and experiences from African-American students' culture," and "promotes Paulo Freire's rhetoric of critical literacy."[6] Now I make sure my creative writing class readings are focused on marginalized or experimental authors within what is considered traditional African-American Literature. Some years I have assigned readings like Audre Lorde's "Biomythography" *Zami: A New Spelling of My Name*, Jean Toomer's *Cane*, Zora Neale Hurston's collected short stories, ZZ Packer's *Drinking Coffee Elsewhere*, or James Baldwin's *Another Country*. I incorporate African diasporic, Hispanic, Asian, and Aboriginal authors in the second level of the fiction writing course (supplemented via the internet or scanned stories; sometimes simply sharing links to author and publisher websites to allow students to explore on their own). Although the majority of my students are assigned equally Afrocentric texts in other classes, at an introductory level, simply reexamining these texts and themes from the view of a fiction writer while simultaneously practicing the craft of writing can be transgressive in itself.

For the next class, students are assigned to read flash fiction from online journals or specific stories that I have provided links to or they have researched. I have students ask themselves questions like: What connected you to the text? What didn't? How did the author develop the character with details? Does the author work with language and/or dialogue in nontraditional ways? How would you use that technique? These questions engage them as writers, not critics. They then have to come up with three questions they would like to ask the authors, and three questions they would ask one of the characters. Additionally, students are always most excited to write when they are reading alternative expression that sounds like or is written by a person of color. A study done in the early nineties shows that in first-year Afrocentric composition classes "[e]ighty percent [of students] felt more positive about writing in general because they had read so many essays by black writers. Seventy-five percent thought they had something worthwhile to say when writing about ... Afrocentric issues."[7]

One reason teaching specifically Afrocentric science fiction becomes innovative in this introductory class is in the way that the genre promotes free imaginative thought and description beyond the "acceptable" standards of writing, as Samuel R. Delaney describes succinctly in his essay "The Jewel-Hinged Jaw," "The particular verbal freedom of SF, coupled with the corrective process [subjunctivity] that allows the whole range of the physically explainable universe, can produce the most violent leaps of imagery. For not only does it throw us worlds away, it specifies how we got there."[8] Isiah Lavender, III in his essay, "Delany Encounters" explains further: "[Delany's] notion of subjunctivity, [is] the word-by-word corrective reading process used to analyze the literal metaphors of science fiction."[9] In other words, this is another form of code-switching—from reality to imagination and vice versa. The culturally appropriate teaching process is, hopefully, a pact of authenticity between student and teacher. It builds trust and heightens the impact of the subject. Butler's story "Book of Martha" is powerful as it focuses on a black woman "given" the powers of God. "Speech Sounds" is about nonverbal communication. "Near of Kin" is a conversation between a young woman and her father/uncle; although the characters are not racially identified, in my class it always leads to a discussion about writing the taboo and how transgressive it is for writers of color because writing itself can be taboo in many cultures. These stories all validate and innovate nontraditional imaginations, giving hope to budding writers who are consistently told their experiences are deviant or nonexistent. Science fiction can give readers hope for a future that is inclusive and does not reflect the current state of oppression; "Hope fuels the fundamental emotional drive that foments resistance, rebellion and subversive writing by and for black people. Hope unsettles the white order of things. Hope also makes allies between the races."[10]

There is so much more to writing culturally authentic text than just describing skin color. All characters need authenticity, depth, and duality, but often characters who are fundamentally different from their writer fall flat on the page. I look forward to including more activities in my class to challenge my students to write outside of a race-binary, traditionally-abled, heteronormative perspective. All students need this type of prompting and respectful experimentation to make their writing more transgressive and transcendent.

***

The bridge approach as described by Redd and Webb "originated in bilingual education," and "... the goal is to teach AAE speakers to write SWE by allowing them to write their early drafts (and sometimes certain finished pieces) in AAE." They explain the nearly forty-year-old concept as it has changed through use in modern composition classes:

> the bridge approach assumes that many AAE speakers fail to "edit out" AAE features in their essays because they are trying to juggle other composing tasks (e.g., formulating a thesis, synthesizing information, and structuring paragraphs (*or creating authentic characters, developing a sustainable plot or dialogue structure*). (italics mine)[11]

I incorporate this methodology into my praxis with one of the first activities I like to do, called "The Eavesdropper." I send students out onto the campus to observe people and listen to their conversations for a half hour, taking down what is said verbatim and recording how it is said through facial cues, hand gestures, and so on without being noticed. They bring their findings back to the class and we discuss the task of transcribing dialect and vernacular speech, especially when many of the students are multi-dialectical themselves.

On the surface, this activity shows that writers must not only read books, they must also be able to read people. What the students find is how hard it is to formally transcribe speech, how each person puts inflections in unique places, how there are a million ways to say the same thing. They've been told for so long that writing in their own dialect was wrong, so here is where I introduce code-switching as a method for effectual character building. Additionally, this helps them understand common issues in SWE.

Redd and Webb also cite numerous studies that have found that translating AAE to SWE is akin to learning a second language; "[f]rom this perspective, AAE speakers ... construct their own interdialect by simplifying SWE forms and overgeneralizing SWE rules."[12] The marked difference between AAE and SWE is that AAE can be spoken and written in a variety of ways and still be authentic, and is never static because of constant infusion of transient popular culture, ethnic dialects, slang, and the dominant social paradigms of local and national speech. SWE has rules that are mostly static and differ from standard spoken English. In a creative writing class, although we are harbored by standards of conventional language, we cannot be anchored to them. In fact, with my students in particular, it is an imperative that I allow for this type of transient infusion of multidimensional dialogue. Alastair Pennycook elaborates:

> We do not write our own scripts, although neither are our lives fully prescripted. This position not only opens up a non-essentialist view of identity, but it also provides the ground for considering languages themselves from an anti-foundationalist perspective by also considering them as multiple, contested, changing, and contingent.[13]

I ask students to go back to "The Eavesdropper" and look at how they translated what was said. Did they truly capture the essence of that person? Did the person use perfect grammar? Of course not. But knowing how people speak and developing a clear understanding of code-switching and vernacular speech is important to developing authentic characters. For my students, it is also critical for validating their voices, the voices of the people they hear every day. If I were to ignore vernacular speech in their writing or to deny them use of switching between Creole or Patois and English, they would be trying to write something other than what is authentic to them, and to me. How we speak is just as important as what we say, sometimes even more so.

By introducing code-switching as a viable method of character development and dialogue, it gives students the chance to embrace their speech and writing. I ask my students to not only understand rules of standard written language, but also to innovate that language by imbuing it with new life. Asking them to have more faith in their reading and writing skills by the end of the semester is something that takes many students from being struggling writers to striving writers, not perfect writers. For an introductory class, this is monumental.

Their next assignment is to write flash fiction that is less than a thousand words, and to include the dialogue they transcribed. This is a diagnostic to assess the levels of writing competency, how well they absorbed "the rules" of dialogue format, how much effort they put into developing a story, and how much time (if any) they put into revision. I can see how much risk they are willing to take in the public online discussion board, and how many of them responded to each other's posts. I'm trying to ease them into a collaborative state of mind and prepare them for the peer critique. Most of the students are writing far below institutional standards, even though they have passed both of the composition courses and I spent a lot of time going over basic formatting. Here are some verbatim examples:

- He thought it would be over for him and then suddenly he hear the voice of the basketball coach Mr. Frankenderp from the recreational center. "Clark I look all over for you". He Continued. I'm surprised you even made it this far, without it."
- James reading Rebecca mind ask, 'if she ready?', ready for what she had no idea, but ready is how she felt. She was stricken with readiness humbled by it.
- "How do you tell someone you love them, without having them looking like you crazy?" stated the slim seventeen years old girl wearing green sweater.

Notice that despite the weakness of SWE skill, there is always description, imagery, and an attempt at depth. This is a low-stakes first draft that allows me to see what each student is working with. Mini or micro-stories are an excellent exercise in word choice and language precision. Although it's diagnostic in nature, it does not assess a student's ability to revise. I compare the first document to their last revisions at the end of the semester to see how and where they have grown.

We spend most of the class learning how to write by revision. Most of the students don't know how to fully use Microsoft Word, so I make a big point of revealing the magic of the REVIEW tab. I show them track changes, comments, and also how to compare and merge documents. "You have to play with it, be willing to make mistakes," I remind them. "I use this to grade and help you edit all of your work." Some nod wearily, but many look like deer in headlights. I ask for a volunteer to have their work revised by the whole class, and we give snaps to the brave soul who, after a few moments of silence followed by threats to pick someone at random, reluctantly raises his hand. I put his work on the screen and zoom in so everyone can see. I see him wince in pain when I read the first sentence because now he can see and hear his SWE errors.

Then we go in with track changes, line by line. I explain how and where the punctuation rules of dialogue must be applied. Then everyone participates, either by reading a line or pointing out where the language could be clearer, where it works the best, how different audiences could interpret it. How he effectively uses descriptive language. We end with more snaps and congratulate the author for his risk-taking. I save the document with track changes and send it to the student to look at and revise further later.

"I wanna be next," a girl in the back frantically waves her hand.

Someone else calls out, "Do mine after hers!"

They actually appreciate it. In fact, they love it. I am showing them how to translate their writing into SWE, but I am also giving them agency to review and revise in a sophisticated way, access to what Audre Lorde might call "the master's tools."[14] Redd and Webb point out that most students want someone to show them exactly the rules of the dominant paradigm in order to understand the language and ultimately empower themselves within their own social system. Although "the master's tools will never dismantle the master's house," they can help to unlock other houses that are even more useful. It is never empowering to lose your native language, but it is empowering to be able to speak and write in multiple languages and dialects, to move seamlessly between cultures yet still be grounded in one's own. Even possessing only one language that I speak and write, I do both in a variety of patterns that are deliberately and inadvertently in adherence with and in rebellion against a multitude of "standards" in order to reach and include a multiperspective audience. The precision of language is a product of years of studying and writing, it is a privilege and yet also a right—the right to speak freely and responsibly.

Code-switching in written and spoken forms are ultimately a use of power and cultural currency, just as much as knowing where the comma goes or knowing how to respectfully address peers, colleagues, and employers. The ability to code-switch effectively and to recognize when, where, and how to do it requires a heightened self-awareness, interpersonal skills and strategy, all of which are valuable for the creative writer. By diminishing the idea of perfectionism in our speech and writing, we become more adaptable and valuable in a variety of communication modes. We all know that language is changing at an exponential rate because of the social context of technology; so, as a teacher of creative writing I need to adapt and embrace the shift or else I will be doing a disservice to my students and to the beautiful complexities of AAE.

Radical imperfection is about releasing oneself from binary thinking, giving up the idea of getting the draft or the sentence "right" at any one point—it's about giving up what is right or wrong as an answer to the construction of written language, especially creatively written language in a classroom context. I try to teach students the importance of understanding form, but more importantly, that revision should become a joyful process, not a fearful, anxiety-ridden task. Radical imperfectionism is wholly accepting students where they are, not where we were; expecting an evolution rather than a revolution within one semester. We still need to push them further, to think differently than we can imagine. To embrace radical imperfection, one must be willing to accept that SWE is only a temporal format. As a creative writing teacher, I had to accept that I was an interloper of sorts; I could not rely on any perceived commonality but I had to gain my students' trust to empower them, coax them into embracing the power of their own words. I am there to nurture their "positive obsession" for words and writing, not squash it or try to fit it into a paradigm meant to oppress them. The true beauty of a sentence is mainly found in the effort it took to write it down.

***

Peer review and collaborative work have always been a difficult task at my college. Students who are already insecure about their skills become more insecure when asked to respond to someone else's work in fear of "doing it wrong." They also don't want to have anyone else "mess up" their work. With twenty-seven to thirty students in each class, grading stories became overwhelming on my own. I began researching rubrics to support and enhance the peer review process. I came up with a few "holistic" rubrics at first, just brief descriptions of what I expected on a scale of 1–10. At first, I was the only one to use the rubric, but I ended up asking students to also rate themselves and their peers. At first the responses were weak (topical and subjective), and everyone gave themselves and their peers nines and tens, which was clearly false. So, I broke down the rubric further to specifically ask the reader to dissect the work numerically and with commentary. The writer also responds to the work with commentary and finally I rate the work numerically and with commentary. The sections are content, development, language, and mechanics (each with subsections), and they have numeric averages that the peer reviewer assigns for each section. I add the peer points to my own, although I gave myself ten extra points to grade with in case the peer reviewer is way off.

The procedure is as follows: Students submit their work via Blackboard, and I randomly assign them into groups of three to four students. Each group is responsible for reading the work of their peers, printing the work, making comments on the page as well as filling out the rubric, which also gets printed and attached to the story, and in class, the groups discuss the work. I found that this frees the writer from the fear of having just one reviewer, allowing them to hear a variety of responses. I get all of the reviewed copies so I can see how students respond to each other and to grade the reviewer for their efforts. In this way, everyone feels as though their input is heard and respected, and I have a little help when grading so my response also isn't subjective or topical. After that, I have private meetings with students and discuss their writing and reviews. We look at their document in Word and I show them again how to do track changes so they have a very clear picture of what they have to work on for the next story. At the end of the semester, students submit a portfolio of at least fifteen pages of work that has been revised; it can be several short pieces or a longer work. They are allowed to revise their flash fiction, their journal writing prompts and/or any of the three to five-page stories they have received peer review feedback. Their final grade is based mainly on their revision skills, but also on the creativity and perseverance they have shown throughout the semester. Obviously, you can do a quick Google search for "creative writing rubrics" and find several examples that you can adapt to your own class, depending on the skill level and purpose of your class. I adapted this one I found from New Paltz high school in New York because it reflects many of my students' needs and utilizes state standards that are familiar to students. I find this rubric gives students a deeper vision for critically critiquing the creative process.

Appendix: Peer review assignment

ENGLISH 301: Intro to Fiction Writing

Author Name:____________________ Draft #______

Peer Reviewer Name:________________________

Date:______________

Rubric Criteria for Peer Creative Writing Review

Please fill in the peer/self-assessment section on the back before handing in this assignment

Estimate an *average* of points for each section (0–10 points each)

	10–9pts	**8–6pts**	**5–3pts**	**2–0pts**
Content: The extent to which the assignment exhibits sound understanding/interpretation/analysis				
Characterization	Develops complex characters through dialogue, narration, and action.	Develops characters through dialogue, narration, and action, adequate description.	Some character development, description.	Characters are flat and undeveloped.

	10–9pts	8–6pts	5–3pts	2–0pts
Content: The extent to which the assignment exhibits sound understanding/interpretation/analysis				
Conflict	Establishes strong and compelling conflict using the 6 types; builds tension throughout.	Establishes limited conflict but needs more tension. Conflict is clear.	Some conflict used but it has weak or cliché elements; little tension.	No conflict or tension developed.

Average of Content Points:________/10

Development: The extent to which ideas are elaborated, using specific and relevant evidence				
Plot	Maintains clear focus; develops ideas clearly and fully; interesting plot; uses a wide range of relevant details; story arc and orchestration utilized.	Develops ideas clearly; focused plot; uses relevant details. Story skips around some but plot is easily understood.	Develops ideas briefly; uses some detail; plot is confusing at times or underdeveloped.	Uses incomplete or undeveloped ideas. No clear plot.
Story structure	Establishes strong plot/ setting/ character/pt. of view.	Establishes plot/setting/ character/pt. of view, clear beginning, middle, and end.	Some elements of story structure; little blending of dialogue and narration. Weak ending.	Few/no story structure elements present, no clear beginning, middle, or end.

Average of Development Points:________/10

Language: The extent to which the assignment reveals an awareness of literary language				
Description	Creative imagery employed; uses literary devices and rich sensory detail.	Assignment uses imagery and concrete language; some literary devices and sensory detail.	Some use of concrete language, literary devices, and sensory detail in assignment.	Minimal or no use of concrete language, literary devices or sensory detail in assignment.

Language: The extent to which the assignment reveals an awareness of literary language				
Dialogue	Little or no format mistakes; dialogue is dynamic, propels plot and supports character development; incorporates action and authentic speech.	A few formatting mistakes (not indenting a few paragraphs, some punctuation outside of quotes); propels plot and supports characterization. Correctly uses some authentic speech.	Several formatting mistakes; dialogue does little to support plot and character development; uses only "he said, she said" etc.; attempts action.	Little or no formatting; dialogue makes reading difficult; does not support or relate to plot or characters; no action.

Average of Language Points:________/10

Mechanics: The extent to which the assignments exhibit conventional grammar/spelling/word usage				
Grammar/ Punctuation	Smooth, fluid, error-free punctuation/ grammar. Uses code-switching correctly in dialogue format.	Mostly correct grammar; errors do not interfere with communication but are noticeable.	Errors occasionally interfere with communication; verb tense errors. Over or under use of punctuation.	Grammatical errors are awkward and interfere with communication.
Spelling and Word Usage	Correct spelling; error-free word usage.	Mostly correct spelling and word usage.	Errors in spelling and word usage.	Misspelled and misused words throughout.

Average of Mechanics Points:_______/10

Peer Assessment:

What this writer does best:

____

____

____

For further revision:

____

____

____

The total peer review points: ______out of 40 possible points (add up your averages)

Writer Self-Assessment:

What I enjoyed most about writing this story:

____

____

____

What I need to remember when I revise:

____

____

____

Professor's Comments:

____

____

____

____

____

____

Professor Points: __________ out of 50 (10 points for writer's peer reviews)
Total Points: __________ out of 100

Notes

1 I use the word "consider" because as a multiracial person, I feel it is up to an individual to label themselves. Clearly, the terms "Caribbean" and "West African" encompass a variety of ethnicities and nationalities, but for many, it is a common mode to identify themselves to outsiders, as are the terms "African-American and/or Hispanic." By no means do I wish to subordinate or diminish the importance of individual identity.
2 Octavia Butler, "Positive Obsession," in *Blood Child and Other Stories*, 2nd ed. (New York: Seven Stories Press, 2005), 134–6.
3 Butler, *Blood Child and Other Stories*, 131.
4 Obviously, the term "AAE" is limiting, but here it is meant to include dialectic and vernacular speech of Caribbean and African cultures.

5 Teresa M. Redd and Karen Schuster Webb, eds, *A Teacher's Introduction to African American English: What a Writing Teacher Should Know* (Urbana, IL: NCTE Teacher's Introduction Series, 2005), 73.
6 Redd and Webb, *A Teacher's Introduction*,94–95.
7 Teresa M. Redd, "Afrocentric," in *A Teacher's Introduction*, 5–9, 100
8 Samuel R. Delany, *The Jewel-Hinged Jaw: Notes on the Language of Science Fiction* (Middletown: Wesleyan UP, 2009), 12.
9 Isiah Lavender III, "Delany Encounters: Or, Another Reason Why I Study Race and Racism in Science Fiction," *Stories for Chip: A Tribute to Samuel R. Delany*, ed. Nisi Shawl and Bill Campbell (Greenbelt, MD: Rosarium Publishing, 2015), 43.
10 Lavender, Isiah III, "Delany Encounters," 45.
11 Redd and Webb, *A Teacher's Introduction*,102–3.
12 Redd and Webb, *A Teacher's Introduction*,65.
13 Alastair Pennycook, "The Rotation Gets Thick. The Constraints Get Thin: Creativity, Recontextualization, and Difference," in *Applied Linguistics* (London: Oxford University Press, 2007), 527.
14 Audre Lorde, "The Master's Tools Will Never Dismantle the Master's House,"' in *Sister Outsider: Essays and Speeches* (New York: Ten Speed Press, 1984).

15

Gender Identity and the Creative Writing Classroom

Ching-In Chen

I am never as nervous as when I enter into a room full of writers who purportedly share the same identity as I do. The stakes are higher, it seems, to connect, to make something of our shared similarity, to identify with each other because this kind of space so rarely happens. When I first arrived at Kundiman, a writing retreat for emerging Asian American poets, I had already been to Voices of Our Nations Arts Foundation (VONA), a writing workshop for writers of color. But there had still been a buffer of enough distance, enough recognizable difference in a way that entering into that first sharing circle at Kundiman did not. The general question is about acceptance and inclusion in a world in which one is often very familiar with not being accepted and included. In some ways, my writing identity has emerged from that sense of making my own path, my own syntax. So going to a space that is built for intentional sharing is one that pushes up against my own writing identity. The other question also arises—we share geography and lineage, but what about other fissures that arise from the body (of ethnic and regional difference, gender, sexuality, class, ability, language, citizenship)?

In this space of so much expectation, there is a kind of raw openness that emerges, a vulnerability that is a choice to break open and to choose to share, to move away from comfort, to explore. This is not to say that creative writing workshops in which the common vector is shared identity (such as Asian/ American at Kundiman, LGBTQI at Lambda Literary Foundation) are utopian spaces. However, I've often found that the engagement among peers and teachers frequently begins at a different location in terms of acknowledgment and understanding of inclusion of such questions as shared identities and what they bring to our creative work. It is a space I have not encountered in the few undergraduate creative writing classes I took at the small liberal arts college I attended—and a space I rarely encountered in graduate creative writing classes. It is a space that has been crucial for me to improve as a creative writer and one I have come to rely on as part of my practice of composing and experimenting with new work.

Many community-led writing communities that converge around a specific marginalized identity were created out of a sense of urgency that mainstream institutions were ill-equipped to support writers of these backgrounds. In the widely circulated and discussed "MFA vs. POC" essay, Junot Díaz argues that many MFA programs "[reproduce] exactly the dominant culture's blind spots and assumptions around race and racism (and sexism and heteronormativity, etc.)."[1] Díaz explains that most of the students and faculty in his MFA program had been educated from the default subject position of the reader and writer as white, straight, and male. Oftentimes, in my experience as a student and teacher in university settings, such questions are left unaddressed though they often flare up as flashpoints when students from varying backgrounds conflict with each other. In those moments, we don't have a shared vocabulary to approach these questions—and there have been times when I've left the classroom biting my words down unsaid. In this situation, so much depends on the comfort and skill of the facilitator—and often times the facilitator is also uncomfortable and/or unknowledgeable about these students' experiences and needs.[2]

The undergraduate creative writing classroom often acts as an incubator for initial explorations of questions of power, authority, and identity for students, especially in classes where students may confront various kinds of experiences different from those they may be familiar with. Even without intentionally setting up the classroom for such conversations around difference and power, the students bring their lived experience as well as assumptions into the classroom. As an instructor, I want to hold space for the possibility of students to be vulnerable in relation to discomfort, which has been a valuable lesson I've learned in community-led writing spaces. The question I've often asked myself as a teacher is which aspects of these practices can be productively altered for use in academic classrooms with different aims and a broader audience.

Though not mutually exclusive, these questions also have to compete for space on the syllabus with other classroom instructions within limited classroom periods.

I have taught at large public universities with more students of color, immigrant students, working-class students, and first-generation college students than the students at the undergraduate liberal arts college I attended. In these classes, I have had students who identify as LGBTQIA, and some within that subset who identify as genderqueer,[3] share creative pieces that explicitly and intentionally include genderqueer and trans content. In these classrooms, I have found the majority of the students to be unfamiliar with experiences of gender-creative people, including creative work by writers across the trans spectrum.

I have not found research on how many writers across the trans spectrum are included on creative writing university syllabi. However, a 2015 count of trans women writers completed by VIDA, an organization that produces data examining gender bias against women at top-tier literary journals and publications, reveals that trans women writers are not being widely published by major journals and publications.[4] Because these journals and publications are " 'feeders' for grants, teaching positions, residencies, fellowships, further publication, and ultimately, propagation of artists' work within the literary community," the lack of inclusion results in more barriers for trans women writers pursuing writing careers, in conjunction with "transphobia, transmisogyny, cissexism, discrimination in jobs, housing and medical coverage, and a continuing widespread lack of education about trans issues and history among cisgender readers who represent 99.5–99.8% of the population."[5]

As a gender-fluid instructor, this is not surprising information to me. In my years as an undergraduate, MFA, and PhD creative writing and literature student, I was not assigned to read any writer who publicly identified as trans or nonbinary in university creative writing and literature classes.[6] Though not always easy, I have found it easier to incorporate writers of color, writers of varying socioeconomic backgrounds, immigrant and migrant writers, and international writers because I have seen more classroom modeling of practices to handle race, gender, and class as part of the creative writing classroom. I have not witnessed creative writing instruction that incorporates the writing of those with gender creative identities, even in writing workshops that are committed to voices of "marginalized" writers. In addition, though I enrolled in pedagogy courses in my MFA and PhD program for teaching composition, creative writing, literature, and general college-level instruction, none provided much guidance for considering questions of power and identity, let alone questions of gender identity.

This type of occlusion is reflected in the larger society's understanding of trans and nonbinary people's lived experiences. Even though familiarity with trans and nonbinary people may be changing due to recent increased media around well-known public trans figures such as Caitlyn Jenner and controversial events such as the recent signing of the North Carolina House Bill 2,[7] increased media focus does not necessarily equate to more understanding of the experiences of students on the trans spectrum. A recent issue of the *Chronicle of Higher Education* "features the voices of many transgender students and academics as they gain visibility on campuses and elsewhere."[8] In this special issue, Genny Beemyn discussed the results of the first national study of nonbinary trans college students conducted in 2015, which showed that:

> All but one of the students felt that their colleges were not doing enough to support them, even though some of the institutions are considered to be among the most "trans-friendly" in the country. The students' most pressing concerns included being regularly misgendered in class, on official documents, and by other students; the absence of safe and comfortable bathrooms; the inadequacy of housing options; the need for gender-identity choices on campus records beyond "male" and "female"; and a general lack of awareness about their lives.[9]

In Julia Schmalz's accompanying video in the same issue, "'Ask Me': What LGBTQ Students Want Their Professors to Know," gender-nonconforming students talk about how these concerns impact their feeling of safety at school and affect their educational experiences.[10] For example, often students' official government-issued documents do not match their gender identity. Some students' gender identities may not conform to a binary of biological male or female categories of identification, which is often what is requested on official forms. Other students may not have the resources to change their gender identity, even if recognized on official forms. In the video, Nate, a queer trans man who also identifies as Christian and white, says: "Getting your legal name changed is really hard or expensive to do, and it's really out of my budget."[11] The resulting consequences for Nate have been that he has skipped classes because of fear for his safety.

Many students also disclosed the need to do extra work before arriving to the first day of class so that there isn't an awkward exchange when roll is called. Prin, a nonbinary trans person says, "My school does not have a preferred-name policy, so a lot of times I feel uncomfortable talking to teachers or other students or even submitting assignments, because it's not the name that I identify with."[12] These students pointed to the ways that the non-accommodating practices of administrators and instructors created extra stress and barriers for their full participation in class. These testimonials are backed up by survey results from a study conducted by Tre Wentling, who distributed an online survey to student participants eighteen years and older who identified with the term transgender. According to Wentling, "educators are in fact less affirming of genderqueer and gender-nonconforming students, at least when it comes to pronoun recognition."[13] Coming out as a gender-fluid PhD student midway through the program required navigating previous assumptions and understandings of identity from both former and current students, peers, instructors, as well as editors. Given my own experiences as a genderqueer writer of color, I wanted to work to create a space within my own creative writing classrooms to support gender-nonconforming students, especially in classrooms where the majority of their peers may not have familiarity with trans and genderqueer voices and experiences.

Starting a job at a new university gave me the opportunity to consider how to better incorporate trans and nonbinary writers into my classroom. I wanted to do this because often when questions of identity and power aren't considered as part of craft discussions, unnamed normative assumptions are often applied to certain pieces of writing and influence the kind of feedback given.

Before arriving on campus, I talked to a colleague about how students would react to my gender-fluid identity as an instructor, especially since I would be teaching at a Southern school that did not have LGBTQIA student resources such as a LGBTQIA Studies program and/or a LGBTQIA student center. My colleague responded that students wouldn't necessarily be hostile, but might be confused, considering that the culture I would be entering was one that was more formal in which students regularly used Ma'am and Sir to address instructors. I would likely be the first nonbinary/genderqueer professor that students had ever had. As such, I decided to take these approaches:(1) to model nonbinaried gender language, (2) to question their preconceived notions around gender binaries and identities, and (3) to introduce students to trans and non-gender-conforming writers as part of the assigned work of the class.

In the first class, to set the tone for the semester, I incorporated a practice that I'm familiar with from many meetings and gatherings run by LGBTQIA folks, especially those who are sensitive to being inclusive to gender creative folks. At the front end of the meeting, it is common practice to ask those present to self-identify and let people know how they prefer to be addressed.[14] I passed out postcards where I asked a series of questions—some intentionally more familiar to the students about recent books they've read and/or favorite books read, and some connected to their identities, especially those that the university system may not be able to process well, including ethnic names, nicknames, and preferred pronunciations as well as gender pronouns.

Because not all students may feel comfortable being put on the spot to be "out" about their gender identity in front of a room of strangers, I decided to give students the option to answer more privately while still introducing the topic of various gender identities for all students. I also modeled these questions by using my own name as an example—that in the university system, I am known by my legal first name, Elizabeth, but that professionally I publish under Ching-In, which is pronounced Chingy. In addition, I used the example of gender pronouns by using myself as an example—that I have a female friend with short hair who sometimes is mistaken for a man because of her hair and androgynous gender presentation, but who doesn't want to be called a man and uses "she/her" pronouns. Then, I explained that since I identify as genderqueer, I use "they/them" pronouns.

In subsequent classes, I incorporated modeling of gender-inclusive language by explaining that I use "they" as a gender-flexible word—and encourage students to use "them" when they do not in fact have enough evidence to assume what the gender of the speaker (or narrator) might be.[15] In many of my teaching documents that I share with students, I give various pronouns (usually some combination of s/he/they) as options. Though I cannot say all of my students automatically and always use nonbinaried pronouns, by introducing these ideas, our classroom workshop has had more conversations around gender expectations and assumptions than it did previously (and how one might know what gender a speaker is or the identity of the speaker). Bringing those discussions back to specific evidence on the page (what constitutes a male voice vs. a female voice vs. a non-gender-specific deity's voice or a voice with no visible gender inflections or markers) has also resulted in a more precise way of analyzing a poem in the classroom. When students automatically revert back to the writer (or character) as male, in early sessions of class, I ask them why they think the writer is male and to point to any evidence on the page, also reminding them not to assume that the persona in the poem is the writer. By the middle of the semester, I noticed that the students either included these kinds of questions within their comments and conversations in workshop, or in talking about the gender and gender identity of the persona they justify their answers with evidence. I believe that this has resulted in a closer reading of peer work, as well as more awareness of what they as writers are laying out on the page for the reader.

In addition, it is important to introduce students to gender creative and trans writers as part of the curriculum so that they can learn how to read and interpret trans literature. Good places to start are Trace Peterson and TC Tolbert's *Troubling the Line: Trans and Genderqueer Poetry*, for its wide range of poets across aesthetic traditions as well as the poetics essay that accompany each poet's creative work.[16] For a prose anthology, check out *The Collection: Short Fiction from the Transgender Vanguard*, edited by Tom Léger and Riley MacLeod, published by Topside Press, which is dedicated to publishing fiction and poetry from trans authors.[17]

I consider these types of classroom practices as important opportunities to produce space for students to consider gender identity in their own work as well as the work of peers. However, I still often feel the inadequacy of the time and space we have to fully address questions of identity, power, and understanding in a 50-minute class period. In this way, the university classroom is a space that is markedly different from the community-based model where those who come to the space have a closer shared understanding of identity and can spend less time coming to a common understanding around certain assumptions or practices.[18] Though these kinds of practices are beginning ways that we can be more inclusive of gender-non-conforming students, the responsibility to create a supportive and nurturing environment for gender-creative students cannot rest only on one creative writing classroom. Instead, creative writing professionals should be working to include trans and genderqueer voices and experiences in an integrated way throughout the curriculum.

One way to start is to take a closer look at the classes we teach, the classes offered by our departments, and to consider which voices we are prioritizing and which voices we are leaving out. As a teacher, I commit myself to incorporate a slate of writers, ranging not only in varying social identities but also aesthetics—and I often do a VIDA-like count among the texts I'm assigning in my syllabi. In my K-12 English education, I primarily read European-American male writers who were taught to me as cisgender and straight. In college, I chose to take classes that trained me in other traditions—including in women's literature, postcolonial literature, and Asian American literature. But I still had gaps in my reading education, which the VIDA-like syllabi count helped me understand. For instance, I had studied a lot of African and East and South Asian diasporic literature, but had much less familiarity with indigenous literature and West Asian literature. Having identified the gaps, I intentionally prioritized reading more authors in those lineages through asking for recommendations from other writer friends and my own research. The critical evaluation of my own training as a writer and adjusting for my own gaps in knowledge has made me better attuned to the community of writers I gather with in my classroom—the students seated in front of me and the experiences that they bring with them into the classroom. I am also a better advocate for the larger community of writers I have invited into the classroom via my syllabus. There's a lot more work to do—in reading and teaching trans and nonbinary literature—and I look forward to doing it with you.

Notes

1 Junot Díaz, "MFA vs POC," in *Dismantle: An Anthology of Writing from the VONA/Voices Writing Workshop*, ed. Marissa Johnson-Valenzuela, Andrea Walls, and Adriana E. Ramírez (Philadelphia: Thread Makes Blanket Press, 2014), 1–8.

2 For more narratives of marginalized students in MFA programs, see Sonya Larson, "Degrees of Diversity: Talking Race and the MFA," *Poets & Writers*, September/October 2015. Available online: http://www.pw.org/content/degrees_of_diversity?cmnt_all=1 (accessed June 13, 2016); Kristine Sloan, "Challenging the Whiteness of MFA Programs: A Year in Confrontations at UW," *The MFA Years*, April 1, 2016. Available online: https://themfayears.com/2016/04/01/challenging-the-whiteness-of-mfa-programs-a-year-in-confrontations-at-uw/ (accessed June 8, 2016).

3 Though terminology frequently shifts in usage and popularity, I use the term "genderqueer" in this chapter to mean "an identity commonly used by people who do not identify or express their gender within the gender binary. Those who identify as genderqueer may identify as neither male nor female, may see themselves as outside of or in between the binary gender boxes, or may simply feel restricted by gender labels." See "LGBTQ+ Definitions," *www.transstudentorg*. Available online: http://www.transstudent.org/definitions (accessed June 20, 2016).

There are many terms used to describe the experience of those who do not identify or express gender within the gender binary, including "nonbinary," "non-gender-conforming," "genderfluid," "agender," and "gender-creative." I use some of these terms throughout the chapter as a way to model using various kinds of inclusive language. For another resource, see Mel Reiff Hill and Jay Mays (2013), *The Gender Book* (Houston: Marshall House Press). Available for download here: http://www.thegenderbook.com/

4 In VIDA's write-up of the trans women count, VIDA included publishing data for writers who are "trans women, trans women-genderqueer/genderfluid, or trans women – transfeminine." For more information, see "The VIDA Count: On Transgender Writers,"*www.vidaweb.org*, 2016. Available online: http://www.vidaweb.org/the-2015-vida-count/ (accessed May 20, 2016).

5 Ibid.

6 Even though I focus on university creative writing classrooms, I have found similar lack of inclusion among most community-based writing classes that have not been taught or organized by another trans or nonbinary writer. In more recent years, trans writers, including Trish Salah, TC Tolbert, and Trace Peterson have offered university classes focused on trans writing and cultural production.

7 North Carolina's controversial House Bill 2 includes a "bathroom bill" that implements state-wide regulation of public restrooms, requiring that a person's use of a restroom be limited to restrooms corresponding with the person's "biological sex," as listed on the person's birth certificate. For more information, see Ulrich, Lana, "Explaining bathroom bills, transgender rights and equal protection," *Constitution Daily*, May 6, 2016. Available

online: http://blog.constitutioncenter.org/2016/05/explaining-bathroom-bills-transgender-rights-and-equal-protection/ (accessed June 20, 2016); Kurtz, David. "What Just Happened in North Carolina?" *Talking Points Memo*, March 24, 2016. Available online: http://talkingpointsmemo.com/edblog/north-carolina-anti-lgbt-bill (accessed June 20, 2016).

8 "Diversity in Academe: Transgender on Campus," *The Chronicle of Higher Education*, October 18, 2015. Available online: http://chronicle.com/specialreport/Diversity-in-Academe-/11 (accessed May 29, 2016).

9 Genny Beemyn, "No Transgender Student Left Behind," *The Chronicle of Higher Education*, October 18, 2015. Available online: http://chronicle.com/article/Leaving-No-Trans-College/233754?cid=cp11 (accessed May 29, 2016).

10 Julia Schmalz, " 'Ask Me': What LGBTQ Students Want Their Professors to Know," *The Chronicle of Higher Education*, October 18, 2015. Available online: http://chronicle.com/article/Ask-Me-What-LGBTQ-Students/232797?cid=cp11 (accessed May 29, 2016).

11 Ibid.

12 Ibid.

13 Tre Wentling, "Trans* Disruptions Pedagogical Practices and Pronoun Recognition," *TSQ: Transgender Studies Quarterly* 2.3 (2015): 469–76.

14 For a good resource for those interested in thinking through approaches to making the classroom more inclusive to gender-nonconforming students, see Harbin, Brielle. "Teaching Beyond the Gender Binary in the University Classroom." Available online: https://cft.vanderbilt.edu/teaching-beyond-the-gender-binary-in-the-university-classroom/ (accessed May 10, 2016).

15 Though I know that not all nonbinary or gender-non-conforming people prefer "they" as a pronoun, in my classroom experience, introducing "they" initially as a gender-flexible pronoun is an easier bridge to other pronouns such as "ze/zir."

16 TC Tolbert, and Trace Peterson, eds, *Troubling the Line: Trans and Genderqueer Poetry and Poetics* (Callicoon, NY: Nightboat Books, 2013). Full disclosure that I'm one of the writers included in the anthology.

17 Tom Léger, and Riley MacLeod, eds, *The Collection: Short Fiction from the Transgender Vanguard* (NY: Topside Press, 2012).

18 Another approach to take in the classroom is to highlight the value of discomfort as a productive and generative activity for students, one that requires the students to potentially stretch outside of their own knowledge base. During a teaching internship, I witnessed students in a community college composition class with a special theme of gender and sexuality assigned a combined research and creative writing project. Each student was assigned a specific identity within the LGBTQIA community such as trans,

genderfluid, lesbian, gay, and asexual and asked to find academic sources about that identity. After they read their academic sources (mostly psychology articles and/or encyclopedia volumes related to LGBTQIA community), they came up with a series of questions about that identity, which were vetted by the professor. The professor of the class, who ran the LGBTQI Student Center, had recruited volunteers who identified with those specific identities and were willing to answer those questions anonymously. Students created a persona (a dramatic monologue or persona poem) based on their research and the questions. Though the students didn't workshop their monologues, they did get individualized feedback from the instructor as well as some peer review—and the best ones were chosen to be performed by a speech class. Most of the students took the assignment seriously and did their due diligence with library research with little resistance to the topic matter. When I talked with the instructor about whether her students were uncomfortable with the assignment and how she dealt with it, she mentioned that two of her students (for whom English wasn't a first language) were not getting the pronouns correct for their assignment (a trans-woman), but she wasn't sure if it was intentional or a language access issue. Because the project was research-based, she was able to point to that as a weakness in the creative project, which invites further reflection and revision. This kind of model—one in which students are asked to produce knowledge by potentially stepping into another's persona (though the student could also be assigned their own identity)—is one that has a lot of potential in terms of opening up that raw space of transformation in the classroom.

16

Pedagogy and Authority in Teaching *The Waste Land*: What We Do With Authorial Voices and the Postcolonial Body in the Writing Workshop

Prageeta Sharma

I am not a critic or scholar. I am a poet and I teach poetry in an MFA program in the American West, in a program that has deep cultural roots in its white canonical traditions, and yet, simultaneously, tries its best to promote the rich tradition of Native American literature produced and celebrated in Montana and the region. The latter cultural project is an attempted reconciliation with the problem of colonial genocide for Native American peoples in America, and thus some work has been done to acknowledge the varieties of writing traditions of the West. Alas, however, what I have noticed is the "celebration" itself can misleadingly prioritize a certain kind of writing or tokenization, either by permitting only a narrow narrative craft—coming out of a particular Americanist mainstream tradition—or a lyric realism to be revered or hailed by white writers of the Americanist traditions. I am of SouthAsian descent. I was born and raised in Framingham, Massachusetts. I lived in New England and New York for most of my life until I moved to Missoula, Montana eight years ago from Brooklyn, New York. When I left New York and teaching in Manhattan at the New School (as well as a progressively-modeled low residency BA program at Goddard College in Vermont), leaving the New York School traditions behind (that's what it felt like leaving St. Mark's Poetry Project and my community of writers and poets), I felt an urgency to bring this specific cultural work with me—the tradition of writing out of polycultural and avant-garde traditions that seek to formulate quotidian and nontraditional writing—to explore the idea that the mainstream is always mining or collecting avant-garde traditions to redefine itself or its future. I believe *The Waste Land* is both an innovative text that came out of an avant-garde tradition, and yet it has become deeply normative in most American pedagogical contexts, and, moreover, has functioned in this particular way for so long that it has now become a confusing poem to teach for the recovery of traditions of innovation and modernity. In some ways, then, its present pedagogical standing renders difficult the recovery of its formal past, particularly in the context of minoritized modernisms. I feel ambivalent about how one might teach the poem responsibly—outside of the criticism by scholars. How do I *really* regard *The Waste Land* in the classroom? What kind of modernity does it have in relation to other (now major) modernist underrepresented modern writers, Langston Hughes? Joaquim Maria Machado de Assis? Djuna Barnes? To say nothing of Rabindranath Tagore or, later, Arun Kolatkar?

As a result of this problematic and ongoing query into teaching and canonical poetry I have found it necessary in my graduate writing workshops to introduce more exploration of reading practices representing diverging traditions and stylistic innovations that have not yet "made it" to the mainstream. These include both avant-garde traditions, "minor poets," and a rereading of canonical texts through literary theory—much like scholars specializing in Shakespearean studies introduce their students to queer readings and theory of Shakespeare's plays and poems. We do this in our English department and I've noticed that here, in my department, some of the more "radical readings" of this caliber exist in the teaching of English literature than in Creative Writing; and we have a strange history here in Montana because of it.

I am reminded of Leslie Fiedler who taught in my English department in the 1950s and fought a battle to advocate for alternative discourses in reading and scholarship practices here, as is done in literary theory as it shifts and changes, but left for Buffalo because it was too hard to do. At that time, I am unsure if there were any creative writers in the department,—but a split soon divided the English department between Creative Writing and Literature, and it is still going strong.

A similar split, I would say, circulates around the question of how to teach canonical texts when they have been reinterpreted and changed due to cultural shifts and changing literary criticism: the kind of historical and interpretive changes represented in the anecdotes from the previous paragraph. A prime example of this pedagogical concern regards the question of how to approach Eliot from a twenty-first-century writer's perspective? More importantly, how to do this when one wishes to examine his modernity in relation to one's own, which may well be from a person of color's perspective and from the vantage of innovative writing by people of color in the contemporary and international landscape. This essay is about the teaching of Eliot from that perspective, in a general way, but not of a close reading of his text, although there is so much to say about the way he collects his references and his Shanti mantra ending. Teaching *The Waste Land* is an opportunity not only to admire the poem but to penalize it; to create a pedagogy and teaching against tradition and about colonial essentialism to discuss creating new/differing/varied traditions in the writing workshop classroom and ultimately give students more to construct out of what might feel innovative because they deepen their discourse of identity in relation to traditions, not in spite of it.

I don't understand why there's such a puzzling, almost bizarre tradition of writers who do not accept the merits of literary theory—as a practice in engaging literature and creative writing—and as a practice of creating such agonism when theory is introduced into the reading experience, study, and practice of writing. Why is theory such an unstable concept or practice for some writers? For many writers of color it might be the only place where their "difference" is articulated as normative or constructed to reflect a particular social reality of experience and theory as it functions.

And so while I have indeed read Eliot, I have largely avoided teaching *The Waste Land* in many of my graduate creative writing workshops because I have a deep ambivalence about its "magnitude" or "greatness" and because of the way the poem tracks something I have found pernicious. I didn't quite understand Eliot's relation to non-Western traditions as an undergraduate, but now I do and have the freedom to explore the merit of the poem on its relationship to those traditions. And no matter how blasphemous some may see me in doing this, I enjoy applying postcolonial theory to Eliot—to examine his consumptive and colonial collection of references and allusions, and to then read out of that experience. He's been amply celebrated, why not bring alternate perspectives to the creative writing graduate students so they can reckon with colonial authority?

Critics and readers have marveled at the form of Eliot's poem, its unreadability or its lack of "transitions," when in fact, from the perspective of the twenty-first century, it feels quite readable and not entirely as imaginative as its authority insists; in all of this cultural shifting, I am forced to fully acknowledge that I am a product of my time, and it is this interpretive slipperiness, in part, which I'd like to examine, because my students, too, are products of their time, and the poem—which might require a formulation of newness to construct and create—becomes the place from which this interrogation of the conferral and challenge to cultural authority arises.

My feelings about Eliot, too, involve a strong reaction to how creative writers like myself, through schooling, are taught to revere narrativity and form and thus to recognize a value in any "fragment," or "experiment" with its tonal authority and its cultural symbolic reach through metaphor, alterity, and allusion as a performance of innovation; and yet, I do see how these great attributes are singularly modern and are therefore innovative. But I wonder how much of this style must I attribute to Eliot and what other work offers much better representation in this form and this style? It seems to me, in thinking about the history of the "fragment" or of parataxis, I can look as far back as Sappho and also to Eliot's more innovative contemporaries, namely Gertrude Stein, who was not uncomfortable with her unreadability. This is what I find as a signal of strength in the poem and its authenticity. Maybe, I want to link this strength to a kind of poetic authority the poem can have and one that we must teach out of to ensure students are comfortable finding tradition and always ongoing innovation as a source of inspiration and not to train them to recognize and uphold one static and individual moment of "innovation," and to then flex authorial ambition in prescriptive style. It seemed that Eliot was terribly anxious about not getting the poem's strength "right" or correct and I think it's his fatal flaw and something I don't want in my workshop—that ethos in the anxiety of failure because you don't know how to ignite the truths of your innovation. You may be incredulous or think me narcissistic to critique Eliot's techniques in such a highly personal and intimate way, but this is actually what I'm most interested in: How are our students reading? Are they reading to engage with how Eliot's mind—with its rising doubts and worries, its specifically Western form of anxiety of influence—is truly working?

As far as literary theory goes, my reading of Eliot comes from both *The Waste Land* and Brooker and Bentley's *Reading The Waste Land: Modernism and the Limits of Interpretation*,[1] which helped me, through its own particular close reading of the poem, to define the interpretative activity of reading the poem's structure and meaning, and find a way to describe the reading experience I seemed to have. It's their theory of the literal interpretation embedded in Eliot that interrupts my teaching—is this word, this line, this stanza literal or symbolic? Such work in these texts and others helped me to articulate the question of why it's hard to stay in the poem's sentiment rather than simply carry the allusions around until they transform into symbols. Brooker and Bentley's premise that *The Waste Land* "calls attention to itself as a text about reading" is interesting to me. Because of this I like to teach the poem as a text about reading and then figure out what it teaches the contemporary creative writing student about writing and about reading.

But I relish in what I perceive as Eliot's discomfort with his imagination and his resulting innovations. Were they his own or what Pound encouraged? Do his other poems perform in this manner? Maybe I don't know how to read *The Waste Land* correctly; and then, for sure, I land on the question of what the fragments do: we know how problematic Pound is as a cultural appropriator, but what is Eliot's hand in this? And, in teaching that long poem, what does it encourage my twenty-first century students to imitate or perform in light of current postcolonial and critical race theory?

Because we are inundated with the literary allusion and reference of modernism's innovation and in a writing workshop we are forced to figure out *The Waste Land*'s significance for our practice of creative writing today, how do I want students to utilize allusion? Do they also need to include notes or footnotes? There's a split about this: do we require them for the reading experience and/or do we think they are stolen texts/words/poems if they are not cited? (I'm not referring to clearly stolen work; that happens and it's indicative of something else entirely–lack of an imagination and not conceptual.) But I think both an experimental text and a more mainstream text that indexes its references and allusions too much can run the risk of seeming glib or unoriginal?

How do we talk about playful allusion and reference in the twenty-first century and let the poems/book inhabit its innovation?

In thinking about *The Waste Land* and its canonical significance as a primary and influential text, how do the references and allusions work as a creative force for the writer? There is much discussion around the uses of Hinduism and Buddhism in the text and in much of Eliot's body of work, such as the question of his scholarship in philosophy, for example. But there is little discussion of how the canonical poem's process of being cowritten by Pound—and Pound's colonial problems—which make some of the edits and the creative process itself seem outmoded. Simply because some of the edits are so highly subjective and insular, and this is not so unusual for a poem today, no poet in a workshop would necessarily redirect the content of the poem to perform more imagination than the poem can offer. Additionally, because *The Waste Land* is taught in relation to its references and allusions in a literature class, there is a kind of confusion for the creative writing professor of color when they try to understand or mine the uses of *The Waste Land* in such a way that the text can go beyond its allusion. Is there a heuristic practice here beyond its referential value? And what does this look like?

Eliot's contemporary critics, readers like Conrad Aiken[2] and others, generated much of their readings of *The Waste Land* on the function of form—its symbolism and lack of cohesion as a problem—so much so that that they neglected the nature and content of what the fragments were ultimately doing. Students today readily absorb the fragments and thus look at *The Waste Land*'s content: the difficulty in Eliot's authority, gendered portrayals, disconnected privilege with class, and the poem's embedded and appropriating colonial discourse; and yet my students have not always encountered enough work outside of this tradition or made enough contact with the radical responses that occur in literary theory or by writers of color who experiment with traditions such as Kamau Brathwaite (who turns away from Eliot's tradition, so to speak, to delve into a deeper, more honest tradition of the speaker's authorial voice and fragment); or other critics such as Foula and Armstrong who unearth the problems of textual boundaries and the abject in Eliot. This chapter functions as a reminder to encourage the writing workshop to engage with the discourse of reading in order to construct and produce work that engages with the possible authorial tensions inherent in voice—a reading practice that allows students to take risks that honor the spaces they want to write into and from, and to "perform" rather than adopt the craft of modernity that pushes them into a writing workshop box, so to speak.

I have found that the way to bring these traditions into the workshop is through the intersection between literary theory and thinking about the politics of poetic authority that contextualize the poem or book and serve to supplement the tropes of the piece, and a way to figure out what our reading and writing practices are and to understand the ever-changing notion of poetic authority. By poetic authority I mean the liberty of the speaker in the poem (see Jane Griffiths' writings on poetic authority in the Renaissance[3]). I therefore try to circumvent the long-standing polarized tradition of the twentieth-century English department that creates a split between reading and writing and engaging with scholarship. Consequently, I champion the discovering of our collective creative processes through close reading and interpretation of literary theory that creates in workshop discussions between students and myself as a lifelong learner, and the resultant stimulating production of poetic interrogation. The majority of students find this approach helpful and exciting. I know I do because it deepens my understanding of how interconnected the reading and writing process is. Through this lens we look at craft, style, and tradition, but we also poke holes in the idea that poetic authority must look a certain way.

What do we do with poetic authority in canonical literature when we have so much literary theory that breaks these poems and our reading practices wide open? How do writers of color bring these discussions to the workshop and the classroom? In my "ideal" workshop or with a certain practice of inquiry, we might explore certain authorial voices and turns in *The Waste Land* that we find "great," or rich with intensity, craft, and innovative language but might also disturb, offend, and engage leisurely "platitudes" that can sometimes be troubling and/or dated. What kind of pedagogy do we invite into our classroom that teaches us historical context (obviously going beyond the old new criticism model) and yet holds concerns or conclusions in current scholarship? What do we do with Eliot's Upanishad ending with its Shanti mantra: "Datta. Dayadhvam. Damyata. Shantihshantihshantih," a closing move that has always baffled me. The "peace that comes" seems really to be an exorcism for the poem's abjection, and it seems to be landing on a polytheistic conclusion in order to reflect Eliot's philosophical enquiry. But it also seems false to his Anglicanism, not that I would take it all too literally, but the poem's authority is grave and serious. Moreover, this kind of poetry ending is not a strong device for our students; and for Pound, it constructed its newness and newness, but is it only new to poet and editor? Much like all of the "Orient" was then?

But first how to define the shifting idea of poetic authority? Or rather, I begin this work in the classroom by defining Eliot's idea of authority and the teaching of his authorial voice while asking the question: is this outmoded or necessary in the workshop? Through this discussion, I hope to make a point about how when language sticks out to a specific reader, say a nonwhite reader of South Asian descent, it might not be seen so much as innovative—but in essence similar to Pound as a kind of appropriation or a way to talk about the cultural moment of that time. And I ask a very problematic question: again, do we need the footnotes? How do they deepen the reading? Where are we with this style in the graduate workshop? I will also say that the split between the teaching of English literature and the creative writing workshop might begin with this: What does the creative writing student learn with these footnotes? The English literature student learns how to think about Eliot's reading experiences and the richness and vastness of them, but the creative writing student, in the imitation of this technique of the footnote, might not learn as much.

I say this because it could encourage the twentieth-century creative writing student to "collect" images and textual moments without thinking too much about how they work on their own. And I would much rather teach Robert Duncan's occultism or backdate Eliot with Hardy or Byron, the former philosophical and the latter hedonistic (albeit both straddle a kind of philosophical alterity that Eliot is uncomfortable with). And while I teach many canonical works in my graduate and undergraduate poetry workshops I do not claim to understand the way in which they are regarded critically and historically by the scholar beyond how they intrigue me, inspire me, and teach me their meanings and structure. But, nevertheless, I have noted what of these works comes in and out of fashion, and I have tried to answer to that historical ebb and flow in the classroom. What I have found over the years is that my students and I become interested in what traditions look like in the face of any contemporary moment, and what comes out of modernism and the avant-garde, but that

I also appreciate a large amount of canonical writing, particularly early and later twentieth-century poets Langston Hughes, Gwendolyn Brooks, Laura Riding Jackson, and later John Ashbery, Frank O'Hara, and Amiri Baraka. Along with those poets are writers publishing today (and in the latter half of the twentieth century): C. D. Wright, Rosmarie and Keith Waldrop, Michael S. Harper, Mei-Mei Berssennbrugge, Alice Notley, Rae Armantrout, and Marjorie Welish, to name a few contemporary poets (many of whom are/were my mentors). Even my peers are now my contemporaries and classmates in my MFA program and community for which I am grateful: Major Jackson, Kevin Young, Rosa Alcala, Camille Guthrie, Jennifer Moxley, Lisa Jarnot, Lee Ann Brown, Thomas Sayers Ellis, Sam Truitt, and Sianne Ngai. It might bear noting that with all of these poets I don't think we once had a conversation about T. S. Eliot while we were in workshop (although Thomas Sayers Ellis's name was surely noted as eponymous). We did talk about Notley, Ted Berrigan, Lucille Clifton, Wallace Stevens, Robert Hayden, Robert Duncan, John Wieners, Allen Ginsberg, Gertrude Stein, and Ntozake Shange among other poets from out of less mainstream traditions, at the time. Most of my mentors in graduate school resisted the term "great" and settled on the idea that to be a poet in the world you must, as poet and mentor, understand why you are writing the way you are writing and that it's a part of you and not a performance you do. As the late C. D. Wright said: "Poetry is a necessity of life."[4] What I have realized, now twenty years later, is how many of the writers believed their lives were plentiful as poets writing their experimental or nontraditional poems—it was enough. Furthermore, the many poets I read and interacted with have become part of new canons, although they were not necessarily so then. I have made note of this and now teach with the idea that we must always look at what is interesting and not necessarily what is to be anointed by the mainstream.

For a long while I wasn't sure how to articulate this conundrum because canonical poems are always markers of their own legitimate cultural moment, warts, erudition, innovation, and all; and yet it was only after I read Nick Selby's *t.s. eliot- the waste land: essays, articles, and reviews* that I began to combine my cursory knowledge of Raymond Williams' positions on Modernism (his antibourgeois stance in literary production) with Selby's accumulated compendium to approach Eliot and the question of authority. Ultimately, I am interested in connecting my own ambivalence in thinking about Eliot's authority with Selby's claim "that the poem still remains deeply problematic and troublesome. Most particularly, what David Craig, Terry Eagleton, and Michael North share in their analyses of the poem is a conviction that *The Waste Land's* difficulties are an index of its problematic politics."[5] These difficulties in their elusiveness give way to the current contemporary poetry culture, which still upholds a bourgeois poem's slippery ethos to appease an apolitical reader that can arbitrate the poem—`a la *The New Yorker*—to a heightened status. This is what I don't want to encourage in workshop. I want the poem to remain difficult in its process and not in its performance of authority.

And so what is admired ultimately in *The Waste Land* is its authority and its perceived innovation. I don't think the innovation is as remarkable as it's treated; rather, it's that the "illegible" fragment became less elusive to its poetry readers and a signal of modernity during its time. So how do our graduate students earnestly manage this signal and the centrality of Eliot's authority when so many other modernist poets are deftly being celebrated for their turning away of aesthetic reproduction of the lyric form? How do we write ourselves into legibility? And how do we understand and construct forms of authority that circumvent the misogyny, anti-Semitism, and colonial installments that constitute a great literature and also further reconstruct an authority that reflects the contemporary moment that seeks to include and insist on a polycultural style of writing? In the spirit of Marx and current theories, we might actively teach in a fashion that resists a hierarchical arm of top-down, good/bad binaries of the poem and celebrate what happens in those poems. What I still have not managed to say yet is that much of Eliot's lyric poem is definitely deconstructing the heroic poem for its inverse, but in managing to succeed, it collapses into its spiral of self-critique at the expense of its subjects and with the perpetuating sweep that a white straight male can leap into and take hold. But let's look more deeply at this incriminating aesthetic grip and thus find an altogether new inverse for the lyric, or its new iteration.

Notes

1 Jewel Brooker and Joseph Bentley, Reading The Waste Land*: Modernism and the Limits of Interpretation*, rev. ed. (University of Massachusetts Press, 1992), 8.

2 Conrad Aiken, "The Anatomy of Melancholy," in *T.S. Eliot The Waste Land: Authoritative Text, Contexts, Criticisms*, ed. Michael North (New York, Norton, 2001), 149.

3 Jane Griffiths, *John Skelton and Poetic Authority: Defining the Liberty to Speak. Oxford English Monographs* (Oxford: Clarendon Press, 2006), xii.214 pp. In this paper, Griffiths, however, considers poetic authority in a broader way, examining how Skelton imagined the foundation of his right to speak as a poet. In the process, she discusses Skelton's multiple ideas: that such legitimacy comes from the king, a patron, God, the poet himself, and the active engagement of readers. Overall, she offers lucid, engaging, deft, and persuasive readings of much of Skelton's work, showing that for him such authority ultimately lies within the poet himself, but depends as well on active and imaginative readers."

4 C. D. Wright. <http://www.poetryfoundation.org/poems-and-poets/poets/detail/c-d-wright>

5 See Nick Selby's *T.S. Eliot: The Waste Land: Essays, Articles, and Reviews* (1999),<AQ: Please confirm year and provide publisher detail.> particularly chapter 4 and 6, "Political Readings: Marx, Ideology and Culture," and "Cultural Readings: Modernism, Ideology and Desire."

List of Contributors

Janelle Adsit is an assistant professor of creative writing at Humboldt State University. Her poetry, reviews, and essays have appeared in literary journals such as *Cultural Society*, *Mid-American Review*, *Colorado Review*, and *Requited*. She is the author of *Unremitting Entrance* and a chapbook *Press Yourself Against a Mirror*. She has published several articles on the teaching of creative writing, including a chapter in *Creative Writing in the Digital Age* (2014).

Mary Ann Cain's fiction, nonfiction essays, and poems have appeared in literary journals ranging from venerable standards such as the *Denver Quarterly*, *The Sun: A Magazine of Ideas*, *The Bitter Oleander*, and the *North American Review* to experimental venues such as *First Intensity* and *LIT*. Her novel, *Down from Moonshine*, was published in 2009. She has received two Indiana Arts Commission Individual Artist grants. Her recent critical work on writing theory and praxis includes a collaborative book (with Michelle Comstock and Lil Brannon), *Composing Public Space: Teaching Writing in the Face of Private Interests* (2010). She has also published a monograph on writing workshops, *Revisioning Writers' Talk* (1995), as well as numerous articles and book chapters about writing and writing instruction. She is currently professor of English at Indiana University–Purdue University Fort Wayne where she teaches fiction, creative nonfiction, rhetoric, and women's studies. Her latest project is a nonfiction book about the legacy of Chicago artist-teacher-activist Dr. Margaret Burroughs.

Ching-In Chen is author of *The Heart's Traffic* and *recombinant* as well as coeditor of *The Revolution Starts at Home: Confronting Intimate Violence Within Activist Communities* and *Here Is a Pen: An Anthology of West Coast Kundiman Poets*. A Kundiman, Lambda, Watering Hole, and Callaloo Fellow, they are part of Macondo and Voices of Our Nations Arts Foundation writing communities. Their work has appeared in *The Best American Experimental Writing*, *The &NOW Awards 3: The Best Innovative Writing*, and *Troubling the Line: Trans and Genderqueer Poetry and Poetics*. They currently teach creative writing, poetry, and world literature at Sam Houston State University and can be found online at www.chinginchen.com.

Michael Dean Clark is an author of fiction and literary nonfiction as well as an associate professor of writing at Azusa Pacific University in the Los Angeles area. A coeditor of the collection *Creative Writing in the Digital Age*, he had also served as a section editor at the *cream city review* and *Relief* in the past. Clark's work has most recently appeared in *Pleiades*, *Whale Road Review*, *Fast Forward*, and *Relief*.

Cathy Day is the author of *Comeback Season* and *The Circus in Winter*. Her stories and essays have appeared most recently in the *Lit Hub*, *PANK*, *The Millions*, and *Inside Higher Education*. She lives in Muncie, Indiana, and teaches creative writing at Ball State University. In addition to her blog "The Big Thing," she maintains blogs about her novel-writing class, her linked stories class, and literary citizenship.

Katharine Haake is the author of five works of fiction, including the future eco-fable, *The Time of Quarantine*; a hybrid California prose lyric, *That Water, Those Rocks*; and three collections of stories. Her writing has long appeared in such magazines as *One Story*, *Crazyhorse*, *The Iowa Review*, *New Letters*, and *Witness*, and has been recognized as distinguished by *Best American Short Stories* and *Best American Essays*, among others. A frequent contributor to the scholarship and theory of creative writing, Haake is also the author of *What Our Speech Disrupts: Feminism and Creative Writing Studies* and, with Wendy Bishop and Hans Ostrom, *Metro: Journeys in Writing Creatively*. She teaches at California State University, Northridge.

Graeme Harper is a professor of creative writing and Dean of the Honors College at Oakland University, Michigan, USA. He is editor of *New Writing: The International Journal for the Practice and Theory of Creative Writing*. Graeme was awarded the first doctorate in creative writing in Australia. From 2008 to 2011 he was the inaugural Chair of the Higher Education Committee at Great Britain's National Association of Writers in Education (NAWE). A former Commonwealth Scholar in Creative Writing, he is an award-winning fiction writer and a scriptwriter. His latest works are the edited collection *Changing Creative Writing in America* (2017) and the novel *There's a Problem with Our Mayor* (2017).

Derrick Harriell is the director of the Master of Fine Arts-Creative Writing Program and Assistant Professor of English and African-American Studies at the University of Mississippi. He is the author of three collections of poetry: *Cotton* (2010), *Ropes* (2013), and *Stripper in Wonderland* (2017). His essays and book reviews have been published widely.

Tonya C. Hegamin, MFA, is the author of *Most Loved in All the World, M+O 4EVR, Pemba's Song*, and most recently, *Willow* (2014). Her honors include the Ezra Jack Keats New Writer Award, the Christopher Award, she was a finalist for the Phillis Wheatley Award and was listed on the Amelia Bloomer Project's Recommended Feminist Readings 2015 and her books have received starred reviews in *Publishers Weekly*, and been featured in *USA Today, The Washington Post, Ebony*, and *Essence*. Her poetry and short fiction have been included in two Cave Canem anthologies as well as in *Yellow Medicine Review* and *Obsidian*. Hegamin currently serves as the Writer-in-Residence for Tengo Sed Writers Retreat in Costa Rica, and is the Diversity and Inclusion section editor for the *Journal of Creative Writing Studies*. Hegamin has received honors for her innovative use of technology in the classroom, and has presented her classroom case study on the use of Digital Game-Based Learning to help build better writing skills for future urban educators at the CUNY Games Fest in January 2016. Hegamin is an assistant professor and the Creative Writing Coordinator at CUNY Medgar Evers College in Brooklyn, New York. www.tonyacheriehegamin.com

Trent Hergenrader, PhD, is an assistant professor in the Department of English at the Rochester Institute of Technology. His fiction has appeared in *The Magazine of Fantasy & Science Fiction, The Best Horror of the Year, The Mammoth Book of Dieselpunk, Weird Tales*, and other publications. He is coeditor of *Creative Writing in the Digital Age* and a senior editor for the *Journal of Creative Writing Studies*. He is cofounder and Secretary of the Creative Writing Studies Organization. He is currently writing a book titled *Collaborative World Building for Writers and Gamers* (2017).

Rachel Haley Himmelheber teaches creative writing at Warren Wilson College in Asheville, North Carolina. Her interest in pedagogy and in the history of creative writing in the academy led to her cofounding the nonprofit

Creative Writing Studies Organization. Her research focuses on the intersection of artistic and social and political forces in the creative writing classroom.

Tom C. Hunley is a professor of English/Creative Writing at Western Kentucky University, director of Steel Toe Books, and lead guitarist/singer for Night of the Living Dead Poets Society. Among his books are the full-length poetry collections *Plunk* (2015) and *The State That Springfield Is In* (2016) and the monographs *The Poetry Gymnasium* (2012) and *Teaching Poetry Writing: A Five-Canon Approach* (2007). With Alexandria Peary, he coedited the essay collection *Creative Writing Pedagogies for the Twenty-First Century* (2015), a nominee for the CCCCs Outstanding Book Award.

Tim Mayers writes poetry and long fiction as well as scholarly work in composition and creative writing studies. He is the author of *(Re)Writing Craft: Composition, Creative Writing, and the Future of English Studies* (2005). He is associate professor of English at Millersville University, where he teaches composition, creative writing, writing studies, and a graduate course in the history and institutional structures of English studies.

Kyle McGinn is a poet. His work has appeared in *Outrageous Fortune*, *Typehouse*, *indicia*, and *Poetry City, USA*. McGinn earned a BS in Creative Writing from the University of Wisconsin–River Falls and placed as a semi-finalist for the 2012 Norman Mailer College Poetry Award. He published his first chapbook of poetry, *Pennies*, with Red Bird Chapbooks in 2014. He is currently pursuing his MFA at Hamline University in St. Paul, Minnesota.

Joseph Rein is coeditor of *Creative Writing in the Digital Age* and *Dispatches from the Classroom: Graduate Students on Creative Writing Pedagogy*. His creative work has been nominated for a Pushcart Prize, and has most recently appeared in the *Pinch Literary Journal*, *Iron Horse Literary Review*, and *Ruminate Magazine*. Short films produced from his screenplays have been featured in film festivals nationwide. He is currently an assistant professor of creative writing at the University of Wisconsin–River Falls.

Prageeta Sharma is the author of four poetry collections: *Bliss to Fill*, *The Opening Question*, *Infamous Landscapes*, and the recent *Undergloom*. She was a recipient of the 2010 Howard Foundation Award. She is the founder and codirector (with Joanna Klink) of the national conference Thinking Its Presence: Race, Creative Writing, and Literary Studies, which has recently been converted to a national board on which she serves as president. She is a professor of English at the University of Montana.

Hazel Smith is a research professor in the Writing and Society Research Centre at Western Sydney University, and is the author of several academic and pedagogical books including *Hyperscapes in the Poetry of Frank O'Hara: Difference, Homosexuality, Topography* (2000), *The Writing Experiment: Strategies for Innovative Creative Writing* (2005), and *The Contemporary Literature-Music Relationship: Intermedia, Voice, Technology, Cross-Cultural Exchange* (2016). She is coauthor with Roger Dean of *Improvisation, Hypermedia and the Arts since 1945*(1997) and coeditor with Roger Dean of *Practice-led Research, Research-led Practice in the Creative Arts* (2009). Hazel is a poet, performer, and new media artist and her website is at www.australysis.com. She has published four volumes of poetry including *The Erotics of Geography: Poetry, Performance Texts, New Media Works*, with accompanying CD Rom (2008) and *Word Migrants*(2016). She has produced three CDs of poetry and performance works and numerous collaborative multimedia works. She is coeditor of *soundsRite*, a creative arts journal of online sound and writing.

Index

accessibility 150–1
adaptability 98, 194
aesthetic 22, 24, 29, 33, 39, 40, 103, 112, 114, 138, 158, 217–18, 232
anthropocentric, anthropocentrism 153, 157
Australia 58–9
authority 3, 24, 47, 79–80, 169, 182, 193, 212, 226, 228–32
autobiogeography 157
autoethnography 157
AWP 1, 35, 170, 175

Bachelor of Arts (BA) 8, 180, 223
Bachelor of Fine Arts (BFA) 8
backdrop 113, 154
basic writing 3, 193, 198
Beasley, Sandra 41
Berman, David 73, 75, 82–3, 85–6
bibliographic essay 169, 171–3
Bishop, Wendy 3, 9, 79, 177, 186

capstone 10, 163, 175
character 12, 38, 40, 45, 46–53, 90, 93, 100–1, 125, 130–2, 133–5, 138, 141–6, 154, 163, 167, 168–73, 186, 188, 199–202, 206–8, 217
characterization 46, 50, 114, 120, 130, 206, 208
cinematography 25, 94
code-switching 194, 199, 201–2, 204, 208
collaboration 11
composition studies 8, 10, 47, 79, 120, 153, 166, 176–8, 198–200, 202, 214
constraints 13, 16, 39, 66, 90–1, 105, 107, 109, 124–5
contact zones 182
craft 1, 37–8, 48, 90, 97–8, 107–8, 111, 114, 133–5, 144–5, 149, 155, 173, 194, 197, 199, 215, 223, 229
creative nonfiction 3, 25, 90, 103–8, 113, 115, 157
creative writing pedagogy 11, 79, 99, 100, 153
creative writing studies 2, 8–10
Creative Writing Studies Organization (CWSO) 2
cultural currency 196, 204
cultural inheritance 152
cultural production 152–3
Culturally Appropriate Teaching (CAT) 198–9
curriculum 24, 29, 93, 142, 151, 156, 175

Dada 59, 112
defamiliarization 150
dialect 48, 200–1
dialectic 136–7, 201
dialogic 111, 124, 136–7, 181
disability 57, 63–4, 68
dissonance 22
diversity 4, 11, 156, 158, 194

ecopoetic(s) 3, 152
ecosocial 154, 157–8
electronic literature 62, 66
elliptical poetry 41
email 27, 36, 74, 85, 134, 179
empathy 2, 45–54
environmentalism 151
ethnicity 57, 63–5, 69, 201, 211, 216
ethos 40, 78, 226

Facebook 177–8
fiction 46, 167, 185, 193–5, 206, 217
first-year writing 177
Freire, Paulo 198
Frost, Robert 37, 188

games 98, 106, 133–6, 138, 141–4
gender 4, 57, 69, 100, 105–6, 138, 152, 171, 181–2, 211, 213–18, 221, 228
genderqueer 213, 215–18

Gordimer, Nadine 154
grading 74, 76, 85, 146, 172, 205

Horton, Randall 34–7, 41

imagery 37, 82, 123, 130, 132, 199, 202, 207
imagination 21, 45, 52, 53, 92, 120, 138, 149, 167, 194–5, 197, 199–200, 227–8
imaginative access 167, 169
inclusion 14, 48, 181, 194, 211–13, 219
individualism 10, 28, 30
innovation 1–2, 11, 108, 193, 194, 199–200, 202, 224–32
inspiration 18, 105, 124, 128, 143, 150, 226
interdialect 201
interdisciplinary 3, 46, 141, 144, 158
introductory courses 2, 8, 10–12, 14, 17, 46, 79, 80, 97, 172, 198, 199, 202
Iowa Writer's Workshop 9

jobs 7, 9, 34, 36, 38, 41, 80, 108, 138, 175, 181
Journal of Creative Writing Studies 2, 177

Kundiman 211

Lambda Literary Foundation 211
LGBTQIA 211, 213–16
literary studies 8, 10, 22, 29, 57, 59, 65
Lorde, Audre 198, 203
low residency programs 33, 223
lyrics 17, 40, 73–85, 103, 106, 112, 223, 232

macro 37–42, 149
manuscript 10, 11, 14, 33–42, 163, 172
marginalization 182
McCann, Colum 167–8
Master of Arts (MA) 8, 58–61, 120, 180
Master of Fine Arts (MFA) 1–2, 7–9, 38–9, 83, 89, 93, 120, 175, 194, 212–14, 223, 231
metonymy 27
Microsoft Word 203
Middletown 164–71, 175
misogyny 182, 232
mnemonics 28
Moxley, Joseph 9
multigenre 2, 8, 10, 12, 14, 17, 80
multimedia 61–2
music 37, 40, 57–69, 73–87

narrative 13, 22, 29, 35, 38, 41, 46, 49, 62, 64, 66, 68, 89–90, 101, 104, 112–14, 126, 129–31, 133–9, 142–3, 145–7, 152
neuroscience 25, 45–8
New Journalism 104
nodes 25, 137, 171
novel (genre) 8, 10–11, 13–15, 24, 62–4, 93, 104, 156, 170, 183–4, 194, 196–7

originality 3, 18, 111
Ostrom, Hans 9
Oulipo 59, 90

parataxis 226
pedagogy 3, 8–11, 17, 47–9, 79, 91, 99, 100, 106, 143, 149–51, 153, 198, 214, 225, 229
PhD 7–8, 58–9, 177–8, 180, 213–15
philosophy 59, 125, 144, 228
place-based pedagogy 3, 149–51
poetry 2, 3, 11–12, 14, 17, 29–30, 33–42, 58, 65, 76, 79–87, 90–1, 156, 157, 194, 217, 224, 230–2
poetry collections 33, 36, 42
portfolio(s) 76, 85, 111–12, 119, 125–6, 129, 131, 163, 175, 206
power reading 196–7
privilege 3, 45, 52, 126, 158, 193, 196, 204, 228
process-oriented pedagogy 10–12, 103
psychology 22, 29, 30, 54, 63, 144, 221
publication 1, 4, 34, 36–7, 94, 98, 109, 166

"reading like a writer" 29
research 3, 4, 25, 46–50, 52–3, 58–61, 98, 110, 112, 114–15, 139, 145, 155–8, 163–70, 172–6, 196, 199, 205, 213, 218, 220–1

scientism 153
screenwriting 3, 90–1, 93–7
scripts, film 90–1
scripts, neuropsychological 110, 201
sense-bound free association 80
sequence 12, 14, 16–17, 38–40, 103, 107, 110

Shields, David 112, 180
social media 30, 33
social science 47–8, 143, 152
songwriting 65, 78–83, 85–7
Standard Written English (SWE) 196, 198–204
Steampunk 3, 138–44
synapses 25–6

technical writing 10, 103
textbooks 14, 80, 82, 85, 89, 105
theory, critical race 227
theory, literary 9, 22, 224–5, 227–9
theory, postcolonial 63, 218, 225, 227
Tumblr 51

unworkshop 2, 21–30

verisimilitude 167, 169
vernacular 201, 209
VIDA 213, 218–19
Voices of Our Nations Arts Foundation (VONA) 211

Wallace, David Foster 52–3
workshop 1, 2, 4, 8–9, 11–13, 17, 22, 26–7, 29–30, 33, 35–42, 57, 59, 67, 73, 89, 92–7, 100, 114, 119–20, 134, 153–4, 157, 172, 175, 184, 188, 194, 211, 213, 217, 221, 224–32

Yagelski, Robert 149, 151, 153, 159–60

CPSIA information can be obtained
at www.ICGtesting.com
Printed in the USA
LVHW05s0155031018
592162LV00007B/105/P